Advances
in
Social Work

Special Issue on
The Futures of Social Work

Indiana University
School of Social Work

Advances in Social Work is committed to enhancing the linkage among social work practice, research, and education. Accordingly, the journal addresses current issues, challenges, and responses facing social work practice and education. The journal invites discussion and development of innovations in social work practice and their implications for social work research and education. Advances in Social Work seeks to publish empirical, conceptual, and theoretical articles that make substantial contributions to the field in all areas of social work including clinical practice, community organization, social administration, social policy, planning, and program evaluation.

The journal provides a forum for scholarly exchange of research findings and ideas that advance knowledge and inform social work practice. All relevant methods of inquiry are welcome.

Advances in Social Work is a peer-reviewed journal that publishes original work. Articles are accepted on the basis of appropriateness, clarity, sound methodology, and utility for social work practice, research, and education. Articles are indexed or abstracted in Social Work Abstracts and Social Service Abstracts.

Subscription Rates: *Advances in Social Work is* published twice each year (Fall and Spring) by Indiana University School of Social Work. Annual subscription is US $30.00 for United States, $40 for international subscriptions. Individual issues cost $15 each. The price includes postage by surface mail.

Order Information: Payment may be made by check or money order in U.S. funds to *"Indiana University School of Social Work."*

Mail orders, request for sample copies, and all other editorial and advertising correspondence should be directed to: Editor, *Advances in Social Work*, Indiana University School of Social Work, 902 W. New York Street, Indianapolis, IN 46202-5156. Telephone: (317) 278-0212; Fax: (317) 274-8630; E-mail: editor@iupui.edu.

Advances in Social Work
Vol.6, No.1.........Spring 2005

CONTENTS

EDITORIAL

This issue is, to date, the most ambitious project of *Advances in Social Work*. The initial idea was to bring together top scholars in different fields of Social Work, challenge them to craft their best vision of the future of that field, and create a highly useful cross-section on the futures of Social Work. The special issue was intended to stimulate readers to consider the different angle that the diamond of Social Work could be viewed. Each angle is not sufficient to rate the quality of Social Work's future but, as a multi-faceted jewel, Social Work can truly shine in its brilliance. We believe that the special issue truly captures that future vision. Each article is unique and adds richly to our understanding of the future. I invite the reader to read each article then think about common themes or what surprises you the most. You are in for a real treat!

The issue is formatted from broader to more defined context. The first three articles are on broad areas: the profession, education, and ethics. The next four articles are still on a larger view: Social Work as a global, multicultural, macro, and policy issues. The next seven articles begin to emphasize frameworks of Social Work: evidence-based practice, strengths-based practice, technology initiatives, spirituality, practice and disabilities, aging, and rural practice. The next seven articles emphasize practice settings: families, child welfare, schools, health care, mental health, addictions, and criminal justice. The final article strives to synthesize the twenty-one articles into a discussion of themes and to suggest some issues to ponder.

The issue is an amazing collection and worthy of each student, clinician, or professor's bookcase. The articles prod us to consider Social Work's future and how we can best position ourselves to navigate the new peaks and valleys to best help our clients and our profession. I look forward in ten years to pulling my well-worn copy of this issue off the shelf and comparing what has actually happened to what was "predicted". But, for now, I believe this issue is our best effort to guide us in preparing for the future.

THE FUTURE OF SOCIAL WORK AS A PROFESSION
Leon Ginsberg

Abstract: *This is an introductory, overview article that summarizes some of the major issues social work will encounter as a profession in the 21st Century. Employment trends are projected. Clinical and other direct services employment appears to be much more pervasive than employment in organization and management of services. Professional employment data show that nonmetropolitan employment will be more prevalent than employment in large cities. Social work in schools will be a major area of growth. So will programs to provide treatment and other alternatives to prison for those involved with illegal drugs. Some of the effects of current political issues and the 2004 elections on social work are also discussed.*

Keywords: Bureau of Labor Statistics, Council on Social Work Education, employment trends, nonmetropolitan employment, social work in schools, illegal drugs, politics

INTRODUCTION

Where is social work going? What social problems will demand our attention? Those are the kinds of questions futurists ponder. They are also the kinds of questions any profession should pose, while also working to influence the answers. In part, our destiny as a profession is within our grasp. However, we are also affected by forces much larger than ourselves.

It is one of the unfortunate truths about social work that we do not always have accurate or comprehensive ideas about where we are going. That is, in part, a reflection of our lack of information about where we have been. Although the history of social welfare is reasonably well-developed and documented by many scholars (For contemporary examples, see Day (2003,), Axinn and Stern (2005,) Jansson (2005,) and Herrick and Stuart, 2005) the social work profession's history is not so well known. In many ways, the decades roughly between the era of the achievements of Jane Addams and Mary Richmond and whoever is currently making major contributions to the field are largely lost. Who still writes or teaches about Chauncey Alexander, Bertram Beck, Mitchell Ginsberg, and Elizabeth Wisner—all of whom were powerful molders of the modern social work profession? We have been through some critical and complicated times and have influenced the ways in which social welfare developed. But much of our information is only sporadically and vaguely retained.

This special issue of *Advances in Social Work* includes articles on most of the seminal subjects in our field. It should be a beacon for those who want to try to understand what is coming and where we are going.

As an introduction, this article attempts to describe some of what we may expect to influence the ways in which social work practice and theory will evolve during the coming decades. These observations are about trends and issues that appear to have the greatest

Leon Ginsberg is Dean and Carolina Distinguished Professor, College of Social Work, University of South Carolina, Columbia, SC 29208.
Copyright © 2005 *Advances in Social Work* Vol. 6 No. 1 (Spring 2005), 7-16

potential for influencing the profession for the first half of the Twenty-First Century.

THE PROFESSION—TRENDS AND PROJECTIONS

Some of our researchers have reported on recent trends in social work as a profession, basing their data on special studies or on surveys of members of our national organizations, especially the National Association of Social Workers (Gibelman and Schervish, 1996, Ginsberg, 2005) However, the most comprehensive information is that provided by the U.S. Department of Labor's Bureau of Labor Statistics (BLS) which engages full time in surveying American occupations and employment. Its Occupational Outlook Handbook (2004) reports on most of the known occupations in the United States and projects their futures. Social work and human services fields related to the profession are among those studied and reported upon in the Handbook.

A Mammoth Occupation

Although we may sometimes tend to think of ourselves as part of a small, almost marginal profession, social work, when we include all the levels at which we practice, is quite large. The BLS (2004) says there were 477,000 social work jobs in 2002. It also reports there were some 300,000 social work and human services assistants at that time.

If one adds the numerous jobs that are not defined as social work but which probably employ many social workers such as drug and alcohol counselors, corrections personnel, and aging services employees, it is probably accurate to say that there are more or less one million broadly defined social work jobs in the United States.

Future Projections

The BLS (2004) says that social work will grow, on average, more rapidly than other occupations through at least 2012. There will be more competition for jobs in metropolitan areas than in nonmetropolitan, but there will be jobs in cities as well as towns. The steady increase in social work employment is based, according to the BLS, on several factors:

1. The increasing proportion of the population that will be elderly, meaning more people will require the kinds of social welfare and health services that social workers provide.

2. A tendency to reorient prevention of and services for those who use illegal drugs from law enforcement to treatment. According to Barrett and Foley (2000) there are some 400,000 people incarcerated in U.S. prisons, for drug convictions, who constitute almost a quarter of the nation's incarcerated population. Treating substance abuse as a criminal issue is much more expensive than providing therapeutic services.

3. Further public efforts to integrate people with disabilities into the mainstream of American society.

4. A growing child and school population, which will demand more services of the kinds social workers provide.

In some ways, the BLS projections make social work's future appear to be similar to its current configuration. The prediction is that almost all social workers will be employed in direct services work—in three categories: child, family, and school social workers, the largest group; medical and public health social workers; and mental health and substance abuse social workers. Although the profession has an historic commitment to work with larger systems, the bulk of employed social workers have always been in the direct services. That is where the employment has been and is likely to continue to be. According to the Council on Social Work Education (Lennon, 2004) over half of all MSW field instruction students are in direct services placements. That group, combined with those that have no field placement definition specified and those in generalist placements, suggests that almost all social work education is in the direct services. Ironically, the best-paying and most prestigious employment in social work is in the organization and administration of such services. (Gibelman and Schervish, 1996) Therefore, although most social workers may be defined now and in the future as "micro" workers, the reality is that the top levels of those services will be in "macro" practice. For the future, community organization and other macro specialization education and practice are likely to remain only small parts of the industry. However, like social group work, which has largely disappeared as a specialty, but is stronger than ever through group services in clinical agencies, organization and management are likely to be important professional roles for social workers in direct practice agencies.

The Political Future

For most of social work's history, government has played a major role in determining how many of us are prepared for practice and how many of us are employed. So we are connected with government in many ways. One of the qualities of social work, and one that separates us from other human services professions, is our formal involvement in government and politics and our commitment to work towards political improvement. We teach about and support movement towards the realization of social justice not only for our profession but in the larger community and in the world. That sets us apart from others engaged in similar work and makes us something more than a self-involved trade or occupation. We take stands on policy issues that affect those we serve. We endorse candidates for office who support the kinds of legislation and administration that benefit people who are disadvantaged or who face disabilities. We encourage our fellow professionals to be politically active, even to seek public office. In the future, we are likely to continue in that posture.

However, we are something of an exception. According to Menand (2004,) ours is a largely non-political nation, when measured in terms of our citizens' political interests and knowledge. Americans are largely ignorant of and bored by politics. Either they don't care or so generally distrust politicians that they don't often bother voting or becoming involved with candidates or campaigns. Menand (2004) cites a number of facts that support the supposition. He suggests that about twice as many people have no political views, at all, as have coherent positions on public issues. A majority cannot name their U.S. senators or representatives. Some of the positions Americans hold are contradictory—believing that taxes should be lower and that government programs should grow; opposing more "welfare" but supporting more help for poor people; between 22 and 44 percent say they don't care who wins presidential elections.

Unless things become terrible—on the order of the 1929 Depression or World War II—American non-involvement and public apathy towards the political process will continue. Although the conventional wisdom views such attitudes as threats to American democracy, it is possible that they may be functional. The Al Gore-George W. Bush 2000 Florida election fiasco, for example, would have led to blood in the streets in some other, more politically involved, nations. The consensus of the Democratic Party leaders was not to make it an issue—that public calm and orderly government were more important than who won the election. In the U.S., keeping politics cool and peaceful is perhaps one of our greatest strengths. Americans, by and large, only become emotionally involved in the political process when they are hurting personally. American government works to avoid agitating the citizenry. Our political sophistication and economic knowledge are such that government can keep the economy from collapsing, from allowing unemployment to become widespread, and, with careful use of medical and public health knowledge, from allowing too many people to become ill at the same time. Social workers and social welfare programs are part of what government uses to keep the populace relatively satisfied. Although political parties reward their friends and punish their enemies, they won't let large numbers suffer too much. It's bad American politics.

Interestingly, the 2004 elections drew more voters than any other in American history. Some commentators suggest that the issues, such as the September 11, 2001, attacks on New York and the war in Iraq, were large enough and the divisions between those who wanted to see President George W. Bush reelected and those who did not were strong enough to encourage voting. It is too early to know whhether or not that election signals a change in the foregoing analysis of American attitudes towards politics and elections.

Voter turnout in 2004 was the heaviest since 1968 with some 60 percent of eligible voters casting ballots. And because the population of eligible voters was the largest in American history, President Bush received more votes than any other president and was reelected by a comfortable majority. (Fineman, 2004) It is likely he and his cabinet, which has changed since his first term, will support policies similar to those of his first four years. Since the National Association of Social Workers supported the Democratic candidate, as it usually does, the profession probably cannot expect strong support from the Bush presidency. That is probably also true of other professional groups, such as journalists. CBS television personality Andy Rooney, commenting on November 7, said that the representatives of the media were split 50-50 between Bush and his opponent, John Kerry. Fifty percent were strong supporters of Kerry and fifty percent intensely disliked Bush, he said.

We'll see gradual political changes but so long as most people are fairly well off, we will not see many grand disruptions. Things will change so incrementally that they may be hard to notice. We won't want to repeat the Depression or the Civil Rights Movement or other such wrenching social changes. Wealth may be gradually channeled away from the poor and the middle classes to the upper; we may see armed international conflicts that not everyone will view as being in our best interests; and these trends may be reversed as one party or another is in power. But the task of our political leaders seems to be keeping us relatively happy and even unaware that public policy changes our personal circumstances. So long as we are, many of us will ignore politics and those in power will be able to stay there.

Humorist P.J. O'Rourke (2004, p. 5) probably summarizes American citizen political thought well. "America is not a wily, sneaky nation. We don't think that way. We don't think much at all, thank God. Start thinking and pretty soon you get ideas, and then you get idealism, and the next thing you know you've got ideology, with millions dead in concentration camps and gulags. A fundamental American question is 'What's the big idea?'" But if 2004 set a trend, some of those comments may no longer be applicable to US politics.

The Primacy of the States

In the last century, some questioned the need for the continued existence of state governments. Communications and transportation were such that the nation could get along with a few administrative districts and save all the costs of operating state governments, some concluded. Of course, American government evolved quite differently. In fact, the states became more powerful than ever, especially in the 1980's under President Ronald Reagan, and have continued to be an important level of governing. That is especially true for social welfare programs, many of which are largely financed through block grants from the federal government to the states. The growing importance of state governments is likely to be one of the most important influences on the future of social work.

State Licensing

The growth of state government power became even more important to social work when every state adopted a program of licensing, certifying, or otherwise regulating social work. (Association of Social Work Boards, 2004) With licensing, the power of the states over social work practice and, ultimately, social work education has shifted away from educational programs and the national organizations such as the Council on Social Work Education and the National Association of Social Workers to the state licensing boards. The licensing boards duplicate many of the functions of our national bodies such as promulgating ethics, exercising quality control, and adjudicating complaints against social workers. Although the boards generally require CSWE accreditation as a way of controlling the quality of educational preparation, that could change. Some states provide some kinds of licenses to graduates of non-CSWE accredited programs.

Over recent years, we have seen the decline and, in some cases, the end of national social welfare organizations. The National Conference on Social Welfare ceased to operate. NASW stopped offering national conferences. In some locales, it has ceased holding regular membership meetings. Of the million or so people who are identified with social work in some ways, only some 15 percent are members of NASW, and that figure includes social work students and retirees. State regulation has rendered much of the program of the national organizations, especially NASW, less relevant than they were in the mid-Twentieth Century, when social work was seeking public recognition. Credentials such as membership in the Academy of Certified Social Workers and the specialty sections of NASW have less relevance than they otherwise might because of licensing and other public regulation. If the existing national organizations are to survive until the end of the current century, they will need to carefully examine and modify their programs and activities. In the current era, much of the money raised by state NASW chapters comes from sponsoring symposia and other continuing education—to which many participants flock because of state licensing continuing education requirements, which is another example of the influence of licensing. Perhaps the most important role of the national organizations is influencing legislation to benefit social workers and social welfare programs. That remains one of NASW's most critical contributions to the profession.

In addition to their role in helping social workers meet continuing education requirements, it almost seems that many of the national social welfare organizations remain in existence because the states and social work students finance social work education programs which, in turn, finance the national bodies. CSWE, the Bachelors Program Directors, the Interuniversity Consortium for International Social Development, the International Association of Schools of Social Work, and the National Association of Deans and Directors, are all largely financed by organizational dues that come from state appropriations, educational and research grants to schools, and student tuition. Only one national organization, the Association of Social Work Boards, which coordinates the state licensing efforts and prepares and administers most of the state licensing exams, seems to have a solid role in social work's future.

IDEOLOGICAL CONFLICTS

Some of the current unsettled social issues that affect social work will be major influences on what we become.

Same Sex Unions

Although President George W. Bush and other leading public officials support a constitutional amendment forbidding marriages between people of the same sex, we probably won't see such an amendment adopted. However, such marriages will be officially forbidden in most states, which hold the ultimate power over family law. That may or may not make a major difference in life styles. Our system of laws enables people who want unions with others of the same sex to do so—to have and adopt children, in many cases, to own property together, and to be each other's benefits beneficiaries. Even the most opposed politicians cannot stop such unions, especially since the U.S. Supreme Court found laws against consensual sex between adults of the same sex unconstitutional. Formal marriage is only one approach to such unions. And formal marriage, as the basis for unions between individuals, has declined throughout the Western world. It is likely that there will be continued same sex unions, legally sanctioned as formal marriages or not, along with further declines in formal heterosexual marriage.

Health Care

An unsettled issue that will likely be settled, in some ways, during the first half of the Century, is the provision of universal health care insurance for Americans. Of course, the issue is complex and politically charged. Health care is a large American industry and the second largest employer of social workers. Medicare and Medicaid, now 40 years old, were the early programs designed to deal with the issue. In more recent years, programs to extend Medicaid to low income children, whose parents may not qualify, covered increasing numbers. A complicated prescription program for Medicare recipients will extend that coverage to more seniors and persons with disabilities.

Much of the discussion about health care deals with the increasing high costs of receiving it—costs that cannot be borne by all but the wealthiest Americans—without some sort of third party coverage. However, the genesis of the high costs is less often mentioned. In fact, the health services and health care have developed more dramatically than have the costs of obtaining them. When Medicaid and Medicare became law, through the 1965 amendments to the Social Security Act, coronary bypass surgery and organ transplants were in their infancy. Even kidney dialysis, which now involves large numbers of social workers, was just becoming available. Health care providers and educators had only recently learned about the use of exercise for heart patients, who had earlier were advised to lead sedentary lives. The HIV/AIDS epidemic was twenty years in the future. Pharmaceuticals for treating depression, psychosis, severe acid reflux, and many other conditions were not yet developed. Although there were antibiotics, their use in treating ulcers, was not known. Modern forms of x-ray did not exist. There was much that was not known and much that could not be diagnosed or treated. We recognize that the life span is longer but don't always connect it with the incredible and expensive advances in health care.

Somehow—through some sort of national health insurance, probably—the health care payment discrepancy between those who have and those who do not have third party coverage will be resolved. As discussed earlier, American politics will not permit such discrepancies to continue. As is currently the case, social workers will continue playing major roles in the organization and delivery of health care—and in dealing with the social elements of the provision of care. Their roles are likely to increase with the advent of extended coverage.

Multiculturalism

Many years ago, this writer suggested that the United States could, in the future, become "Latinamericanized." I had just returned from a sabbatical in South America and concluded that instead of the Latin American nations becoming more like the United States, the United States was becoming more like Latin America. The diminution of the middle classes and the increasing division of the population into rich and poor was much like Latin America's distribution of wealth. The growth of the security industry and the belief among many people that they needed alarm systems and police patrols was another similarity. Since that time, those trends have continued but a new phenomenon also has influence. That is the widespread movement of people from Latin America into every part of the United States. My state of South Carolina had barely enough Latinos in its population to count them when I came here 20 years ago. Now the bank toll free numbers offer Spanish as well as English menus. Stores stock favored Latino food products. And bilingual social workers, who know Spanish as well as English, are aggressively sought by employers.

This multicultural trend is likely to continue, although by mid-Century, it is likely that the Latin American immigrants as well as those from the rest of the world will become well-integrated into the U.S. mainstream, such as the forbearers of those of who were born here did in the last Century. The integration of the large immigrant population will continue to make demands on social workers, especially those who speak languages other than English.

Religious and Political Fanaticism

Because much of social work originated in religious initiatives, it is difficult to view religious behavior as a potential social problem. However, religious and political fanaticism—or the translation of religious commitment into political and public action—have the potential for exacerbating and sometimes causing social problems.

Perhaps the best known and most often cited example of violent problems that emanated from religious-political zealotry is the September 11, 2001, attacks on New York and Washington by members of groups identified with radical Islamic movements. Although the best known among them is Al Qaeda, in more recent times the Ansar al-Sunna Army, operating in Iraq (MSNBC, 2004,) was identified as murdering a dozen Nepalese hostages and threatening to kill two kidnapped French journalists, if France refused to lift its ban on children wearing Muslim head scarves to school. Kidnapping and taking hostages is perhaps the most effective and least demanding of terrorist acts because it requires few financial or personnel resources as well as few weapons. And one need not be a combatant to be taken hostage or beheaded. Most of the hostages have been ordinary citizens engaged in construction projects or food services. Beheading hostages is no more deadly than other forms of execution but it terrifies people—especially when those bloody acts are telecast. Of course, the overwhelming majority of Muslims condemns such acts, taken in the name of the religion.

However, the other two Mosaic religions, Christianity and Judaism, also include groups that pursue policies in conflict with much of what social work supports. A small, Texas-established, with a California address, Christian group, ChristianExodus (August, 2004) expresses alarm at the directions in which the United States is moving, especially the separation of church and state as manifested in bans on school prayer and the public display of the Ten Commandments. They want the repeal of the 14th (equal protection of the law,) 16th (the income tax,) and 17th (direct elections of Senators,) to the Constitution as well as an end to tolerance of homosexuality and federal funding and influencing of education. Their action plan is to move thousands of Christians who agree with them to South Carolina in groups of 12,000 who would, in turn, change the state to one in which its philosophy would prevail. This is only one of many small groups proposing quite radical changes in the United States. However, even the Southern Baptists, the largest Protestant denomination, have a vocal minority that proposes that Christians remove their children from public schools because they are "secularized." (Knauss, 2004)

What some may call fundamentalist Jewish groups opposed the founding of Israel as being impious while others equally fervently believe that it is the sacred duty of Jews to take all of the area now occupied by Palestinians as well as Israelis and preserve it for the coming of the Messiah. (Ruthven, 2004)

These examples of religious fanaticism coupled with political agendas affect broader and broader bands of world society and will be important influences on social work programs and services in much of human society.

CONCLUSION

Clearly, social work has a secure future. In some ways, it prospers under diverse conditions—when times are good, governments want to spend more for social services. When times are bad, we want to spend more to address human problems. Social workers are involved in both.

The issues will be different in the second half of the 21st Century than they were in earlier years. However, great social change is such that it may not be detectable except in retrospect.

And some of the pervasive, historical phenomena that continually affect human society—politics, family life, and religion, will be among the more important influences on the evolution of that future as well as the ways in which social workers discharge their responsibilities.

References

Association of Social Work Boards (retrieved September 1, 2004) *www.aswb.org*

Axinn, J. and Stern, M.J. (2005) *Social welfare: A history of the American response to need, 6th ed.* Boston, MA: Allyn and Bacon.

Barrett, S. and Foley, G. (August 24, 2000) "400,000 Now Imprisoned in Endless U.S. 'Drug War' *www.ptreyeslight.com.* Point Reyes, California: Point Reyes Light. (Retrieved June 22, 2004)

Christian Exodus, *www.christianexodus.org,* (Retrieved, August 31, 2004)

Day, P.J. (2003) *New history of social welfare. 4th ed.* Boston, MA: Allyn & Bacon.

Fineman, H. (November 15, 2004) A sweet victory. *Newsweek.* pp. 23-26.

Gibelman, M. and Schervish, P. (1996) *Who we are: A second look.* Washington, DC: NASW Press.

Ginsberg, L. (2005) *Thinking about a social work career, 2nd edition.* Boston, MA: Allyn and Bacon.

Herrick, J. and Stuart, P. H. (2005) *Encyclopedia of social welfare history in North America.* Thousand Oaks, CA: Sage.

Jansson, B. S. (2005) *The reluctant welfare state: American social welfare policies: Past, present and future.* Belmont, CA: Brooks-Cole.

Knauss, C.L. (2004) Area man backs call to pull children from public schools. *The Columbia State.* pp. B1, B5.

Lennon, T.M. (2004) *Statistics on social work education in the United States: 2001.* Alexandria, VA: Council on Social Work Education.

Menand, L. (August 30, 2004) A critic at large: The unpolitical animal. *The New Yorker.* Pp. 92-96.

MSNBC (Retrieved August 31, 2004) *www.msnbc.msn.com* 12 Nepali hostages purportedly slain in Iraq.

O'Rourke, P.J. (2004) Parliament of whores. New York: Atlantic Monthly Press.

Ruthven, M. (2004) *Fundamentalism: The search for meaning.* London: Oxford University Press.

U.S. Department of Labor, Bureau of Labor Statistics (2004) *Occupational outlook handbook: 2004-2005 edition.* Washington, DC: Author.

Author's Note

Address correspondence to: Leon Ginsberg PhD, College of Social Work, University of South Carolina, Columbia, SC 29208. e-mail: Ginsber@gwm.sc.edu.

SOCIAL WORK EDUCATION: A FUTURE OF STRENGTH OR PERIL

Julia M. Watkins
Dean Pierce

Abstract: *In a dynamically changing world and one in which higher education generally is challenged by a scarcity of resources and the ever present need to justify the results of its mission and purpose, social work education faces an uncertain and perhaps perilous future. But rather than succumbing to pessimism, one should consider the strengths that social work education brings to the academy. The authors suggest the major challenges that face social work education in the coming decade and tie these to active initiatives on the part of social work educators in shaping a positive and dynamic future within the academy.*

Keywords: Social work education trends, future, teaching

INTRODUCTION

Social work education has enjoyed healthy respect and substantially positive development within the academy for at least the past 50 years of existence of the Council on Social Work Education (CSWE). Although there are the expected tensions among universities with differing missions and purposes as well as degree levels, social work education has maintained a long term focus on education for the profession while at the same time struggling to define its theoretical and knowledge base, its practice competencies, its research priorities, and its strength within the academy. In a healthy educational and professional environment, these tensions and struggles are not only to be expected, but they serve as an essential element in the process of academic and professional renewal.

The numbers of CSWE accredited social work programs have grown dramatically over the past two decades from a total of 427 in 1985 to 617 in 2005, an increase of 44 percent (CSWE, 1985, & CSWE, 2005). At the master's level in the past four years alone, there has been an increase of 29 programs or an increase of 17 percent with an additional 18 programs in candidacy status. At the baccalaureate level the corresponding numbers are 21 new programs or an increase of almost 5 percent and 20 programs in candidacy status (CSWE, 2000, & CSWE 2005). Reference frequently is made to a "proliferation" of programs as being highly questionable or outright negative with respect to decreasing market share and educational quality. On the other hand, this expansion can be viewed as a healthy step toward meeting market demand and ensuring educational access to a more place bound and older student population. The fundamental tension between matters of access to education and quality of education reaches far beyond social work and will continue to occupy a prominent position in academic discourse for the foreseeable future. For our purposes, the unanswered question is what is it about social work education that makes it so attractive to institutions to initiate new programs even under conditions of fiscal distress?

Julie M. Watkins is Executive Director, Council on Social Work Education and Dean Pierce is Director of the Office of Social Work Accreditation and Educational Excellence, Council on Social Work Education, Alexandria, VA 22314.

Copyright © 2005 *Advances in Social Work* Vol. 6 No. 1 (Spring 2005), 17-23

Although the numbers of programs has increased, it is factually accurate, however, that the number of students enrolled as well as the number of degrees granted annually at the master's and the baccalaureate levels since 1998 has remained fairly stable at approximately 25,000 in 1998 and 25,683 in 2003. At the same time that overall student enrollments have inched slowly downward, the number of social work faculty members has increased in the aggregate (across all educational levels) by approximately 1,000 (about 16 percent between 1998 and 2003), perhaps in part as a result of the increased numbers of programs. Therefore, overall, one might infer that with increased numbers of programs and stable numbers of students and graduates, supply has outstripped demand and prompts caution about the future. It is worth noting that student enrollments are not the only variable of value in determining institutional or program viability, but they certainly are not ignored by university and college administrators whose responsibility is to fund programs in their institutions that they determine serve effectively and efficiently, the broader educational purposes of the institution. In spite of how wonderful programs may be perceived by students, the community, and the faculty, small programs with low enrollments are highly vulnerable in most colleges and universities especially in today's environment.

QUESTIONS AND FIVE KEY CHALLENGES FOR THE FUTURE

From this brief overview of the statistics reported annually by social work education programs and the Commission on Accreditation, is the emergence of a number of questions having serious implications for the future of social work education: Are potential students seeking other educational opportunities for preparation to work in the human services sector; are social work curricula and their formats relevant to the 21st Century, based, for example, on such dynamics as physiological clinical advances, globalism and the rapid transformation to a digital information society; is social work a primary stakeholder in the academy with appropriate administrative recognition and allocation of the necessary resources to achieve its goals and objectives; and fundamentally, is the social work education enterprise sustainable in a dynamic new century and a higher education environment that values research over teaching, cost containment over intellectual and curricular innovation, and digitization over traditional pedagogy and human resource development?

Unmasking these questions suggests several issues that must be the focus of our ongoing dialogue and discussion to ensure the future strength of social work education. In the briefness of this paper, we will highlight several of the most pressing issues and suggest the major steps to dissuade from peril and ensure a strong future for social work education.

The first issue is spelled out in a recent article by the late Frank Newman, et. al. (Newman, Couturier & Scurry, 2004) in which it is asserted that higher education is not meeting the public's needs. Relevancy is compromised by the academy's difficulty, for whatever reasons, in attending to efficiency and productivity, its inattention to degree attainment, and the overall failure to reward teaching in ways similar to that of research. The latter observation is an especially blunt critique, and suggests that social work educators must engage in a robust dialogue about the respective relevance of teaching and research in professional social work education. Do we serve the public trust and do we serve in the public interest? If so, then how is social work education meeting the needs of the 21st Century? Do we educate students with our lens on educational outcomes, educational attainment, and do we do it in an efficient as well as effective manner? Does our research provide sufficient evidence that our practice interventions are effective? If we are not able to articulate and demonstrate that our programs are relevant to the 21st Century, we certainly will be challenged more vigorously by the encroachment of other degree programs into our domain and we will be starved financially by our institutions as they look to fund programs that have broad public support and perceived relevancy.

Second, if social work education is seen as irrelevant to the 21st Century, that is, in its preparation of practitioners and scholars, this challenge could not come at a more troubling time, a time of severe financial distress characteristic of many colleges and universities. Financial distress affects our ability to adequately fund institutional financial aid – including graduate student stipends and research fellowships, salaries and benefits, and operations, including research and technology – all of the commonly agreed upon quality indicators in higher education. Organizational economies in shaping delivery and governance structures suggest the trend toward more social work programs becoming part of larger administrative units. Resource scarcity is the most prevalent reason documented by the CSWE Commission on Accreditation (COA), for actual social work program non-compliance issues or program closure as opposed, for example, to changes in the institutional mission. Certainly mission may be changed in order to bolster the financial picture of an institution or create a new relevancy for the institution, but this is a related issue for yet another discussion.

To deal overall with this financially troubling situation will require innovative and flexible strategies in teaching and learning and a consistent demonstration of relevance to the 21st Century. It is also no secret that tensions exist between teaching and learning and research productivity, further heightening the internal disharmony in a fiscally distressed institution. In fact, the financial crisis intensifies the demand on faculty for externally funded research, and further undermines the emphasis on quality teaching by regular faculty.

A third major challenge for the future of social work education is the preparation of doctoral educated faculty. It is clear that although the numbers of doctoral programs has increased by 25 percent (from 53 to 66 programs) in the last decade, the annual production of doctoral degree recipients has increased only slightly from 229 in 1993 to 289 in 2002, (Lennon, 1993, & 2002). At the same time, the average number of degrees awarded per program has increased from 4.3 to 4.6 annually. While there may be an expected upturn in these numbers as newly developed programs award their first doctoral degrees, we will be hard pressed to meet the demand, now estimated to be 3-4 academic positions open for each doctoral degree recipient in any one year. The demand will be particularly acute with many academics preparing to retire within the next five years and the requirements of so many institutions to hire doctoral prepared faculty.

The fourth challenge we face has to do specifically with how our educational programs are structured and what is taught in them – the curriculum. At all levels of social work education and in all programs, regardless of geographic location, concentrations, or defined outcomes and objectives, the fundamental task is to educate students with the intellectual competencies for practice relevant to the 21st Century. Yet, we as educators have only recently embarked upon that discussion – of what are the intellectual competencies, what is relevant to this Century? What is the fit between what we teach in our social work programs and the competencies required in the practice setting? This important work is being developed by the CSWE Commission on Curriculum and Educational Innovation (CO-CEI) as it prepares for the revision of the Education Policy Statement and, subsequently, the next edition of Accreditation Standards. Our task is to fully understand the intellectual competencies that will be required for practice in the coming decades and to translate those understandings into appropriate curriculum content and delivery structures.

At the baccalaureate or entry level of practice, it is specifically to the liberal arts that we should be turning our attention. Although the liberal arts form the base for further education, the substance and processes should be a purposeful part of the entire four years of the student's educational experience. The liberal arts are key to developing the habits of mind that contribute to appropriate intellectual competencies including critical thinking, problem solving, team work, creativity, intellectual honesty, evidence seeking, question formation, and ethical behavior. Moreover, social work students, at the baccalaureate as well as the master's levels, must be intellectually driven by ideas as opposed to ideology. The intellectual competencies, requiring our attention in definition and substance, must be based not only in academically rigorous curricula, but serve as the groundwork for entry level social work practice as well as graduate education at the master's and doctoral levels. It is essential that students be adequately prepared for intellectual discovery as well as the challenges faced by social workers as part of a global community.

At the master's level, how we define foundation content, how we envision concentrations, how we incorporate and reinforce the values and skills of rigorous research and intellectual inquisitiveness are fundamental to our success in being relevant to the 21st Century.

One final challenge to the traditional social work curriculum is the increasing importance of on-line learning, especially web based course delivery. In the 2000 – 2001 academic year, about ninety percent of America's public institutions of higher education offered electronic learning and around sixty percent participated in a consortium (or virtual university) of Universities offering such learning opportunities (Epper & Garn, 2003). On-line and other forms of distance learning challenge several traditional, core academic values including autonomy, collegiality, liberal education and related degrees, the authority of the faculty over the curriculum, and a site based community of learning. Distance and on-line learning disperses faculty and students; emphasizes proprietary coursework and standardized courses; focuses on part-time faculty; favors training and specialized credentialing over the granting of a traditional degree; and puts lessened importance on place in learning (Eaton, 2000). Social work education must address these challenges to its traditional academic values, especially in terms of student socialization and faculty control of the curriculum.

Social work and other professions, however, have been slow to adopt distance learning methods. As reported in a survey of specialized accreditors, about 76 percent of the 50 specialized accrediting bodies report that at least some of their programs use distance learning. When individual programs are examined, however, only about 18 percent of the total number of accredited programs report offering such instruction (CHEA, 2002).

Among distance education methods, on-line learning will have an especially profound impact on social work education. Fully on-line accredited programs in nursing and counseling offered by proprietary institutions serve as models for those who wish to study social work on-line and whose lives require flexibility and greater accessibility to learning than what is offered by traditional institutional arrangements. Questions for social work education regarding on-line education include how to teach, what to teach, and how to adapt it to field education.

Our own task at intellectual discovery for future relevant practice is an enormous challenge that will require the very best thinking and creativity on the part of social work educators. But this task it is not in a context of isolation. The fifth challenge is acknowledging, facing and influencing a rapidly globalizing environment. The world in which we live and work is one where geographic boundaries are permeable and where access to information is both rapid and almost universal. Given observational as opposed to values consensus on this point, then social work students must be well prepared, not only in the liberal arts, social and behavioral theory, research and knowledge dissemination, they must have cross cultural practice and policy experiences based in a complex of international academic and work experiences that not only expose them to but require of them new ways of thinking, behaving, and understanding. The study of foreign languages, cross-cultural content, international politics, peace studies, history and the cultural heritage of non-Western societies help form an appropriate intellectual base for the 21st Century (Healy, 1990).

Yet such a base is not highly prevalent. For example, in U.S. higher education generally, there are approximately 160,000 U.S. students who study abroad in any one academic year and there are slightly more than half a million foreign students who study annually in the United States. Because of the current situation related to U.S. national security and the prevailing isolationist view, this number has dropped by 5 percent in the most recent years since September 11, 2002. In social work, the percent of international students receiving doctoral degrees annually hovers around 10 percent and has not varied substantially over the past decade (Lennon, 1995 – 2003). Through the newly launched CSWE Katherine A. Kendall Institute for International Social Work Education (KAKI) and the CSWE Commission on Global Social Work Education (CGSWE), social work education will have new avenues for support of its international and global initiatives as well as a base and guidelines for determining the substantive relevance of internationalism in social work education.

CONCLUSION: CAN WE OVERCOME THE CHALLENGES?

These mounting challenges are significant enough independent of one another and if not addressed, they will place social work education in a perilous position for the coming decades. But more importantly, however, they test the capacity of social work education to create effective leadership and establish external and internal partnerships of strength and opportunity. Multiple opportunities exist within social work education to provide leadership. Examples include deans and directors of graduate programs, directors of BSW programs, field education directors, and elected and voluntary positions within social work and multidisciplinary professional organizations. The leadership that is required to meet the challenge, however, is within the academy itself. Social work education needs to assume positions of influence within their colleges and universities, serving on campus wide search and curriculum committees, participating in strategic planning initiatives and institutional accreditation efforts. Recognizing this need for leadership development, the CSWE has created a Commission on Professional Development and within it, a Council on Leadership Development. The primary anticipated goal of the newly formed Council will be the establishment of a Leadership Institute to serve the current and emerging needs of social work educators for fulfilling leadership positions in the academy.

Is our professional and educational survival at stake? It is clear that it certainly is being challenged. But our greatest strength of leadership will be found in the incorporation of the preeminence of partnership into the very fabric of all social work educationally related organizations and the construction of closer partnerships within our individual colleges or universities. This strategy underscores the need to acknowledge the strengths and the shortcomings that each organization brings to the agenda, to develop a common consensus about our future, and act to achieve that commonly held consensus. We must think and act differently within the context of the larger national and international issues to be addressed, otherwise we risk becoming irrelevant to the 21st Century. Our conversations must transcend the artificial and antagonistic boundaries of we and they often spoken in ideological terms and focus on the big ideas that will give meaning to the future and ensure our professional survival. Isolation will not help our cause; it will only exacerbate the risks to our survival. Social work education has a future of strength if we focus our energies on being the future leaders in the academy and understand that that future is highly dependent on what we do today in conceptualizing social work education in the promotion of diversity, human rights, social and economic justice and global peace and security.

References

Council for Higher Education Accreditation. (2002). *Specialized Accreditation and Assuring Quality in Distance Learning*. CHEA Monograph Series 2002, Number 2. Washington, DC.

Council on Social Work Education. (1985). *Colleges and Universities with Accredited Social Work Degree Programs*. Alexandria, VA.

Council on Social Work Education. (2000). *Directory of Colleges and Universities with Accredited Social Work Degrees*. Alexandria, VA.

Council on Social Work Education. (2005 Spring/Summer). *Commission on Accreditation Decisions, February 2005*. Social Work Education Reporter: In press.

Eaton, J.S. (2000). *Core academic values, quality, and regional accreditation: The challenge of distance learning*. Retrieved March 30, 2005 from the CHEA Web site: http://www.chea.org/Research/core-values.cfm.

Epper, R.M., & Garn, M. (2003). Virtual College & University Consortia: A National Study. Retrieved March 30, 2005 from the Western Cooperative for Educational Telecommunication Web site: http://www.wcet.info/resources/publications/vcu.pdf.

Healy, L.M. (1990, February 8). *The International Curriculum Content: The Challenge of Relevance for Social Work*. Paper presented at the Proceedings of an International Symposium at Hunter College School of Social Work in New York, New York.

Lennon, T.M. (1993, 1995— 2003). *Statistics on Social Work Education in the United States*. Alexandria, VA: Council on Social Work Education.

Newman, F., Couturier L., & Scurry J. (2004, October 15) *Higher Education Isn't Meeting the Public's Needs.* Chronicle of Higher Education.

Author's Note

Address correspondence to: Julia M. Watkins, Ph.D., Executive Director, Council on Social Work Education, 1725 Duke Street, Suite 500, Alexandria, VA 22314. e-mail: jwatkins@cswe.org.

Note

Parts of this article have been excerpted from presentations given by the senior author to the Annual Meeting of the Group for the Advancement of Doctoral Education (GADE), October, 2004, and the Annual Conference of the Association of Baccalaureate Program Directors (BPD), November 2004.

SOCIAL WORK VALUES AND ETHICS:
REFLECTIONS ON THE PROFESSION'S ODYSSEY

Frederic G. Reamer

Abstract: *Social workers' understanding of ethical issues has matured significantly. This article traces the evolution of the profession's approach to values and ethics. During its history, social work has moved through four major periods—the morality period, the values period, the ethical theory and decision-making period, and the ethical standards and risk-management period. The author argues that the profession's current emphasis on ethics risk management (the prevention of ethics complaints and ethics-related lawsuits) is diverting social workers from in-depth exploration of core professional and personal values, ethical dilemmas, and the nature of the profession's moral mission. The author encourages the profession to recalibrate its focus on values and ethics.*

Keywords: ethics, values, risk management, ethical dilemma, ethical decision-making

INTRODUCTION

In October, 1976 I embarked on my personal efforts to wrestle with social work's most daunting ethical issues. At the time I was a Ph.D. student at the University of Chicago, School of Social Service Administration. I clearly remember the day when the ethics light bulb, which for me had relatively few watts, turned on in my head. I was actively engaged with a fellow student in a spirited discussion about the relative merits of incarceration and community-based care of juvenile offenders; my colleague and I were employed as research assistants in a national program evaluation sponsored by the U.S. Department of Justice.

Our energetic dialogue took an unexpected turn. We moved from discussion of social policy issues and empirical evidence concerning recidivism rates to a very principled, intellectually challenging exchange of ideas about "right" and "wrong" in juvenile justice. We pulled and pushed apart a range of arguments about moral culpability, punishment, retribution, freedom, justice, and self-determination. We debated about the extent to which juvenile offenders are morally responsible for their actions and whether they deserve punishment. I recall feeling energized by our efforts to unearth a variety of ethical issues that are germane to juvenile justice and, more broadly, social work.

I left that discussion with more questions than answers. To what extent have social workers thought about and analyzed the ethical dimensions of practice and policy? What guidelines has the profession cultivated to help social workers conceptualize about, and attempt to resolve, ethical issues? In what ways do social work values shape the profession's practice principles and policies?

I recall visiting the school's library later that week to search the literature; in those pre-Internet days I was limited to the dusty card catalogue and tomes of journal abstracts in

Frederic G. Reamer is Professor, School of Social Work , Rhode Island College, Providence, RI 02908.

Copyright © 2005 *Advances in Social Work* Vol. 6 No. 1 (Spring 2005), 24-32

the stacks. I assumed, naively it turns out, that I would find volumes of publications on the subject of social work values and ethics. I was surprised to discover relatively little. Most of what I came across focused on the nature of social work values and the profession's value base. I found a handful of discussions of social work perspectives on clients' right to confidentiality and self-determination.

It was then that I decided to broaden the contours of my doctoral education to include this broad arena related to professional ethics. It seemed clear to me that social work, as a profession, was rife with ethical challenges in direct and clinical practice, community practice, administration, supervision, policy and planning, and research and evaluation. I resolved to spend some time learning about the broad subject of ethics – as conceptualized by moral philosophers – and applying my new knowledge to the practical challenges and dilemmas in social work.

That is how my ethics journey in social work began. In the earliest years I spent considerable time learning the theories, concepts, and argot that formally trained ethicists use to understand and think about moral problems. I brought myself up to speed on the core subjects of meta-ethics and normative ethics. I started at square one with foundation literature in moral philosophy on relatively arcane meta-ethical theories of cognitivism, intuitionism, emotivism, prescriptivism, and naturalism (Rachels, 2002). I moved on to classic ethical theories related to deontology, teleology, egoism, act utilitarianism, and rule utilitarianism. My mind began to explode with ideas about how these abstruse concepts – which originated in the works of Socrates, Plato, and Aristotle and found currency in the later works of luminaries such as Immanuel Kant, Jeremy Bentham, John Stuart Mill, and John Rawls – might help social workers think more clearly about, and respond to, ethical dilemmas in the profession.

LOOKING BACK TO PLAN THE FUTURE

In retrospect, it is clear to me that my early musings about social work ethics – in the mid-to-late 1970s – occurred midstream in the profession's complex attempts to develop a core set of values and ethical standards. Viewed broadly, social work has traveled through four major periods, and now needs to embark on a fifth.

The morality period

When social work practice and education began formally in the United States in the late 19th century, many practitioners paid more attention to the values and morality of clients than to the morality or ethics of the profession and social workers themselves. Paternalistic concern about clients' moral virtues and rectitude (especially preventing "waywardness" and responding to "shiftless" tendencies) often dominated social workers' efforts during the Charity Organization Society phase of the profession's history (Brieland, 1995; Leiby, 1985; Lubove, 1965). Scholarly discussions of social work's history typically note practitioners' relatively patronizing and judgmental preoccupation with clients' personal morality.

The values period

A critical mass of scholarship on social work ethics per se did not emerge in the U.S. until the 1950s, although certainly the subject was explored in several earlier publications (Elliott, 1931; Frankel, 1959; Johnson, 1955). After a half-century of development in the U.S., the social work profession began to explore in earnest the development of a core set of nationally endorsed values and ethical standards (Emmett, 1962; Pumphrey, 1959; Varley, 1968). Clearly, the social foment of the 1960s, including intense and widespread focus on social justice issues, inspired a number of social workers to highlight and analyze social work values and construct conceptually-based typologies (Gordon, 1965; Levy, 1976).

In addition to exploring the profession's core values, some of the literature during this period reflected social workers' attempts to examine, clarify, and critique their own personal values and professional practice (Hardman, 1975; McCleod & Meyer, 1967; Varley, 1968). Many social workers developed a rich appreciation of the relationship between their personal values and professional practice, especially with respect to controversial issues such as welfare reform, abortion, homosexuality, substance use and abuse, and race relations.

Ethical theory and decision-making period

In the late 1970s and early 1980s, social workers in the U.S. embarked on another stage in the evolution of professional values and ethics, due largely to the emergence of a new field of applied and professional (or practical) ethics. The applied and professional ethics field began primarily with the development of the bioethics field in the 1970s, when a small group of scholars and practitioners began to explore moral ethical issues in health care. This was a watershed period in the ethics field, in that it entailed, for the first time, the deliberate, systematic, and explicit application of moral philosophy, ethics concepts, and ethical theory to the practical ethical challenges in diverse professions, such as medicine, law, business, journalism, engineering, nursing, the military, psychology, and social work (Chadwick, 1998; Reich, 1995; Sloan, 1980). The emergence of the applied and professional ethics field directly influenced the development of social work ethics. Beginning in the early 1980s, a small number of U.S. social work scholars began writing about ethical issues and dilemmas, drawing in part on literature, concepts, and theories from moral philosophy in general and the newer field of applied and professional ethics (Loewenberg & Dolgoff, 1982; Reamer, 1982; Rhodes, 1986). Using somewhat different approaches, these authors explored the relevance of moral philosophy and ethical theory and concepts to the analysis of ethical dilemmas faced by social workers. Since the early 1980s several social work scholars have developed frameworks for ethical decision-making (Congress, 1998; Linzer, 1999; Reamer, 1999).

Ethical standards and risk-management period

In the early 1990s several social workers began to explore the nature of formal, codified ethical standards in social work and related risk-management issues. One key event was the ratification in 1996 of a new National Association of Social Workers <u>Code of Ethics</u>, only the third code in NASWs history (Reamer, 1998). The complex national process required to develop this new code stimulated widespread discussion and analysis of maturing ethical standards in the profession. Further, the ratification of new ethical standards also led many social work licensing boards to examine and refine their ethical guidelines.

One of the explicit purposes of the new NASW <u>Code of Ethics</u> was to prevent ethics complaints and ethics-related lawsuits, in addition to the primary purpose of protecting social workers' clients. Since the mid-1990s social workers have paid much more attention to ethical issues broached in licensing board complaints and lawsuits filed against social workers (Houston-Vega, , Nuehring, & Daguio, 1997; Reamer, 2003). As a result of practitioners' growing awareness of ethics-related risk management issues, many social work education programs, social service agencies, and professional organizations began to sponsor special training and education on ethical issues with an emphasis on risk management.

AN AGENDA FOR THE FUTURE

One of the outcomes of social workers' increased focus on ethics-related risk-management issues is growing concern that ethics education is now preoccupied with "defensive ethics," that is, teaching social workers about ethical standards primarily to prevent ethics complaints and lawsuits. Understandably, many social workers are concerned that the profession's ethics ballast has shifted from primary concern about protecting clients to primary concern about protecting practitioners.

In my opinion, the principal challenge facing social work in the 21st century is to design and deliver ethics education in a way that retains client well-being as the centerpiece and, in addition, provides appropriate risk-management instruction as an important, but secondary, goal. Toward this end, I claim that ethics education and training – in undergraduate and graduate programs, agency settings, and continuing education curricula – needs to be strengthened considerably to include several core components (Reamer, 2001a):

Values in social work practice

Contemporary ethics education and training should focus especially on the core values and virtues that constitute the profession's moral foundation and mission. In addition to acquainting social workers with traditional social work values (particularly as they are reflected in the profession's literature and the current NASW <u>Code of Ethics</u>), educators and trainers should also encourage practitioners to constructively critique the profession's enduring, shifting, and emerging values. Practitioners must continually examine and critique the validity of social work's values and their relevance to contemporary life.

Further, educators and trainers should highlight values-related concepts from the broader field of applied, practical, and professional ethics. This especially includes study of <u>virtue theory</u>, which entails analysis of core professional virtues such as honesty, respect, trust, fairness, responsibility, autonomy, nonmaleficence, beneficence, justice, fidelity, faithfulness, forgiveness, generosity, compassion, and kindness (Beauchamp & Childress, 2001; MacIntyre, 1981).

Several issues related to social workers' values deserve special attention. First, practitioners sometimes face tension between their own personal values and those held by clients, employers, or the social work profession itself (Goldstein, 1987; Hardman, 1975; Hodge, 2003; Siporin, 1992). Social workers may have strong reactions to the ways in which some clients parent their children, engage in self-destructive behavior, violate the law, or treat spouses or partners. Some social workers object to the profession's official or formal positions on reproductive rights and welfare reform. How social workers respond in these situations – whether they challenge the profession's values stance, share their views with clients, or try to influence clients' behavior and values – depends on practitioners' views about the role of their own personal values and opinions.

A related and critically important issue concerns social workers' values or beliefs with respect to the determinants of clients' problems, such as poverty, unemployment, substance abuse, domestic violence, and emotional distress. Social workers sometimes make values-based assumptions about the causes and malleability of clients' problems and shape interventions accordingly (McDermott, 1975; Reamer, 1983). Practitioners' values in this regard are likely to have important bearing on their response and intervention, that is, the extent to which social workers believe that clients are responsible for their difficulties in life and "deserve" help.

A particular challenge related to values involves practitioners' and clients' religious and spiritual beliefs. On the one hand, social workers are becoming increasingly aware of the importance of religion and spirituality in clients' lives and the need to acknowledge and be sensitive to clients' values and beliefs (Canda & Furman, 1999). Appropriately, spirituality and religion have become critically important issues in professional practice.

On the other hand, social workers must pay close attention to possible ethical challenges involving religion and spirituality. Specific challenges involve social workers' decisions to share and discuss with clients the practitioners' personal beliefs; attempt to influence clients' religious and spiritual beliefs; and participation in religious or spiritual rituals with clients.

Ethical dilemmas

Many ethical issues in social work are not particularly complicated. However, there are many situations where social workers' professional obligations and values are, or appear to be, in conflict, for example, when a client's right to confidentiality or self-determination conflicts with a third party's well being. To enhance social workers' grasp of ethical dilemmas – those instances where professional duties and obligations clash – practitioners should be acquainted with three major themes involving: (1) the delivery of services to individuals, families, couples, and small groups (for example, ethical dilemmas related to limiting clients' right to confidentiality and privacy, interfering with clients' right to self-determination, conflicts of interest, and professional boundaries and dual relationships), (2) "macro" practice involving social policy and planning, administration, community practice, advocacy, supervision, and research and evaluation (for example, social workers' use of deception or coercion for benevolent purposes, decisions about whether to violate an unjust law or regulation, and attempts to allocate scarce agency resources in a just manner); and (3) relationships between social workers and their colleagues (for example, instances when social workers must decide how to respond to impaired colleagues or colleagues' involvement in unethical or illegal activities – the ethics of "whistle blowing").

Ethical decision making

Since the early 1980s, all of the professions have enhanced their understanding of ethical dilemmas and ways for practitioners to address them deliberately and systematically. Consistent with this trend, practitioners have paid increased attention to decision-making steps and protocols they can use when they encounter ethical dilemmas. Typically, these frameworks include a series of conceptually-based steps social workers can follow in their efforts to address and resolve complex ethical challenges (for example, identifying the ethical issues, including the values and duties that conflict; identifying the individuals, groups, and organizations who are likely to be affected by the ethical decision; tentatively identifying the possible courses of action, along with potential benefits and risks; and examining the reasons in favor of and opposed to each course of action, considering practitioners' values, ethical theories and principles, codes of ethics, legal guidelines and regulations, and social work practice theory.

Ethics risk management

In some instances, ethical issues present social workers with more than difficult decisions. At times these issues are accompanied by practical risks – in the form of lawsuits filed against social workers and ethics complaints filed with licensing boards and professional associations – that can threaten practitioners' careers (in extreme cases social workers are charged with criminal offenses, such as insurance fraud, embezzlement, or sexual involvement with a client).

To minimize these risks, social workers should be acquainted with prevailing standards related to professional malpractice, liability, and negligence, particularly as they pertain to common risks involving client rights; confidentiality, privacy, and privileged communication; informed consent; delivery of services and interventions; conflicts of interest; dual relationships and boundaries; defamation of character; documentation; client records; supervision; consultation; client referral; fraud, termination of services and client abandonment; and evaluation and research (Reamer, 2001b).

Special attention should be paid to the issue of impaired social workers. Some ethics complaints and lawsuits are filed because of mistakes, judgment errors, or misconduct engaged in by social workers who are, in some way, impaired. Common forms of impairment – which occurs when social workers are unable or unwilling to adhere to professional standards or are unable to control personal stress and psychological dysfunction – include emotional disability, substance abuse, or severe burnout (Coombs, 2000; Katsavdakis, et al. 2004; Kilburg, Nathan, & Thoreson., 1986). Ideally, social workers would become familiar with the nature of professional impairment and possible causes, warning signs, and practical strategies to prevent, identify, and respond constructively to impairment.

BALANCING VIRTUE ETHICS AND RISK-MANAGEMENT

Social workers' increasingly mature grasp of ethical issues represents one of the most impressive and important developments in the profession's history. Over time, social workers have moved from a relatively paternalistic preoccupation with clients' morality to concern about ethical dilemmas, ethical decision making, and ethics-related risk management.

Most recently, ethics instruction in social work education programs and, especially, continuing education offerings has emphasized ethics risk management in an effort to prevent lawsuits and ethics complaints. Focus on social work's values, ethical dilemmas, and ethical decision making has faded some.

The current emphasis on ethics risk management is understandable, particularly in a litigious culture. However, preoccupation with ethics risk management has the potential to divert social workers from their core mission: to examine and wrestle with ethical issues that affect social workers' ability to "enhance human well-being and help meet the basic human needs of all people, with particular attention to the needs and empowerment of people who are vulnerable, oppressed, and living in poverty" (NASW, 1999). Social workers cannot afford to lose sight of the fact that, first and foremost, their duty is to understand the impact that personal and professional values, ethical dilemmas, and ethical decision making have on their ability to assist people in need. Ethics risk management – while an important and compelling issue – must always be a secondary concern.

Toward this end, I believe the social work profession must recalibrate its focus with respect to values and ethics. It is time to shift the weight of the profession's emphasis back toward issues involving core professional and personal values, ethical dilemmas, and ethical decision making, with an eye toward what social workers need to know in order to serve people in need and carry out the profession's noble mission. Ethics risk management is important, but it is hardly the heart of the matter. After all, social work's raison d'etre is rooted in practitioners' service to others, not to themselves.

References

Beauchamp, T.L. & Childress, J.F. (2001). *Principle of biomedical ethics* (5th ed.). New York: Oxford University Press.

Brieland, D. (1995). Social work practice: History and evolution. In R.L. Edwards (Ed.-in-Chief), *Encyclopedia of social work* (19th ed., Vol. 3, pp. 2247-2258). Washington, DC: NASW Press.

Canda, E., & Furman, L. (1999). *Spiritual diversity in social work practice: The heart of helping.* New York: Free Press.

Chadwick, R. (Ed.-in-Chief). (1998). *Encyclopedia of applied ethics.* San Diego, CA: Academic Press.

Congress, E. (1998). *Social work values and ethics.* Chicago: Nelson-Hall.

Coombs, R. (2000). *Drug-impaired professionals.* Cambridge, MA: Harvard University Press.

Elliott, L.J. (1931). *Social work ethics.* New York: American Association of Social Workers.

Emmett, D. (1962). Ethics and the social worker. *British Journal of Psychiatric Social Work,* 6, 165-172.

Frankel, C. (1959). Social philosophy and the professional education of social workers. *Social Service Review,* 33, 345-359.

Goldstein, H. (1987). The neglected moral link in social work practice. *Social Work,* 32, 181-186.

Gordon, W. (1965). Knowledge and value: Their distinction and relationship in clarifying social work practice. *Social Work,* 10, 32-39.

Hardman, D.G. (1975). Not with my daughter, you don't! *Social Work,* 20, 278-285.

Hodge, D. (2003). Value differences between social workers and members of the working and middle classes. *Social Work,* 48, 107-119.

Houston-Vega, M., Nuehring, E., & Daguio, E. (1997). *Prudent practice: A guide for managing malpractice risk.* Washington, DC: NASW Press.

Johnson, A. (1955). Educating professional social workers for ethical practice. *Social Service Review,* 29, 125-136.

Katsavdakis, K., Gabbard, G., & Athey, G. (2004). Profiles of impaired health professionals. *Bulletin of the Menninger Clinic,* 68, 60-72.

Kilburg, R., Nathan, P., & Thoreson, R. (Eds.). (1986*). Professionals in distress: Issues, syndromes, and solutions in psychology.* Washington, DC: American Psychological Association.

Leiby, J. (1985). Moral foundations of social welfare and social work: A historical review. *Social Work,* 30, 320-330.

Levy, C. (1973). The value base of social work. *Journal of Education for Social Work,* 9, 34-42.

Levy, C. (1976). *Social work ethics.* New York: Human Sciences Press.

Linzer, N. (1999). *Resolving ethical dilemmas in social work practice.* Boston: Allyn and Bacon.

Loewenberg, F., & Dolgoff, R. (1982). *Ethical decisions for social work practice.* Itasca, IL: F.E. Peacock.

Lubove, R. (1965). *The professional altruist: The emergence of social work as a career.* Cambridge, MA: Harvard University Press.

MacIntyre, A. (1981). *After virtue.* South Bend, IN: University of Notre Dame Press.

McCleod, D., & Meyer, H. (1967). A study of values of social workers. In E. Thomas (Ed.), *Behavioral science for social workers* (pp. 401-416). New York: Free Press.

McDermott, F.E. (Ed.). (1975). *Self-determination in social work.* London: Routledge and Kegan Paul.

National Association of Social Workers (1999). *Code of ethics.* Washington, DC: Author.

Pumphrey, M.W. (1959). *The teaching of values and ethics in social work* (Vol. 13). New York: Council on Social Work Education.

Rachels, J. (2002). *The elements of moral philosophy* (4th ed.). New York: McGraw Hill.

Reamer, F.G. (1982). *Ethical dilemmas in social service.* New York: Columbia University Press.

Reamer, F.G. (1983). The free will-determinism debate in social work. *Social Service Review,* 57, 626-644.

Reamer, F.G. (1998). *Ethical standards in social work: A review of the NASW Code of Ethics.* Washington, DC: NASW Press.

Reamer, F.G. (1999). *Social work values and ethics* (2nd ed.). New York: Columbia University Press.

Reamer, F.G. (2001a). *Ethics education in social work.* Alexandria, VA: Council on Social Work Education.

Reamer, F.G. (2001b). *The social work ethics audit: A risk management tool.* Washington, DC: NASW Press.

Reamer, F.G. (2003). *Social work malpractice and liability (*2nd ed.). New York: Columbia University Press.

Reich, W. (Ed.-in-Chief). (1995). *Encyclopedia of bioethics.* New York: Macmillan.

Rhodes, M.L. (1986). *Ethical dilemmas in social work practice.* London: Routledge and Kegan

Paul.

Siporin, M. (1992). Strengthening the moral mission of social work. In P. Reid & P. Popple (Eds.), *The moral purposes of social work* (pp. 71-99). Chicago: Nelson-Hall.

Sloan, D. (1980). The teaching of ethics in the American undergraduate curriculum: 1876-1976. In D. Callahan & S. Bok (Eds.), *Ethics teaching in higher education* (pp. 1-57). New York: Plenum.

Varley, B.K. (1968). Social work values: Changes in value commitments from admission to MSW graduation. *Journal of Education for Social Work, 4*, 67-85.

Author's Note

Address correspondence to: Frederic G. Reamer, Professor, School of Social Work, Rhode Island College, Providence, RI 02908. e-mail: freamer@ric.edu.

THE FUTURE OF GLOBAL SOCIAL WORK

Miriam Potocky-Tripodi
Tony Tripodi

Abstract. *This article addresses social work within the context of internationalism and globalization. Based on an examination of published documents on international social work in the past decade, the authors make an evidence-based projection of what is likely to occur in the future of global social work. Finally, the authors make a social work values-based projection of what should occur.*

Keywords: global, social work, future

INTRODUCTION

During the past twenty-five years, two contemporary forces have impacted the context in which social work is practiced: (1) internationalism, that is, the increasing involvement of society and social work in international activities, and (2) globalization, that is, global interdependence, with its positive and negative consequences for societies. In contemplating the future of global or international social work, at least two possible projections come to mind: what is *likely* to occur (reality), and what *should* occur (ideal). Indeed, the role of social work in the global arena has always been characterized by a disconnection between ideals and reality (this may, of course, characterize many other aspects of social work apart from its global dimension). On one hand, scholars of international social work note the opportunities and indeed the imperative for an international perspective in a globalized society (Healy, 2001; Hokenstad & Midgley, 2004; Ife, 2001). On the other hand, scholars (often the same ones) lament the marginalized position of social work in influencing global affairs. Similarly, calls for increased international content in social work scholarship and education are not uncommon, yet such content remains largely ghettoized to a minority of professional journals, schools, and interested individual practitioners, educators, and researchers.

In recognition of this duality between ideals and reality, in this article we address both types of future projections. The projection of what is likely to occur is derived from social work knowledge; that is, it is evidence-based. The projection of what should occur is derived from social work values.

EVIDENCE BASE: WHAT IS LIKELY TO OCCUR

Prediction of the future from an empirical basis necessitates an examination of the past in order to discern patterns that serve as forecasts. While there are many ways to gather such empirical data, due to resource constraints, we decided to base our analysis on an examination of published documents on international social work over the past decade. Clearly, such an approach has its limitations, in particular, that what is written does not

Miriam Potocky-Tripodi is Associate Professor, School of Social Work, Florida International University, Miami. Toni Tripodi is Dean, College of Social Work, Ohio State University, Columbus.

necessarily reflect what is practiced. Nonetheless, some degree of insight into the future of global social work may be gained from this approach.

We examined four major types of documents on international or global social work: (1) books; (2) policy statements of the International Federation of Social Workers (IFSW); (3) the IFSW Action Plan for 2004-2006; and (4) journal articles on international social work appearing during the past decade. Each of these is addressed below.

Books

A number of books on international or global social work have appeared during the past decade. These include *International Social Work: Professional Action in an Interdependent World* (Healy, 2001); *Lessons from Abroad: Adapting Social Welfare Innovations* (Hokenstad & Midgley, 2004); and *Human Rights and Social Work: Towards Rights-Based Practice* (Ife, 2001).

Healy (2001) provides a definition of international social work as "international professional action and the capacity for international action by the social work profession and its members. International action has four dimensions: internationally related domestic practice and advocacy, professional exchange, international practice, and international policy development and advocacy" (p. 7). Internationally related domestic practice includes working with refugees and immigrants, international populations, international adoptions, and so forth. Professional exchange involves communication of knowledge and sharing of experiences. International practice involves direct work in international agencies, such as relief and disaster work. International policy development and advocacy involves the formulation of policy positions and actions to resolve global social problems. Healy's book addresses each of these issues in detail, with many global examples.

Hokenstad & Midgley (2004) address the challenges and opportunities of globalization and examine the role of social work in this context. The chapters in this edited volume provide examples of social policies and programs from other countries that can be used as models in the United States. Thus, this book is a direct example of the international professional exchange described by Healy.

Ife (2001) provides a conceptualization of social work as a human rights profession. Grounded in the fact that human rights are universal, this therefore means that social work must have a global or international perspective. Throughout the book, Ife provides many examples of how rights-based practice is affected by global interdependence. He addresses three generations of human rights (civil and political rights; economic, social, and cultural rights; and collective rights) and describes how social work interfaces with these in both theory and practice.

Together, these representative books demonstrate an increasing recognition within the profession to the issues of global or international practice.

IFSW Policy Statements

"The International Federation of Social Workers (IFSW) is a global organization striving for social justice, human rights and social development through the development of social work, best practices and international cooperation between social workers and their professional organizations" (IFSW, 2004a, p. 1). This organization has issued fourteen policy statements for the purposes of "address[ing] some basic concepts from a social work perspective" and "provid[ing] social workers globally with practical as well as philosophical guidelines on a number of particular issues" (IFSW, 2004b, p. 1). The fourteen topics are:

1. Health
2. HIV/AIDS
3. Human rights
4. Migration
5. Older persons
6. The protection of personal information
7. Refugees
8. Conditions in rural communities
9. Women
10. Youth
11. Peace and Social Justice
12. Displaced persons
13. Globalization and the environment
14. Indigenous people

Presumably, the choice of these fourteen particular issues can be taken as a reflection of what the global representatives of the profession collectively consider to be the major social challenges facing the international community now and in the near future.

IFSW Action Plan for 2004-2006. This plan (IFSW, 2004c) addresses nine goals for IFSW as a whole:

1. The IFSW has a contemporary, well-researched and articulated policy position on critical social issues and matters central to social justice and the aims of IFSW.

2. The IFSW has a human rights orientation for all its activities.

3. Social work practice is governed by an internationally-recognized and accepted statement of Ethical Principles and Code of Ethical Conduct.

4. Establish an organizational structure which is contemporary, transparent, democratic, and best meets the needs of the IFSW and its membership.

5. Ensure the effective and efficient management of the federation's finances.

6. Develop, publish, and maintain high quality publications serving practice and information needs of members and the international social work community.

7. Increase the access of individuals and other interested groups to the work of IFSW.

8. Represent the profession and IFSW on an international level by establishing relations with relevant and key international organizations.

9. Seek strategic partnerships that will assist IFSW in strengthening the voice of social work.

As can be seen, about half of these goals (i.e., 4, 5, 7, 8, 9) are concerned with the maintenance and promotion of the organization itself, rather than directly addressing the social problems of the world. However, it is not known what amount of time and effort the organization expends on each of the goals. In may be that indeed most of the work does go into those goals directly addressing global problems.

Journal Articles

We conducted a content analysis of article abstracts that were retrieved from the Social Work Abstracts database for the period 1995-2004, using the key term "international social work" in any search field. This yielded 279 articles (excluding editorials and commentaries). (A search using the term "global social work" yielded only 9 articles, all of which were also retrieved in the prior search). Clearly, this search method excludes some relevant articles and includes some irrelevant ones. Again, resource constraints played a role in this decision.

We coded all the abstracts in five content areas: (1) topic; (2) level of practice; (3) whether the article concerned one or more than one country; (4) the region of the world that the article addressed; and (5) the research methodology used. The results are presented below.

Topic

For purposes of convenience, the topic areas used by the Society for Social Work and Research (2004) to identify members' research interests were used to categorize the abstracts. The results are shown in Table 1. As can be seen, the highest numbers of articles addressed social work education and social work practice. These two topics together accounted for almost 30% of all the articles. In the area of social work education, the articles typically concerned the development of social work education programs in various countries, particularly those that were recently formed democracies (i.e., the former Soviet Union, Eastern Europe, and South Africa). Other education-focused articles addressed student and faculty exchanges between countries, and the inclusion of international content into existing curricula. In the area of social work practice, most of the articles addressed the role of the social work profession in various countries.

All of the other topic areas were substantially less represented. Among these, the most frequently appearing were child welfare; immigrants; international social work; poverty and social/economic development; and women's issues. However, each of these had less than half the articles as were devoted to social work education or practice. Thus, similar to the IFSW Action Plan, the published scholarship on international social work appears to be focused somewhat more on the maintenance of the profession (including education for the profession) rather than on addressing global social problems themselves. In general, the fourteen topics identified earlier by the IFSW policy statements are minimally represented in the published social work literature of the past decade.

We further examined these data year by year to determine whether there were any changes in topic frequency over time (i.e., increases, decreases, or cycles). No such changes were readily apparent. Thus, a continued pattern of steady maintenance within each topic area would be expected in the future.

Table 1. Topic areas in articles on international social work, 1995-2004.

Topic	n (%)
Social work education	44 (16)
Social work practice	36 (13)
Child welfare	19 (7)
Immigrants	19 (7)
International social work	17 (6)
Poverty/development	16 (6)
Women's issues	15 (5)
Mental health treatment and services	14 (5)
Ethnic minority groups	12 (4)
Civil society	11 (4)
Social policy	10 (4)
Social work research and scholarship	9 (3)
Health and illness	7 (3)
Spirituality	7 (3)
Aging	4 (1)
Drug use/abuse	4 (1)
Ethical issues	4 (1)
Cultural competence	3 (1)
Domestic violence	3 (1)
HIV/AIDS	3 (1)
Community development	3 (1)
Criminal justice system	2 (1)
Homelessness and housing	2 (1)
Theory	2 (1)
Violence in communities	2 (1)
Environment	2 (1)
Military	2 (1)
Adolescent delinquency	1 (0)
Disability	1 (0)

Level of Practice

Social work practice in the United States has been criticized by some for straying from its roots and overly focusing on micro practice, an approach that is seen as irrelevant to most of the rest of the world. We therefore examined the extent to which the selected abstracts addressed micro (individuals, families, small groups), meso (organizations, service delivery systems, communities), or macro (nations, policies) practice. As seen in Table 2, the overemphasis on micro practice that dominates in the U.S. is not evident in the international literature. There was an approximately equal number of micro- and macro-focused studies, and a large number of studies that addressed all or none of the levels (for example, generic studies on social work education were coded into this category). Meso practice was the least represented.

Country and Region

As seen in Table 2, sixty percent of the studies concerned only one country and the remainder concerned more than one. Many of the former could not really be considered "international social work" according to the definition given earlier, even though they were retrieved under that search term. That is, they involved strictly domestic practice, not internationally related domestic practice as previously defined. The articles were fairly evenly distributed across the regions of the world, with the exception of the Latin American/Caribbean region, which had relatively few articles.

Table 2. Characteristics of articles on international social work, 1995-2004.

Characteristic	n (%)
Level of Practice	
Micro	76 (28)
Meso	26 (10)
Macro	73 (27)
All/none	95 (35)
Country	
1 country	158 (60)
2 or more countries	105 (40)
Region	
Africa	27 (10)
Asia/Pacific	54 (19)
Europe	40 (14)
Latin America/Caribbean	14 (5)
North America	39 (14)
Middle East	36 (13)
All/None	71 (25)
Research Method	
Conceptual	126 (47)
Survey	67 (25)
Case study	54 (20)
Phenomenology	6 (2)
Program evaluation	5 (2)
Ethnography	4 (1)
Content analysis	4 (1)
Grounded theory	1 (0)
Narrative	1 (0)
Instrumentation	1 (0)

Research Methods

The research methods utilized in the articles were coded according to a list of methods used by the Society for Social Work and Research (2004). The category of "conceptual" was added to the list of empirical methods. As seen in Table 2, almost half the articles were conceptual rather than empirical. Among the empirical articles, by far the most dominant methods were the survey and the case study. The latter were not clinical case studies, but organizational, community, and country case studies.

WHAT IS LIKELY TO OCCUR

Newton's first law of motion states that a moving object will continue on its established path unless acted upon by an outside force; this is known as the law of inertia. The same principle applies to social phenomena. Thus, the evidence reviewed in this article suggests that, in the absence of outside forces – i.e., unforeseen events or intentional actions – global social work will continue into the future along the same pathways that have been followed over the past decade. Specifically:

1. *There will continue to be an increased interest in the impact of globalization and internationalism upon social work, and continued arguments for the inclusion of global and international perspectives.* This is evidenced by the recent books on the topic.

2. *Much of the literature will continue to be preoccupied with issues of professional education, roles, and identity.* This is suggested by the evidence from the journal articles showing that about one-third of the articles in the past decade focused on these issues.

3. *The social problems of the world will continue to be addressed largely within national borders, rather than globally.* This is likely because although two-thirds of the articles in the past decade did address substantive social problems, many of them did not examine these problems from an international perspective. In other words, they focused on the problems within their countries rather than placing the problems in a context of internationally related domestic practice, professional exchange, international practice, or international policy development.

4. *The international association representing social workers will continue to devote a not insubstantial amount of its efforts toward its own organizational maintenance.* This is because the IFSW Action Plan has more than half of its organizational goals devoted to these issues.

This forecast is based on the empirical evidence derived from the methods described earlier. Naturally, these methods do not provide a complete picture. For example, since the review of journal articles was limited to the past decade, there remains the possibility that some meaningful change in article content has occurred in the past decade in relation to earlier ones. It is also possible that practitioners within countries do indeed make practice decisions that are informed by social work in other countries, but if so, these experiences are not widely documented in the literature that was accessed. Finally, it is also possible that the observed focus on educational and professional issues has been a necessary precursor to real social work action, which will now occur.

VALUE BASE: WHAT SHOULD OCCUR

In contrast to what is likely to occur, well-established social work values of human rights and social justice as articulated and advocated by the IFSW dictate that social workers should take direct actions to address global social problems. The definition of social work recently adopted by IFSW (2000) states that, "The social work profession promotes social change, problem solving in human relationships and the empowerment and liberation of people to enhance well-being.... Principles of human rights and social justice are fundamental to social work" (p. 1). From this it follows that the purpose of social work is to improve social problems; therefore, global social work should have as its primary aim the alleviation of global problems, rather than the current apparent aims as previously described – i.e., issues of professional education, identity, and maintenance. Further, since human rights violations and social injustices are global, rather than local, problems, all social workers should consider the international dimensions of their practice. Thus, the following are some actions that should occur in the future of global social work:

1. *A global perspective should inform all social work practice.* It should be evident that social problems in one country have their counterparts, causes, and/or effects elsewhere in the world. Practice that is informed by events elsewhere is more likely to be effective than practice conducted in isolation. For example, consider a social worker addressing the problem of disproportionately high rates of HIV infection among Black women in the United States. Certainly, this scenario has its counterparts elsewhere in the world, such as Africa. Social technologies for decreasing infection within these two regions would provide useful lessons to each other, if for no other reason than not to reinvent the wheel. Further, the problem clearly has global causes and effects. Among one of the causes is the use of illicit intravenous drugs among these women's male sex partners. These drugs, in turn, are imported from other world regions, which in turn export these products in order to generate revenue for their economies, which in turn are constrained from development by policies and practices of intergovernmental organizations and multinational corporations, and so on. Among the global effects of the problem is lost productivity among these women, which affects the local economy and in turn the global one. Thus, failure to target interventions to any of these multiple inputs and outputs would be tantamount to failure to address the problem at all, since the cycle would be perpetuated. An analogous scenario of interconnected causes and effects can be constructed for virtually any social problem faced by any nation.

2. *The professional organizations and professional literature should focus on developing solutions to the world's major social problems, particularly the fourteen topics identified in the IFSW policy statements.* As noted, much of the reviewed literature focused on peripheral issues rather than direct action to improve social problems. If global social work is to undertake more direct work, it seems reasonable to begin by focusing on those areas that have al-

ready been identified as important by the profession's elected global leaders. As well, any casual perusal of any newspaper will reveal that the fourteen identified topics pose significant social concerns facing the world.

3. *Social workers who utilize knowledge from other countries should document the process and outcomes of their work, in easily accessible forums (e.g., a centralized Internet resource).* As previously noted, it is possible, and indeed seems likely, that much global social work is occurring but is either not documented or not readily accessible. Thus, all social workers should heed the ethical mandate, present in some national codes of ethics, to contribute to the knowledge base. For example, the U.S. National Association of Social Workers Code of Ethics (2005) states that "Social workers should promote and facilitate evaluation and research to contribute to the development of knowledge" (Sec. 5.02b). Production of knowledge is only one part of its adoption, however; it must also be easily accessible. For example, the IFSW publishes "Social Work Around the World" (2004d), which appears to be a potentially rich information resource. However, the text is not available in an on-line format, nor is it available in the authors' institutional libraries. Thus, access to the knowledge therein would require a personal expenditure and a wait (likely several weeks) for delivery. While this would not cause a hardship for the present authors, it almost certainly would for many other social workers around the world. Thus, a centralized Internet resource would solve some (although certainly not all) knowledge accessibility barriers.

4. *Social work researchers should focus more on determining what interventions (macro, meso, and micro) work for whom under what conditions, through methods of policy, program, and practice evaluation.* Since direct action to improve social problems is the primary aim of social work, clearly knowledge is needed about how best to do so. Yet, only 2% of the articles reviewed herein were program evaluations, and none were policy or practice evaluations. The need for more evidence-based knowledge is evident.

References

Healy, L. M. (2001). *International social work: Professional action in an interdependent world.* New York: Oxford University Press.

Hokenstad, M. C., & Midgley, J. (2004). *Lessons from abroad: Adapting international social welfare innovations.* Washington, DC: NASW Press.

Ife, J. (2001). *Human rights and social work: Towards rights-based practice.* Cambridge, UK: Cambridge University Press.

International Federation of Social Workers (2000). *Definition of social work.* Retrieved December 8, 2004 from www.ifsw.org.

International Federation of Social Workers (2004a). *Welcome to IFSW.* Retrieved January 4, 2005 from www.ifsw.org.

International Federation of Social Workers (2004b). *Policy statements and other documents.* Retrieved

ADVANCES IN SOCIAL WORK 6(1), Spring 2005

December 8, 2004 from www.ifsw.org.

International Federation of Social Workers (2004c). *IFSW Action Plan 2004-2006: Draft.* Retrieved December 8, 2004 from www.ifsw.org.

International Federation of Social Workers (2004d). *Social Work Around the World III.* www.ifsw. org.

National Association of Social Workers (2005). *Code of Ethics.* Washington, DC: Author. Retrieved May 9, 2005 from www.socialworkers.org.

Society for Social Work and Research (2004). *SSWR Membership Information Update Form.* Retrieved December 8, 2004 from www.sswr.org.

Author's Note

Correspondence should be addressed to Miriam Potocky-Tripodi, School of Social Work, Florida International University, University Park, HLS-II, Miami, FL 33199; e-mail potockym@fiu.edu.

THE FUTURE OF MULTICULTURAL SOCIAL WORK
Rowena Fong

Abstract: *Multicultural social work has been evolving over the last forty years despite challenges in limited knowledge, insufficient resources, and inadequate infusion into the curriculum. Discussions continue about appropriate conceptual frameworks, culturally sensitive terms, traditional and indigenous practice approaches and treatments, and relevant outcome measures and evaluation methods. Future directions foster the inclusion of cultural values as strengths. Intersectionality guides practice approaches and systems of care. Service learning requirements, national ethnic resource centers, and ethnic studies dual degree programs are innovative initiatives yet to be fully integrated into social work curriculum.*

Keywords: immigrants, refugees, intersectionality, biculturalization of interventions

INTRODUCTION

Multicultural social work has been evolving over the last 40 years since the Council on Social Work Education, in the 1960's, set forth standards of nondiscrimination in schools of social work (Newsome, 2004). Over time the struggle has been to establish cultural diversity requirements in the schools of social work, despite encountering the challenges of limited knowledge, insufficient resources, inadequate infusion, inconsistent application, and resistance from administrators and educators who do not fully support building curriculum on minority groups of color (Newsome, 2004; Gutierrez, Zuniga, & Lum, 2004). However, since social work is a profession committed to oppressed populations and social justice issues, the advances in multicultural social work education during this era are noteworthy.

Terms and definitions related to multicultural social work have evolved. In the 1970's the dual perspective (Norton, 1978) challenged the notion that there was only one way of viewing things—that the perspective of minority persons of color does differ from the majority worldview. In the 1980's the concept of the cross-cultural system of care (Cross, Bazron, Dennis, & Issacs, 1989) forced social work providers and agencies at the macro level of practice to take into account ethnic minority clients' needs and offer culturally appropriate treatments across different systems of care in the various human service disciplines and organizations (Delgado, 1998; Lecca, Quervalu, Nunes, & Gonzales, 1998). In the 1990's the notion of cultural competence (Fong & Furuto, 2001; Lum, 2003; Sue, Arredondo, & McDavis, 1992) closely examined the characteristics of the social worker's self-awareness, ethnic sensitivity, and approach to practice (Devore & Schlesinger, 1999; Fong, Boyd, & Browne, 1999). It also forced practitioners to review the appropriateness of treatments to see if they reflected the cultural values and indigenous interventions of the ethnic minority populations served (Fong, Boyd, & Browne, 1999).

Discussions continue about appropriate conceptual frameworks, culturally sensitive

Rowena Fong is Professor and Director, Center for Asian American Studies, School of Social Work, University of Texas Austin, Austin, TX 78712.

terms, definitions, and assessments, indigenous micro-, mezzo- and macro- practice approaches, and relevant outcome measures and evaluation methods (Fong & Furuto, 2001; Guadalupe & Lum, 2005). Newsome (2004) summarizes the state of the art in dilemmas still confronting multicultural social work, "Although identified as important more than 2 decades ago, multicultural education and competence remain a hot topic for the new millennium. While every author or educator may not agree on how this process should be carried out, most concur that it is important for the helping professional" (p. 5).

CURRENT CONTEXT

American society is becoming increasing multiracial with growing immigrant and refugee groups (Balgopal, 2000; Fong, 2004; Delgado, Jones, & Rohani, 2005; Segal, 2002). Census data for the year 2000 identify the number of nonwhites in the United States in the year 2000 as 211, 460, 626 total white, including Hispanic / Latino (U.S.Census Bureau, 2000). Foreign-born individuals now constitute 1 out of 10 members of the population in the United States, with the largest growing population Latino and Mexican Americans (Zuniga, 2004).

This rise of ethnic diversity in the population has forced social workers to increase their knowledge base about peoples and countries outside of the United States. Interpreters and translations are routinely included in assessment tools and ways of interviewing clients. Despite limited resources, services have been expanded to include undocumented immigrants, refugees, asylees, unaccompanied refugee minors, and victims of human trafficking (Busch, Fong, & Williamson, 2004; Potocky-Tripodi, 2002; Webb, 2001).

Poverty, lack of financial and social supports, tendencies towards substance abuse and domestic violence plague these families (Cohen, 2000; Ewalt, Freeman, Kirk, & Poole, 1996). Immigrants and refugees join an already economically challenged population of American-born ethnic minority families (Choi, 2001; Fong, 2004; Dhooper & Moore, 2001). Underemployment, racial profiling, glass ceiling discriminations, and model minority stereotypes are also often problematic for American-born families of color who are middle class and part of the workforce (Kivisto & Rundblad, 2000; See, 1998).

Problem-solving approaches to these issues may preclude natural and indigenous ways of handling problems in each ethnic group's context. Evidenced-based practices, while important to ascertain effective outcomes, may not include strategies recognizing shamans, acupuncture, and peyote as valid treatments or acceptable social services (Choi, 2001; Jung, 1998; Weaver, 2005). These are only a few of the current unresolved dilemmas still inadequately addressed in the area of multicultural social work..

FUTURE DIRECTIONS

We can build on these 40 years of progress as we advance the issues of multicultural social work in years to come. In the next quarter century attention needs to be focused more intensively on the complex diversity of the makeup and identity of the multicultural people served (Rockquemore & Brunsma, 2002; Winters, & DeBose, 2003). Assessments and interventions need to be better integrated with clients' cultural values and indigenous practices (Fong, Boyd, & Browne, 1999; Fong, 2004; Webb, 2001). Evaluations of practices need to be more creative in allowing for natural helping processes used in the ethnic communities. Finally, better linkages need to occur between the systems of services and among the educators, practitioners, and researchers who interact with these diverse groups (Guadalupe & Lum, 2005; Fong, McRoy, & Ortiz Hendricks, in press).

Complex Diversity of Multicultural Persons

Multicultural, for the sake of this discussion, focuses mainly on race and ethnicity although the characteristics related to gender, sexual orientation, social class, and religion are also important as intersecting variables. In defining multicultural one must, in addition, note the between-group differences and within-group differences in ethnic groups. Historically people of color were divided into white and non-white. The recent Census of 2000 offers six race categories with an option for "two or more races" (p.1), which allows for those who are mixed or multiracial persons to self-classify their identification (U.S. Census, Bureau, 2000; Winters & DeBose, 2003). The identity of the multicultural individuals warrants much more attention since clients are frequently classified into convenience categories, heedless of complexities, resulting in a social work practice process, which lends itself to result in poor and inaccurate assessments and interventions.

Ethnic groups themselves embody variations, as between African Americans, Asian and Pacific Islander Americans, Latino and Mexican Americans, and First Nations Peoples and Native Americans (Delgado, 1998; Fong, 2001; See, 1998; Weaver, 2005). Within the Asian American group alone are East Asians (Chinese, Japanese, Korean, Filipinos), South Asians (Indian, Pakistani, Bangladeshi), and Southeast Asians (Vietnamese, Cambodians, Laotians, Thai, Burmese, Malaysians and Indonesians) and in each of these sub-groups are further—often quite radical—distinctions.

Immigrants and refugees are a growing population differentiated by their statuses, such as documented or undocumented, asylee, and unaccompanied refugee minor (Busch, Fong, & Williams, 2004; Delgado, Jones, & Rohani, 2005). The human trafficking situation compounds the issue when the victim is incorrectly labeled as illegal rather than treated with the protective rights due her or him (Busch, Fong, & Williams, 2004). Even the American-born children of such families are still very tied to homelands with transnational issues compounded by generational issues.

The distinctions between American-born, immigrant and refugee (Fong & Mokuau, 1994) are likely to become increasingly critical, and assessments, interventions, and evaluations will have to reflect this complexity. As for any other client, ethnicity, race, and status are to be taken into account, along with social class, gender, sexual orientation and religion. In sum, there are many more, and more complex, variables to consider in understanding the multicultural client than social work practitioners may be accustomed to.

Assessments and Interventions with Cultural Values and Indigenous Practices

Theoretical frameworks, which guide the practice of doing assessments and implementing interventions, will have to be changed beyond the more commonly used strengths perspective (Saleeby, 1997) and ecological model (Germain, 1979). Social environments of origin are affecting the human behaviors of our clients and more attention is needed for culturally diverse human behaviors and social environments (Fong, 2004). Additional theory building is needed to reflect the multicultural social environments, especially of the homelands, from which many immigrants and refugees come.

Cultural values (Lum, 2003; Fong, 1999) are important assets and resources to multicultural clients. These have routinely been ignored in the intake and investigative assessment processes of social work. Fong, Boyd, and Browne (1999) advocate using cultural values as strengths and assets to be assessed and used in treatment planning and intervention implementation. They also write of the need for culturally competent interventions using the biculturalization of interventions, which combine indigenous practices with western interventions.

Evaluation of Practice and Natural Helping Processes

By incorporating more indigenous treatments and interventions, the evaluation system of practice needs to be carefully chosen and often times modified to accurately measure the effectiveness of these nontraditional practices. Delgado (1998) writes, "These principles reinforce the importance of flexibility, innovation, and the critical role "nontraditional setting play in the lives of Latino elders" (p.33). He cites Heath and McLaughlin (1993) who "validate these perspectives: 'Effective programs often provide activities in nontraditional settings, at nontraditional hours, and with nontraditional personnel, and pay little attention to orthodox boundaries of this service sector, bureaucratic compartments, or professional parameters. The program and the terms on which they are offered take their shape from the needs and contexts of those with whom they work rather than from bureaucratic guidelines, accountability precepts, or objectives formulated at geographic and culturally remove from the local contexts...."(p.62). Delgado (1998) concludes "Researchers must be prepared to engage in activities and enter arenas/settings that are totally new to them!" (p. 33).

Linkages Between Systems of Services

Because the problems for multicultural clients are becoming more complex, the social service delivery system can no longer afford to not collaborate more intensively and extensively. For example, problems in child welfare regularly overlap with issues in substance abuse, domestic violence, or mental health (Straussner, 2001; Fong, McRoy, Ortiz Hendricks, in press). Since the child welfare system serves a disproportionate number of African American children (McRoy & Vick, in press) and the need for kinship care is evolving, sustaining partnerships must be developed between social work practitioners in child development, child welfare, gerontology, substance abuse, domestic violence, and mental health.

A developing concept and practice of linking these systems is intersectionality. Fong (2004) writes about culturally competent contextual social work practice and intersectionality. She advocates the need take all the informal and formal services used to help multicultural clients and use an intersectionality framework, which includes cultural values, biculturalization of interventions, indigenous helping strategies, and nontraditional practices and services as guideposts to link the services. Lum (2003) speaks of internal and external intersectionality, focusing on individuals, families and social group memberships, which are interconnected and interrelated. Intersectionality needs to be adopted as the standard approach to offering services and linking systems integrally and consistently.

Linkages Among Educators, Practitioners, and Researchers

Educators, practitioners, and researchers in social work need to have better linkages than what currently exists. This can be done through requiring service learning projects, strengthening affiliations with national ethnic research centers, and developing joint degree programs between social work and ethnic studies.

Service learning is a means by which students, from elementary school level to higher education, can be educated and serve the community. The National Service Learning Clearinghouse offer resources to students, faculty, practitioners, community leaders, policy makers, and researchers in various areas in which students can be involved in communities outside the classroom and receive educational credit. Unlike field practicums and volunteer placements, service learning requirements in the classroom force instructor and student to engage in critical thinking dialogue during the service learning experience. Teachers can immediately integrate the community learning experiences into discussions, assignments in class. Student, teacher, and agency practitioner are all concurrently responsible for the students' learning. This integrative approach is necessary with multicultural clients and reflects intersectionality of classroom and community.

Besides service learning requirements in social work courses focused on multicultural clients, another way to link educators, practitioners, and researchers is to develop or strengthen the affiliations to the national ethnic research centers. Social work departments should have collaborations doing joint research projects with ethnic research centers such as, the National Resource Center for Asian American Mental Health at the University of California at Davis or the Center for African and African American Studies at The University of Texas at Austin, or the University of Kansas's Center for Indigenous Nations Studies. National social work research societies, such as the Society for Social Work Research (SSWR) and the Institute for the Advancement of Social Work Research (IASWR) should continue to seek and develop ongoing research collaborations with the national ethnic research centers.

A final suggestion for future developments in multicultural social work education is for schools of social work to develop degree programs with ethnic studies departments. Social work has successfully established many collaborative degree programs between professional schools of law, business, public health, and religion. But what are yet to be explored are joint programs between social work and ethnic studies. There are many undergraduate and graduate degree granting ethnic studies programs on campuses throughout the United States. Both ethnic studies and social work believe in tenets of social justice, activism and advocacy. Linking social work with ethnic studies makes for a better informed, stronger educator, practitioner, or researcher ready to be involved in social justice issues concerning the multicultural clients.

CONCLUSION

Multicultural social work has progressed in the last 40 years but must yet move deeper into acknowledging the complexity of the populations and using the correct terminology, which reflects the multicultural clients' differential statuses and identities.

Assessments and interventions need to incorporate more indigenous cultural values and natural helping modalities. Field components need to develop more multicultural settings and integrate international placements as a normal part of field and classroom teaching. Social systems of care need to always include the intersections of agencies rather than the current approach of operating in isolation. Linkages between education, practice, and research are going to require more of an emphasis on using the multicultural client as the main guide and informant.

Creative collaborations need to occur between schools of social work, national ethnic research centers, and ethnic studies departments. Clients have been the persons acted upon – that role needs to be reversed so that multicultural clients become co-consultants in assessments, interventions and evaluations. Multiculturalism, in brief, needs to be more of an equal playing field. The diversity of the population, with growing numbers of immigrants, refugees and interracial marriages, is going to mandate that social work education move to another model of perspective-taking. Fong (2001) proposes a shift toward making indigenous and traditional "cultural values the foundation of performing assessments, implementing interventions, and conducting evaluations. It also requires a biculturalization or multiculturalization of practice methods, incorporating the norms and practices of the appropriate ethnic groups, which will then be supplemented by Euro-practices. This is the shift in perspective that needs to guide the development on cultural competency as the helping professions move into the twenty-first century" (p.7).

References

Balgopal., P. (Ed.). (2000). *Social work practice with immigrants and refugees.* New York, NY: Columbia University Press.

Busch, N. & Fong, R. & Williamson, J. (2004). Human trafficking and domestic violence: Comparisons in research methodology needs and strategies. *The Journal of Social Work Research and Evaluation. 5, 2,* 137-148.

Choi, N. (Ed.). (2001). *Psychosocial aspects of the Asian-American experience: Diversity within diversity.* New York, NY: The Haworth Press.

Cohen, N. (Ed.). (2000). *Child welfare: A multicultural focus.* Boston, MA: Allyn and Bacon.

Cross, T.,Bazron, B., Dennis, K., & Issacs, M. (1989). *Towards a culturally competent system of care.* Washington, D.C.: CASSP Technical Assistance Center.

Delgado, M. (1998). *Social services in Latino communities: Research and strategies.* New York, NY: The Haworth Press.

Delgado, M., Jones, K., Rohani, M. (2005). *Social work practice with refugee and immigrant youth in the United States.* Boston, MA: Allyn and Bacon.

Dhooper, S. & Moore, S. (2001). *Social work practice with culturally diverse people.* Thousand Oaks, CA: Sage.

Devore, W. & Schlesinger, E. (1999). *Ethnic-sensitive social work practice.* (5th ed.). Boston, MA: Allyn and Bacon.

Ewalt, P., Freeman, E., Kirk, S., & Poole, D. (Eds.). (1996). *Multicultural issues in social work.*

Washington, D.C.: NASW Press.

Fong, R. (2001). Culturally competent social work practice: Past and present. In R. Fong & S. Furuto (Eds.). *Culturally competent practice: Skills, interventions, and evaluations.* (pp. 7). Boston, MA:Allyn and Bacon.

Fong, R. (Ed.). (2004). *Culturally competent practice with immigrant and refugee children and families.* New York, NY: Guilford Press.

Fong, R., Boyd, T. & Browne, C. (1999). The Gandhi technique: A biculturalizationapproach for empowering Asian and Pacific Islander families. *Journal of Multicultural Social Work. 7,* 95-110.

Fong, R. & Furuto, S. (Eds.). (2001). *Culturally competent practice: Skills, Interventions, and Evaluations.* Boston, MA: Allyn and Bacon.

Fong, R., McRoy, R. & Ortiz Hendricks, C. (Eds.). (in press). *Intersecting child welfare, substance abuse, and family violence: Culturally competent approaches.* Alexandria, VA: Council on Social Work Education.

Fong, R., & Mokuau, N. (1994). Social work periodical literature review of Asians and Pacific Islanders. *Social Work, 39*(3), 298-312.

Germain, C. (1979). *Social work practice: People and environments.* New York: Columbia University Press.

Guadalupe, K. & Lum, D. (2005). (Eds.). *Multidimensional contextual practice: Diversity and transcendence.* Belmont, CA: Brooks/Cole.

Gutierrez, L., Zuniga, M., & Lum, D. (2004). (Eds.). *Education for multicultural social work practice: Critical viewpoints and future directions.* Alexandria, VA: Council on Social Work Education.

Heath S. & McLaughlin, M. (1993). Identity and inner-city youth: Beyond ethnicity and gender. *New York:Teachers College Press.*

Jung, M. (1998). *Chinese American family therapy.* San Francisco, CA: Jossey Bass Publishers.

Kivisto, P. & Rundblad, G. (Eds.). (2000). *Multiculturalism in the United States: Current issues, contemporary voices.* Thousand Oaks, CA: Pine Forge Press.

Lecca, P. Quervalu, I., Nunes, J., & Gonzales, H. (1998). *Cultural competency in health, social, and human services: Directions for the twenty-first century.* New York, NY: Garland Publishing, Inc.

Lum, D. (Ed.). (2003). *Culturally competent practice: A framework for understanding diverse groups and justice issues.2nd Ed.* Pacific Grove, CA: Brooks/Cole.

McRoy, R. & Vick, J. (in press). Intersecting child welfare, substance abuse and domestic violence In R. Fong, R., R. McRoy, & C. Ortiz Hendricks. (Eds.). *Intersecting child welfare, substance abuse, and family violence: Culturally competent approaches.* Alexandria, VA: Council on Social Work Education.

Newsome, Jr., M. (2004). Analysis of past and present movements in cultural competence theory and practice knowledge in social work education. In L. Gutierrez, M. Zuniga, & D. Lum, (Eds.). *Education for multicultural social work Practice: Critical views and future directions.* (pp.3-18). Alexandria, VA: Council on Social Work Education.

Norton, D. (1978). *The dual perspective.* New York: Council on Social Work Education.

Potocky-Tripodi, M. (2002). *Best social work practice with refugees and immigrants.* New York, NY: Columbia University Press.

Rockquemore, K. & Brunsma, D. (2002). *Beyond black: Biracial identity in America.* Thousand Oaks, CA: Sage Press.

See, L. (Ed.). (1998) *Human Behavior in the social environment from an African American perspective.* New York, NY: The Haworth Press.

Segal, U. (2002). *A framework of immigration: Application to Asians in the United States.* New York,

NY: Columbia University Press.

Saleebey, D. (Ed.). (1997). *The strengths perspective in social work practice.* (2ⁿᵈ ed.). New York: Longman.

Straussner, S. (Ed.). (2001). *Ethnocultural factors in substance abuse treatment.* New York, NY: The Guilford Press.

Sue, D., Arredondo, P., & McDavis, R. (1992). Multicultural counseling competencies and standards: A call to the profession. *Journal of Counseling and Development. 70*, 477-486.

U.S. Census Bureau. (2000). *Methodology and assumptions for the populations projections of the United States. 1999-2100.* Washington, D.C.:Author.

Weaver, H. (2005). *Explorations in cultural competence.* Belmont, CA: Brooks/Cole

Webb, N. (Ed.). (2001). *Culturally diverse parent-child and family relationships.* New York, NY: Columbia University.

Winters, L. & DeBose, H. (2003). *New faces in a changing America: Multiracial identity in the 21st century.* Thousand Oaks, CA: Sage Publishers.

Zuniga, M. (2004). Latino children and families. In R. Fong. (Ed.). (2004). *Culturally competent practice with immigrant and refugee children and families.* (pp.183-201). New York, NY: Guilford Press.

Author's Note

Address correspondence to: Rowena Fong PhD, University of Texas, School of Social Work, 1 University Station D3500, Austin, TX 78712-0358. e-mail: rfong@mail.utexas.edu

THE FUTURE OF MACRO SOCIAL WORK
F. Ellen Netting

Abstract: *Macro social work is social work. History tells us that the profession was birthed from diverse traditions in which relief work, reform work, and radical work interfaced. Yet different traditions were grounded in different assumptions, spurring different ways of knowing and doing. This versatility is a hallmark of the field and it will serve macro social work well into the future. A profession that seeks to sustain, advocate and change, with the intent of increasing quality of life, will always need practitioners who can recognize diverse worldviews, understand multi-layered contexts, deal with limitless inter-connections, and be invigorated by conflict.*

Keywords: Advocacy, Change, Sustainability, Quality of Life, Multiparadigmatic practice

INTRODUCTION

Macro social work *is* social work. A profession that defines itself as based in a person-in-environment perspective is "macro" because the larger environment must be considered in every practice decision-making process. A professional education is "macro" when its' purpose is "to prepare competent and effective professionals, to develop social work knowledge, and to provide leadership in the development of social delivery systems" (CSWE, 2001), encouraging expansion "beyond interpersonal direct practice foci" (Wagner, Newcomb, & Weiler, 2001, p. 114). Therefore, the future of macro social work lies with every person who carries the title of social worker regardless of setting or role.

For the purposes of this article, macro social work is defined as *efforts within and outside organizational, community and policy arenas intended to sustain, change, and advocate for quality of life.* These efforts are "in concert with vulnerable and underserved populations [since] macro practice skills are necessary to confront inequalities. If the social worker is unwilling to engage in some macro practice types of activities relating to [various] environments, he or she is not doing social work" (Netting, Kettner, & McMurtry, 2004, p. 10).

In this article, a brief historical and current context is provided, followed by an examination of critical factors influencing macro social work for the next twenty-five years.

HISTORICAL & CURRENT CONTEXT:
MULTIPLE WAYS OF KNOWING & DOING MACRO SOCIAL WORK

Before the dawn of social work as a U.S. profession, feminist historians identify three traditions of women's organizing: benevolence, reform, and rights. Missionary work and orphan asylums to address immediate needs emerged in the late 1700s as benevolent efforts, followed by reformers in the 1830s who created organizations to advocate for causes such as abolishing slavery or eliminating brothels. In the 1840s and 50s a third tradition focused on women's rights. Each tradition of organizing held different sets of assumptions and goals, attracting different members, and often fraught with tension. Each tradition

F. Ellen Netting is Professor, School of Social Work, Virginia Commonwealth University, Richmond, VA 23238.

sought to advocate for populations at risk and to change organizations, communities, and policies – but in different ways (McCarthy, 2003; Scott, 1993).

In searching for the role of advocacy in the history of the profession, Schneider and Lester (2001) identify "three separate and distinct social work movements [that emerged] in the last 20 years of the 19th century, [each with] a different perspective about wealth and poverty as well as the responsibilities one owed to the other and to the developing social systems" (p. 10). Charity organizations focused on *community justice*, settlement houses focused on *social justice*, and the third movement out of the University of Pennsylvania Wharton School focused on *distributive justice* (Schneider & Lester, 2001, p. 10).

Reisch and Andrews (2002) write an alternative history of social work in *The Road Not Taken*. Their focus on radical social work gives "voice to the effects of nonmainstream social service and social work organizations on the creation of U.S. social welfare and the emergence of social work theories and methods" (p. ix). They reveal a complex array of strongly held beliefs about the target(s) of change, ranging from social reform within the system to direct assaults on societal structures.

Similarly, Reamer (1993) explores the various ideologies regarding the provision of social welfare, revealing widely varying conceptions and multiple models that have influenced the profession's development. The history and context of social work macro practice continues to be written and rewritten as new analyses reveal important diverse perspectives on the profession, its underlying philosophy, and the methods used to carry out strongly held assumptions.

In these writings are important messages for the future. First, there are multiple pre-existing traditions within and outside the field that converged in the early 1900s as the profession emerged. Their convergence does not imply agreement about one best way, but reflects different beliefs about what the profession should be and do. This diversity of thought will continue into the future and is a strength of the profession. Second, since histories are filtered through each writer's lense, some voices are more privileged than others. The interpretation of different traditions reveal diverse perspectives within the context of the times. Thus, feminist historians, advocates, and radical social workers felt the need to write their own histories so that alternative voices are heard. Historical reflections, representing different views, will continue to contextualize the profession. Third, the conflict among strongly held beliefs about what actions are necessary in order to do social work were divergent in the beginning of the profession, just as they are divergent today and will be tomorrow. Within continuously changing contexts there are and will be divergent views, perspectives, and strongly held beliefs about what actions should occur in order to perform the work of the profession. Last, perhaps it is through the divergence of assumptions, thoughts, and actions that the future of macro social work lies and which reflects the profession's contribution to the larger society. The future of macro social work, thus, is tied to expecting and respecting the inevitability of difference.

CRITICAL FACTORS INFLUENCING MACRO SOCIAL WORK

It is impossible to predict the future and perhaps that is a key to the future of macro social work. For a profession diverse in its traditions, interpretations of traditions, and alternative methods, social workers are curious, adaptable and continually faced with the unexpected. This facility at dealing with and instituting change will be particularly helpful as we face the future.

Given rapid contextual changes, in twenty-five years social workers will have unimaginable tools to use in the conduct of their practice. Yet, whatever technological advances may occur, there will be unexpected and unintended consequences. It is the need to be savvy in assessing complex situations, understanding context, forming connections, and living with conflict that must characterize macro social work in the years to come.

Assessing Complexity

Assessing situations is a hallmark of macro social work. Just as there have been divergent assumptions about the purpose of social work, there are diverse, deep underlying philosophical assumptions held by individuals and groups in organizational and community settings. Reamer identifies five areas about which philosophical assumptions vary: 1) the goals of government, 2) the rights of citizens in relation to the state, 3) the obligations of the state toward its citizens, 4) the nature of political or civil liberty, and 5) the nature of social justice (1993, p. 2). The 2004 U.S. presidential election revealed just how deeply various assumptions are held and how diverse they may be. The conflict between groups who hold divergent views will continue and social workers must be adept at assessing these assumptions, many of which may be so deeply felt that they are difficult to articulate.

It is encouraging to see social work writers focusing on assumptions at the world view or paradigmatic level, in attempts to emphasize the importance of assessing complexity at its roots. For example, Mullaly (1997) argues that "social work must engage itself in ideological analysis and become more cognizant of various theories of the state" (p. x). He then presents four paradigms (neo-conservatism, liberalism, social democracy, and Marxism) that offer different explanations for social problems, the ideal social welfare system and the interpretation of social problems, and the nature and form of social work practice (p. x-xi).

At the organizational level, Netting and O'Connor (2003) build on Burrell and Morgan's (1979) four paradigms (functionalism, radical structuralism, interpretivist, and radical humanist) as do Martin and O'Connor (1989). The intent of these writers is to encourage social workers to recognize that words and actions are only artifacts of deeply held views. Thinking that a person can change another's actions is one thing, but recognizing that these actions are tied to views of the world that form a person's, group's, program's, organization's, or community's identity reveals the difficulty one may encounter in approaching, much less making, change. The future of macro social work is dependent on recognizing what one is up against (what the profession is up against) in carrying out social work values. Being able to assess the situation means being able to recognize when worldviews are clashing and to distinguish between views that can be changed and those that may require years (if ever) to change. Assessing the situation also requires recognizing that diverse assumptions are often embedded in the same structures, leading to paradoxical situations. For example, a program may be designed by planners with one set of assumptions, only to be located within an organization whose staff have different assumptions and in a community with even different assumptions about the population to be served.

There is no room for naivete in the future of macro social work, but there is great room for self awareness about the worldview one holds and with which one feels most comfortable. Equally important is for macro social workers to be able to step out of their comfort zones and work multiparadigmatically, and live with paradox (Netting & O'Connor, 2003).

Understanding Context

The future of macro social work depends on being able to take what is learned from the assessment of situations and move toward understanding context. Whatever actions or in-actions are identified in the assessment process need to be viewed within a larger context.

In macro social work the arenas in which and with which one operates are typically group, organizational, interorganizational, community, and policy settings. It is encourag-ing to see social workers writing about community organization and including content that just as likely might be included in management or policy textbooks. For example, Hardina (2002) talks about legislative analysis, program planning, and budgeting as part of community organization, not allowing practitioners to engage in compartmentalizing skills needed in program design and development from policy analysis. Contextually, it is important to see one's program design as the implementation of policy decisions or one's budget as highly political.

The recognition that interorganizational relationships, collaboration, partnering and re-lated terms are not just verbiage but require seeing the organization in context reveals the connectedness among organizations. Mulroy (2004) introduces a conceptual framework of "Organization-in-Environment" having implications "for a future-oriented practice that emphasizes external relations and their political dimensions: strategic management, interorganizational collaboration, community building, regional action, and a commit-ment to social justice" (p. 77). She explains that this model helps in understanding con-textual complexity in a global economy. She refers to research by Alter and Hague (1993) in which "they contend that the growing number of partnerships, alliances, joint ventures, consortia, obligational and systemic networks represent a stunning evolutionary change in institutional forms of governance. They predict that interorganizational networks are the future institution" (Mulroy, 2004, p. 89).

Thus, macro social work will be performed in a dizzying array of changing structures and program designs that do not always conform to one's experience, yet open opportunities for alternative and virtual relationships. For example, Roberts-DeGennaro (1997) identi-fies "five different types of coalitions, each serving a different purpose and each requiring a different structure and different activities" (Waysman & Savaya, 2004, p. 124). Social workers can gain from recognizing that considering context generates the emergence of diverse approaches. Being versatile is a prerequisite for macro social work.

Forming Connections

If structural arrangements will emerge in which new connections are made, there are also trends toward relationship building between different roles, disciplines, and profes-sions. In elaborating on directions for the *Journal of Community Practice*, the editors look to the future as one of increasing interdisciplinariness. "Barriers fall, silos collapse, and insights emerge from new combinations – whether these combinations are admixtures of disciplines, expertise, methodologies, or even characteristics of those who understand a particular scholarly enterprise" (Alvarez, Gutierrez, Johnson, & Moxley, 2003, pp. 2-3). The editors continue with emerging themes relevant to community practice, calling for humanists, artists, social scientists, life scientists, and others to join with social workers in facing hard issues of community practice. In their presentation, they recognize what macro social work brings to community practice – a commitment to facilitation and process – a classic theme that informs the future. Knowing what to "do" in process is an important legacy to carry into the future – macro social workers risk turning multiple ways of knowing into *doing*.

Mancini, Mare, Bryne, and Huebner (2004) allude to the connections that must be made between the worlds of program professionals and evaluators. These connections must occur within increasingly complex systems in which context is pivotal, manifested "in many communities [in which] there is interaction across systems, as well as interactions between levels within systems" (p. 10). Similarly, Lennon & Corbett (2003) link policy intent to program implementation and impact analysis, recognizing that accountability requires asking questions about how policies are implemented and evaluated for their effectiveness. Again, these approaches focus on the implementation process, not stopping with an enacted policy or a program design, but pushing macro social workers to figure out how to carry out intent – to move to action.

Mixed methods research, university-community partnerships, interdisciplinary relationships, interorganizational collaboration, and a host of other concepts jump from the pages of professional journals and from conversations with practitioners. Although the terms may be used differently, the message is clear. Whether approaching groups, programs, organizations, coalitions, or communities social workers have to consider multiple contexts in which diverse stakeholders interact, and they must be able to evaluate those interactions and impacts in an accountable manner.

Living with Conflict

With such complexity, multiple contexts, and diverse connections social workers will find macro practice to be increasingly conflictual. This conflict goes beyond ambiguity and uncertainty, but fully reflects the possibilities that any movement toward change may be met with strong clashes of values because someone's or some group's worldview may be challenged. Additionally, as the number of nonprofit organizations grow, as government seeks to devolve responsibility to the local level, as the push for accountability escalates, macro social workers face practice challenges.

Macro social workers face an increasingly challenging dilemma in the future. Advocacy programs and organizations attempt to formalize the more radical language of social work into action. They are typically formed around a "cause" and often attempt to empower diverse groups who are oppressed. Such organizations may be called social movement, social change, alternative, and social reform organizations. They may engage in activities such as lobbying, campaigning, even social protest to achieve their goals. If they are truly advocacy organizations, they likely depend on nontraditional funding sources and to their dismay they may see mirrored images of their methods in organizations and groups that are advocating just as strongly for the status quo. The methods used by radical groups do not belong to radicals of one political persuasion. Thus, the competition among interests will likely continue apace as diverse organizational forms emerge within local communities. Some will be hybrid organizations that identify as both service providers and as advocacy organizations. Others may consider advocacy their single mission. Campbell's (2002) study of nonprofit organizations examines the paradox that occurs when program leaders focus on direct service outcomes "over which they have control and for which indicators are readily available, they risk default on the larger question of accountability to publicly valued goods. On the other hand, if they try to demonstrate the impact of their particular projects on community wide outcomes, they risk taking credit inappropriately or shouldering the blame for indicators beyond their control" (p. 243).

Reisch and Andrews (2002) reveal a number of struggles that have occurred in the history of radical social work in the U.S. These include the move from cause to function, tension between liberals and radicals, and perceived incompatibilities between radicalism and professionalization. They conclude that "it is not enough . . . to use words like 'empowerment,' 'multiculturalism,' 'oppression,' and 'social justice.' The test of social work's commitment to its underlying values lies in the willingness to struggle on an often mundane, day-to-day basis to translate these values into deeds, as our professional forebears did individually and collectively" (p. 231).

IMPLICATIONS: SUSTAINABILITY, CHANGE, ADVOCACY, & QUALITY OF LIFE

Earlier, macro social work was defined as those efforts within and outside organizational, community and policy arenas intended to sustain, change, and advocate for quality of life. In light of the factors highlighted in the previous section, what does it mean for macro social work to sustain, change and advocate for quality of life?

Sustainability

Sustainability is a word used often by community practitioners. According to Hart (1999) sustainable communities develop natural, human, social, and built capital. Natural capital is everything from trees to waterways, whereas human capital involves people's skills and well-being. Social capital focuses on connections as individuals, groups, friends, and organizations come together. Built capital focuses on infrastructures such as roadways and housing. Together, these four types of capital can be strengthened and sustained to protect and restore communities for future generations. Therefore, macro social workers must know how to assess natural, human, social, and built capital within communities, understand the context, form connections, and live with conflicts that are inevitable in any situation involving multiple people.

Change

Change is a concept well known to social work. Social workers know that any change, no matter how small, may be met with resistance. The future of macro social work lies in recognizing that change, like power, can be used in positive as well as in destructive ways. Change can be incremental or radical or anywhere in between. In the future, macro social workers will witness changes that they are resistant to, as well as work toward changes that have unanticipated consequences. Whether one is working toward policy, organizational, programmatic, or community change (or all of the above), it will be important to assess the complexity of the situation, understand the context, form connections with anyone who will be affected by the change, and expect conflict.

Advocacy

Everyone is doing advocacy but some persons are advocating for the status quo (Ezell, 2000). There is a mythology about advocacy that must cease. Advocacy is a codeword in social work for change, sometimes for radical change. Yet, advocacy can be for sustaining and maintaining what is, for not losing more ground when current programs are threatened, for keeping a community intact when a highway is designed to cut it in half, for keeping a plant open when a small town's citizenry will lose their jobs, and a host of other possibilities. Macro social workers will also find that they are faced with advocates who hold different worldviews, different philosophies, and opposite values from their own. Advocating carries so many meanings that future social workers will have to be clear about which form it is taking in a world in which everyone is advocating for something.

Quality of Life

Quality of life is a complicated concept because no one's quality of life may be identical to anyone else's. Yet, the push toward outcome-based measurement tends to lump quality of life outcomes into groups, making assumptions about individuals that may or may not fully increase their self-perceived quality of life. Outcome-based measurement is part of an accountability movement that will continue apace in the years ahead. It will be incumbent upon macro social workers to be certain that persons served have a voice in determining those outcomes, that measurements are sensitive, that alternative methods of measuring success are used, that outcomes are not always determined by persons one or two steps removed from consumers, and that being accountable means being accountable to consumers, as well as to decision-makers and funders.

A strength of macro social work is in the knowledge of direct practice that professionals bring to the public arena. Social workers (unlike their colleagues in business, political science, sociology, public administration, health administration and other macro programs of study) engage in work with individuals and groups in the field, under professional supervision, in order to graduate as a social worker. Thus, social work professional education requires seeing the faces of the persons with whom and for whom one advocates. This exposure gives voice to direct practice experience (sometimes called clinical or micro) that is not always required of other non-clinical professionals who are educated to manage, plan, and change organizations, communities, policies, and even societal structures. Conversely, to perform the role of direct practice or clinical social work, exposure to macro content is part of one's professional education, mandating that practitioners always consider context rather than focus solely on the individual. Exposure of all professional social workers to person(s)-in-context is critically important to the future of macro social work.

CONCLUSION

Macro social work *is* social work. History tells us that the profession was birthed from diverse traditions in which relief work, reform work, and radical work interfaced. Yet different traditions were grounded in different assumptions, spurring different ways of knowing and doing. This versatility is a hallmark of the field and it will serve macro social work well into the future. A profession that seeks to sustain, advocate and change, with the intent of increasing quality of life, will always need practitioners who can recognize diverse worldviews, understand multi-layered contexts, deal with limitless inter-connections, and be invigorated by conflict.

References

Alter, K., & Hague, J. (1993). *Organizations working together.* Newbury Park: Sage Publications.

Alvarez, A. R., Gutierrez, L. M., Johnson, & A. K., Moxley, D. P. (2003). The Journal of Community Practice: A social work journal with an interdisciplinary perspective. *Journal of Community Practice, 11*(3), 1-12.

Burrell, G. & Morgan, G. (1979). *Sociological paradigms and organizational analysis.* London: Heinemann.

Campbell, D. (2002). Outcomes assessment and the paradox of nonprofit accountability. *Nonprofit Management & Leadership, 12*(3), 243-259.

Council on Social Work Education.(2001). *Educational policy and accreditation standards.* Alexandria, VA: The Author.

Ezell, M. (2000). *Advocacy in the human services.* Belmont, CA: Brooks/Cole.

Hardina, D. (2002). *Analytical skills for community organization practice.* New York: Columbia University Press.

Hart, M. (1999). *Guide to sustainable community indicators.* North Andover, MA: Sustainable Measures.

Lennon, M.C., & Corbett, T. (Eds.). (2003). *Policy into action: Implementation research and welfare reform.* Washington, D.C.: The Urban Institute Press.

Manicini, J. A., Marek, L. I., Byrne, R. A., & Huebner, A. J. (2004). Community based program research: Context, program readiness, and evaluation usefulness. *Journal of Community Practice, 12*(1/2), 7-21.

Martin, P. Y., & O'Connor, G. G. (1989). *The social environment: Open systems applications.* New York: Longman.

McCarthy, K. D. (2003). *American creed: Philanthropy and the rise of civil society 1700-1865.* Chicago: The University of Chicago Press.

Mullaly, Bob (1997). *Structural social work.* Ontario, Canada: Oxford.

Mulroy, E. A. (2004). Theoretical perspectives on the social environment to guide management and community practice: An organization-in-environment approach. *Administration in Social Work, 28*(1), 77-96.

Netting, F. E., Kettner, P. M., & McMurtry, S. L. (2004). *Social work macro practice* (3rd edition. Boston: Allyn & Bacon.

Netting, F. E., & O'Connor, M. K. (2003). *Organization practice: A social worker's guide to under-*

standing human services. Boston: Allyn & Bacon.

Reamer, F. G. (1993). *The philosophical foundations of social work.* New York: Columbia University Press.

Reisch, M. & Andrews, J. (2002). *The road not taken: A history of radical social work in the United States.* New York: Brunner-Routledge.

Roberts-DeGennaro, M. (1997). Conceptual framework of coalitions in an organizational context. *Journal of Community Practice, 4,* 91-107.

Scott, A. F. (1993). *Natural allies: Women's associations in American history.* Chicago: University of Chicago Press.

Schneider, R. L. & Lester, L. (2001). *Social work advocacy.* Belmont, CA: Brooks/Cole.

Wagner, M., Newcomb, P., & Weiler, R. (2001). The 2001 educational policy and accreditation standards: Implications for MSW programs. *Advances in Social Work, 2*(2), 112-118.

Waysman, M. & Savaya, R. (2004). Coalition-based social change initiatives: Conceptualization of a model and assessment of its generalizability. *Journal of Community Practice, 12*(1/2), 123-143.

Author's Note

Address correspondence to: F. Ellen Netting, School of Social Work, Virginia Commonwealth University, 1001 West Franklin Street, Richmond, VA 23238-2027. E-mail: enetting@vcu.edu

SOCIAL WELFARE POLICY IN AN INFORMATION AGE:
NEW VISIONS OR MORE OF THE SAME?

John G. McNutt

Abstract: *As we move into the 21st Century, the social policy enterprise stands at the nexus between technological, political and social forces that will undermine the base that contemporary programs and policies depend upon. Assumptions about work and the workforce, the nature of governance and the role of technology will radically change. If our social welfare system is to remain relevant, changes will be needed. This paper explores these changing systems and examines how they will influence the current system. It will also speculate on the types of changes that will be necessary if social welfare is to remain relevant to the society of the future.*

Keywords: Social Policy, Social Welfare, Technology, Information Society

INTRODUCTION

The past few decades have been trying times for those involved in with the American social welfare policy enterprise. Massive cutbacks, the impacts of a world wide trend toward devolution, a conservative political climate and a number of emerging social problems make the social policy world seem both chaotic and threatening. Many social workers long for the good old days of the 1960s and 1970s and fear that decades of progress toward an American welfare state are being undercut and destroyed by shortsighted, wrong headed and destructive economic and political actors.

Political and economic change has done real damage to the social safety net and called into question programs once considered secure. It is easy to explain these developments as the fortunes of political battles and the outcomes of conflicts between money and greed vs. virtue and truth. While there is definitely some truth to this argument, it is far from the whole story.

American social policy is at the convergence of an economic and political transition that is changing the playing field within the social welfare system and within society as a whole. This is a process that has been developing for several decades and we ignore it at our peril. In this paper we will explore this transition and provide some ideas about how if might evolve. More importantly, we will examine the implications for the future of the American welfare state and for social welfare policy.

THE WELFARE STATE IN THE INFORMATION ECONOMY

The American welfare state, as we know it, is a product of industrialization and the aftermath of the institutional changes necessary to support the various aspects of that process. Wilensky and Lebeaux (1965) note that industrialization not only created the need for a welfare state in the United States, but also the economic capacity to create a welfare state. As we transition yet again to an information society, some of underpin-

---

John G. McNutt is Associate Professor, College of Social Work, University of South Carolina, Columbia, SC 29208. The author would like to thank Dr. Thomas Meenaghan for his advice on this paper.

nings of an earlier economic order are going to be radically altered, as will the problems that are created by the transition.

While industrialization leads us to one type of social order, the information economy leads us in other directions. The growth of the factory system and the assembly line were key features of the industrial economy. These systems required a large number of workers to be concentrated in one place, which led to immigration and ultimately to the growth of urban areas (Garvin & Cox, 1987). It also led to the creation of formal jobs as a social construct (Bridges, 1994) because of the need to have continuous access to workers. Employment was often life long (although lives were shorter) and secure, save for retirement and occasional unemployment. Benefits were provided not only to maintain the workforce, but also to encourage employee loyalty[1]. This was the beginning of the occupational welfare system in America. As Titmus (1974) observed, occupational welfare was one of the major components of the welfare state. The benefits that employers provided eventually eclipsed those provided by government for many workers.

Against this backdrop, the American social welfare system evolved. Most social workers would agree that the centerpiece of this process was the Social Security Act of 1935 (Trattner, 1998). When this watershed legislation was passed, it addressed many if not most of the most pressing problems of the day. As long as things remained as they were, there was reason to believe than many of the problems were being addressed. Social policy activity refined and expanded the existing model.

In the 1970s, things were beginning to change in dramatic ways (McNutt, 1996a; 1996b; Beniger, 1988; Williams, 1988; Dillman, 1985; 1991; Cleveland, 1985; Porat, 1977; Huey, 1994). The information sector began to push for dominance, reducing the industrial sector's importance. We saw some of the result of this transition in the 1980s as plant closings and capital flight became commonplace. Unemployment compensation, designed for downturns in the industrial sector, was no longer an adequate response. Several states exhausted their unemployment compensation funds in the 1980s and 1990s and required additional funds from the federal government.

We began to see a movement from the industrial economy, based on manufacturing, to an information economy, based on knowledge work. Knowledge work is different from industrial factory work. This changes many of the dynamics that any social welfare policy enterprise must address. While the social welfare system of the 1950s and 1960s could count on long-term, relatively stable industrial employment, by the 1980s and 1990s, that was no longer the case.

The knowledge economy has less of a need to concentrate workers in a given place. This means that pressure toward urbanization may be less and that firms can locate operations wherever they want. Knowledge work also requires more advanced skills than manufacturing work. This means that more poorly educated workers are excluded from the more desirable jobs, a situation identified by dual labor market theory. Knowledge workers are often needed for a brief span of time, and then are off to other assignments (Bridges, 1994). Firms in an information economy have less need for a consistent workforce and more need to be able to change the organizational skill mix to meet new competitors. The pace of change is much quicker in an information economy and organizations must adapt to this more volatile environment.

This change has lead to the growth of virtual organizations and a theater model of employment. A virtual organization is one that has a small permanent group of employees and out sources most of its functions to other organizations or individuals (Voss, 1996). This means that the virtual organization can easily restructure itself to meet new environmental threats. While this was always an option, information technology makes the considerable coordination burden far lighter. In a theater model of employment, workers are employed on a project for as long as their skills are needed. After that, they move on to other projects. There are often no benefits provided and workers are responsible for maintaining and upgrading their skills. Formal jobs may no longer exist (Bridges, 1994; Rifkin, 1995). This, of course, creates a good deal of insecurity on the part of the workers and separates them from employer paid benefits in many cases.

This is not a possibility for a distant future--this is a change that is occurring now. A considerable portion of the US Workforce is made up of part time, temporary and contingency workers (Bluestone & Rose, 1997). These are people who often fall outside the eligibility structure for many workforce based income support programs. Not only do they often lack security in the workplace, but they even lack security in the social safety net.

This situation will describe work life for people who have the appropriate range of skills, education and most critically, the ability to use information technology. While this is certainly not desirable, a far worse fate awaits those who cannot become part of the information revolution because they lack these characteristics. Unfortunately, for many, we have the digital divide (Mossberger, Tolbert & Stansbury, 2003; Norris, 2001; McNutt, 1998; Ebo, 1998; McConnaughey, Everette, Reynolds & Lader, 1999) that creates two groups--those who can participate in the information economy and those who cannot. Many of our current workers lack the skills and access to technology and networks that will allow them to have inclusion in the information sector of the economy. Because information technology infiltrates the other economic sectors, many current jobs will be out of reach as well (Beniger, 1988). They will become the information poor and will be shut out of all but the most menial work situations. Research into the digital divide suggests that most disenfranchised groups in the industrial society will remain disenfranchised in the future.

The social welfare implications of these developments are enormous. One of the reasons that the United States has been able to maintain a rather minimalist formal welfare state is the occupational welfare system. Firms are under great pressure to reduce benefits in order to cut cost. As this occupational welfare system recedes, tax expenditures and the small formal welfare system will have to cover additional ground. This comes at a time where soaring deficits and ideological pressure for tax reform cloud the political agenda. In addition, the digital divide will create a new underclass that will add to the one that was inherited from the industrial order. This situation might be described as the "perfect storm" of post-industrial social welfare.

In addition, the global reach of the information economy appears to weaken the state, as governments compete for economic activity and jobs. While this is especially true at the state and local level, the ability of nation states to deal with large multinational organizations is open to question. Pressure to reduce taxes and created a good business climate has lead many states to drastically cut benefits and services. This also leads to outsourcing and governmental efficiency efforts. Some political scientists have offered the opinion that this will lead to a hollow state that only taxes and minimally regulates, leaving services to third parties (Peters, 1994). As states grow weaker, the ability of social welfare groups to mobilize and pressure government to increase services and benefits is constricted.

One way that government has tried to cope with this situation is the rise of electronic government (West, 2001; Fountain, 2001). This has a number of aspects including electronic government information, government services (including social services), e-procurement and digital democracy. The latter term includes wired legislators, e-rulemaking, electronic voting and town meeting and a range of other electron participation techniques. While the aim of all of this is to make government more user-friendly and less expensive, it can also have the impact of moving government out of the reach of those who are on the wrong side of the digital divide. This applies to individuals and organizations.

The reduced power of government, coupled with efforts to move deliberation in government on line, can create new challenges for those who advocate for social welfare programs. This is especially true for those who plan to use only traditional advocacy techniques (McNutt, 2003).

While social welfare systems are products to the times they evolved and the economies that support them, there are usually choices that can be made about the direction of change. It is critical that social workers carefully examine the social welfare system and their role within it as society evolves.

TOWARD A POST INDUSTRIAL SOCIAL WELFARE SYSTEM

Social policy can take many paths in the future. We may decide on a minimalist social welfare system that is characterized by declining traditional benefits and services. This system will meet fewer needs while over spending for those who were needier in the industrial society of the past. Public support of social welfare will continue to decline because people will see it as less and less relevant. Social workers will find themselves more marginalized and frustrated because the policy context will not support them and will fit poorly with the problems that developed. This path represents the stay the course alternative in American social policy.

On balance, we might make choices that lead to a better place for society and for the profession. This creates a social welfare system that enjoys public support because it meets current needs and fits well with other elements of society. It also requires some hard choices and political skill. We must recognize that the workforce of 2005 is not the workforce of 1935. A social welfare program that is supported will fit well with the economy that we have today and not the economy that our grandparents experienced. What would this program look like?

We might consider that replacing Social Security, unemployment compensation and most our public welfare programs with a global income security blanket program makes more sense. The majority of these programs were designed for another time with a different society and a much different economy. A more broad-brush effort would provide a minimal income floor across the life span. It would address the problems of child poverty, unemployment and poverty after retirement.

In addition, National Health Insurance might form the second major pillar of a future-oriented approach. Health care is a large part of the cost of employee benefits and the number of uninsured people in the United States is a national embarrassment. If people move quickly from employer to employer, health insurance is likely to become even more of a major survival issue than it is today. Many of the problems that we currently experience are a consequence of taking a piecemeal approach. A more comprehensive and preventative approach will be more cost effective and ultimately more successful.

These are policies that have had a hard time finding acceptance in the past. As time progresses and the situation with employment and benefits becomes more apparent, resistance should decrease.

The digital divide must be considered a priority social policy issue for the future. Assuring that every American has access and that every American has the skills and technology to make proper use of that access is critical. It is as essential as free public education, universal phone services or any of the things that we are sure everyone need to live a successful life.

One might expect that, aligned with the movement toward e-government, more and more social services would be moved on line. This will allow for greater access and more immediate response to human needs. It will also allow cost savings and more flexibility for agencies and workers. This should lead to a revitalization of the professional association as access to training, insurance and so forth become detached from the workplace.

It is also likely that human services will follow the trend toward more part time and contract employment. In addition, many human service organizations will also become virtual organizations. In this new world of human services employment, social workers will work for a number of organizations on an as needed basis. They will need both appropriate supports and again, professional associations can fill these roles.

It is also likely that various forms of e-practice will develop and will eventually dominate many practice environments. The growth of virtual communities and virtual environments will require practice that can deal with those emerging areas of life. If agencies move toward a virtual organization form, technology based practice will fit well into these reconstructed organizations. Appropriate policy instruments in terms of licensing laws and vendorship requirements will support these new work environments. Social work can resist this change but the results will be damaging to the profession's credibility and ability to control its own practice settings.

Perhaps the most serious ramifications will be for managers in the social services. Managers will find themselves working with networks as opposed to hierarchies (O'Toole, 1997). This will require a different mindset and new skills. It will be a different world for those who are learned to manage bureaucracies.

Technology will also be a critical part of making policy (McNutt & Boland, 1999; Hick & McNutt, 2002; West, 2001). The legislative body of the future will continue the significant progress made so far and use technology to support deliberation, citizen participation and public information. Administrative organizations will use it to create new regulations and facilitate the growth of public participation. Interest groups, lobbyists and social movement organizations will use it to gather information, inform the public, organize supporters and pressure decision makers (McNutt & Boland, 1999). On balance, those individuals and interest groups that do not make use of technology will find themselves left out of the discussion--other victims of the digital divide (McNutt, 2003).

The policy framework will undoubtedly be more reflective of a mixed economy of care (Smith & Lipsky, 1993). Responsibility for policy making will continue to be shared, not only by different levels of government, but by nonprofit and profit making organizations. While some regard devolution as simply a move from federal to state responsibility, it is already apparent that the trend continues to local government and non-governmental organizations. It is also unclear what the role of multinational organizations will be in the future. Networks are becoming more important than organizations Cleveland,1985) . These networks will not stop at national boundaries.

All of these changes occur and will continue to occur at mind numbing speed. The pace of change creates problems at all levels in society and the dislocations are often deeply felt. Perhaps one of the underlying themes in the cultural battles occurring within the United States is that people deeply fear for their future when familiar institutions are crumbling because of economic and social change. The backlash created by these irresistible forces can be both unsettling and threatening.

This raises a final issue, but one of particular importance for social workers--one of social justice. Our conception of social justice is strongly rooted in industrial thinking. What constitutes fairness in the future may be very different than it is today. The movement toward an information society could very well eliminate many familiar threats to social justice, while imposing even more ominous situations that we might find it hard to recognize. Expect that some of the battles will be fought in unfamiliar venues: privacy, copyright and patents, telecommunications policy, intellectual property and access (McNutt, 1996a, 1996b; 1998). This is certainly not a time to let the profession's guard down.

CONCLUSIONS

We are entering a world with many new opportunities and challenges. Social Work, a child of the industrial revolution, now finds itself dealing with new realities. We helped shape the policies that give form to the industrial welfare state. We can provide this same assistance to the welfare system that will emerge as our society enters the information society.

Our task is not to recreate or ever preserve the programs of the past. We have a responsibility to create new opportunities to advance social welfare and well being in the coming age.

We will also change as a profession. Our technology will be different, as will our organizations and the policies that provide a framework for our practice. Social work has, however, always been about creating the future. Sometimes we build a better future for a single client. Later we create a new future for entire societies. The goal is the same if the task is different.

We are faced with all of the exciting possibilities and difficult challenges that were faced by the first members of our profession decades ago. It is our mandate to build social welfare policy for the future.

References

Beniger, J. (1988). Information society and global science. *Annuals, 495,* 14-29.

Bluestone, B. & Rose, S. (1997) Overworked and underemployed. The *American Prospect. (31),* 58-69.

Bridges, W. (1994). The end of the job. *Fortune. 129,* 62-74.

Cleveland, H. (1985). The twilight of hierarchy: Speculations on the global information society. *Public Administration Review. 45,* 195-195.

Dillman, D. (1985). The social impacts of information technologies in rural north America. *Rural Sociology. 50.*(1), 1-26.

Dillman, D. (1991). Information society In Borgetta, E. & Borgetta, R. (eds.). *The Encyclopedia of Sociology.* New York: Macmillian.

Ebo, B.(ed.) (1998*). The Cyberghetto or Cybertopia: Race, Class, Gender & Marginalization in Cyberspace.* New York: Praeger.

Fountain, J (2001). *Building the digital state,* Washington, DC: Brookings.

Garvin, C. And Cox, F. (1987). A History of Community Organization Since The Civil War with Special Reference to Oppressed Communities. in Cox, F. , et.al (eds.) *Strategies of Community Organization.* [Fourth Edition] Itasca: F. E. Peacock.

Hick, S. & McNutt, J. (eds.) (2002). *Advocacy and Activism on the Internet: Perspectives from Community Organization and Social Policy.* Chicago: Lyceum Press.

Huey, J. (1994). Waking up to the new economy. *Fortune. 129.*(13) 36-46.

McConnaughey, J. Everette, D.W. Reynolds, T. & Lader, W. (1999). *Falling through the net: defining the digital divide,* Washington, DC: National Telecommunications and Information Administration, U.S. Department of Commerce.

McNutt, J. G. (1996a). National information infrastructure policy and the future of the American welfare state: Implications for the social welfare policy curriculum. *Journal of Social Work Education. 6* (3), 375-388.

McNutt, J.G. (1996b). Teaching social policy in the information age: Innovations in curriculum content and instructional methods. *Tulane University Studies in Social Welfare. 20.* 71-85.

McNutt, J.G. (1998). Ensuring social justice for the new underclass: Community interventions to meet the needs of the new poor. In Ebo, B.(ed.) (1998*). The Cyberghetto or Cybertopia: Race, Class, Gender & Marginalization in Cyberspace.* New York: Praeger, pp. 33-47.

McNutt, J.G. & Boland, K.M. (1999). Electronic Advocacy by Non-Profit Organizations in Social Welfare Policy. *Non-profit and Voluntary Sector Quarterly. 28* (4), 432-451.

McNutt, J.G. (2003). *Advocacy Organizations and the Organizational Digital Divide.* Presented at International Perspectives on Social Welfare, Social Justice and Technology" University of Calgary, Calgary, Alberta, Canada May 14 to 16, 2003

Mossberger, K., Tolbert, C., & Stansbury, M. (2003). *Virtual inequality: beyond the digital divide.* Washington, DC: Georgetown University Press.

Norris, P. (2001). *Digital divide.* New York: Cambridge University Press.

O'Toole, L.J. (1997). Treating networks seriously: Practical and research based agendas in public administration. *Public administration review. 57* (1), 43-52.

Peters, B.G. (1994). Managing the hollow state. *International journal of public administration. 17* (3 & 4), 739-756.

Porat, M. (1977).*Information Economy: Definition and measurement.* Washington: US Department of Commerce.

Rifkin, J. (1995).Vanishing jobs. *Mother jones.20*, 58-64.

Smith, S.R.,& Lipsky, M. (1993) *Non Profits for Hire: The Welfare State in the Age of Contracting.* Cambridge, MA: Harvard University Press.

Titmuss, R. (1974). *Social policy: An introduction.* London: Allen and Unwin.

Trattner, W. I. (1998). *</SPAN>From poor law to welfare state.* [Sixth Edition] New York: The Free Press.

Voss (1996) Virtual Organizations. *Strategy and Leadership, 24*(2), 12-16.

West, D.M. (2001). *E-government and the transformation of public sector Service delivery.* Paper prepared for delivery at the 2001 Annual Meeting of the American Political Science Association, San Francisco, CA. August 30-September 2, 2001.

Wilensky, H. & Lebeaux, F. (1965). *Industrial Society and Social Welfare.* New York: Macmillian.

Williams, F. (1988).The information society as an object of study. In Williams, F. (ed.). *Measuring the information society.* Newbury Park: Sage Publications.

Author's Note

Address correspondence to: John G. McNutt, Associate Professor, College of Social Work, University of South Carolina, Columbia, SC 29208. e-mail: mcnuttjg@gwm.sc.edu.

THE FUTURE OF EVIDENCE-BASED SOCIAL WORK:
AN OPTIMISTIC VIEW?

Barry R. Cournoyer

Abstract: *This abbreviated article contains a brief overview of the contemporary state of evidence-based social work (EBSW) and projections of its likely future. The forecast is based upon a review and analysis of the current trends and themes reflected in books, journal articles, dissertations, conferences, university programs, centers, and resources available through the World Wide Web. The analysis suggests that the future of evidence-based practice (EBP) in social work is likely to be characterized by further evolution, clarification, and explication of the EBP perspective; continued growth in popularity and a commensurate increase in the number of publications about EBP; modest increase in the number of practice-relevant research studies conducted by social workers; slight decrease in the gap between research-based knowledge and actual practice; and continued polarization within the profession about the relative value and utility of evidence-based social work.*

Keywords: Evidence-Based Practice, Evidence-Based Social Work, EBP, EBSW, Future

WHAT IS EVIDENCE-BASED SOCIAL WORK?

The term evidence-based practice has been defined in various ways in social work (Mullen, 2002). Most definitions include reference to the quality or strength of evidentiary support for a particular practice. From this perspective, an "evidence-based practice is considered any practice that has been established as effective through scientific research according to some set of explicit criteria" (Mullen, 2004a, p. 8). Typically, these evaluative criteria include reference to the degree to which research studies that support the efficacy or effectiveness of a practice control for various threats to internal and external validity. In general, research designs that involve random selection and assignment processes and the comparison of treatment versus control groups are highly valued. Contemporary definitions, however, also incorporate reference to professional expertise, ethical principles, and clients' values, needs, and preferences. For example, McNeece and Thyer (2004) suggested that "Evidence-based practice can be defined as the integration of the best research evidence with clinical expertise and client values in making practice decisions" (p. 9). Cournoyer (2004) proposed the following definition of evidence-based social work:

Evidence-based social work is the mindful and systematic identification, analysis, and synthesis of practice effectiveness as a primary part of an integrative and collaborative process concerning the selection and application of service to members of target client groups. The evidence based decision-making process includes consideration of professional ethics and experience as well as the personal and cultural values and judgments of consumers. (p. 4)

These definitions reflect the importance of searching for, analyzing, and applying the

Barry Cournoyer is Professor, School of Social Work, Indiana University, Indianapolis 46202.
Copyright © 2005 *Advances in Social Work* Vol. 6 No. 1 (Spring 2005), 68-78

currently available best evidence in an attempt to serve clients in an effective manner. A several step, sequential process is involved: (1) Questioning, (2) Searching, (3) Analyzing, and (4) Applying and Evaluating (Cournoyer, 2004). In effect, these steps involve critical thinking and scholarship. They also reflect values of integrity and altruism. Social workers are expected to place the interests of clients before their own, base their professional activities on an established knowledge base, and incorporate clients' needs, values, and preferences in the decision-making process. Indeed, evidence-based social workers are highly interested in both *ideographic* and *nomothetic* knowledge (Cournoyer & Powers, 2002).

Ideographic information is typically gained through the use of individualized and standardized scales along with client and constituent reports within the context of single-system research designs. Research-mindedness is needed during the working and evaluating processes to ensure that services shown to be generally effective through nomothetic research are also effective when provided to a particular individual, couple, family, group, organization, or community.

Gilgun (2005) encouraged professionals to view evidence—whether nomothetic or ideographic—as tentative or provisional, to actively seek information that contradicts or "falsifies" currently held positions, and to willingly revise conclusions on the basis of all relevant knowledge. She argued that, "Processes of falsification lead to inclusiveness and are a check on bias and blind spots, which is one of the main purposes of a scientific approach and a goal of EBP" (p. 52). This openness to unlearning and relearning based upon evidence may be contrasted with "authority-based" (Gambrill, 1999, 2001) attitudes through which information remains essentially unexamined and often unchallenged—perhaps due to tradition or the status of the source.

ANTICIPATING THE FUTURE OF EVIDENCE-BASED SOCIAL WORK

Based upon current and historical trends in the profession, the future of evidence-based practice in social work is likely to be characterized by several themes. These include: (1) evolution and clarification of the EBP perspective to further explicate decision-making processes in general and especially the means by which clients participate as informed consumers and collaborative partners; (2) continued growth in the popularity of EBP and the number of books, book chapters, practice guidelines, treatment manuals, and theoretical and practical articles about EBP and its application in practice and education; (3) modest increase in the number of practice-relevant research studies conducted by social workers accompanied by a continued dramatic growth in those conducted by professionals in medicine, psychology, nursing, and allied health; (4) increased ease of access to the research literature; and (5) slight decrease in the gap between research-based knowledge and actual practice.

Evolution and Clarification of the Evidence-Based Perspective

Evidence-based practice in social work will evolve conceptually and empirically to incorporate greater attention to the processes by which decisions about the quality, value, relevance, and applicability of evidence are made. The means by which social workers attend to the idiosyncratic needs, values, and preferences of specific individuals and diverse population groups will be further explicated as will the processes by which potential clients become informed consumers who participate actively in collaborative decision-making.

A fundamental principle of the informed consent process in evidence-based practice involves the provision of accurate information to potential clients about the potential risks and benefits, and the likely effectiveness of applicable services. Of course, many consumers independently seek information about the efficacy of various programs and practices to empower themselves as they "comparison shop" for services offered by different professionals and organizations. Unfortunately, many people remain information illiterate and depend solely upon professionals to provide information upon which to base decisions about the likely safety and effectiveness of various services. The processes by which potential clients become genuinely informed consumers will be clarified and explicated as EBSW evolves (Entwistle, Sheldon, Sowden, & Watt, 1998).

Growth in Publications about and Popularity of the Evidence-Based Social Work

Evidence-based practice has generated enormous attention throughout the social work global community during the last decade. In the United Kingdom especially, numerous organizations have been created to promote EBP throughout the social care system (e.g., Be-Evidence-Based, Research in Practice: Supporting Evidence Informed Practice with Children and Families, Social Care Institute for Excellence (SCIE), Social Work Research Center at the University of Stirling, Electronic Library for Social Care (eLSC), and the Centre for Evidence-Based Social Services (CEBSS):

Evidence-based social work in the United States has grown more slowly than in the United Kingdom. However, many social work educators, policy makers, agency administrators, and some practitioners are becoming increasingly interested in EBP. This growing popularity may be accounted for by several factors. For example, many social workers now consider it their ethical obligation (Myers & Thyer, 1997; NASW, 1999) to inform clients about the potential risks, benefits, and likely effectiveness of applicable services (Joint Initiative of Mental Health Professional Organizations, 2000) and, whenever possible, to provide services that reflect the greatest probability of helping consumers achieve agreed-upon goals. Mandated by accreditation standards (CSWE, 2001), a growing number of schools and departments of social work are attempting to evaluate the effectiveness of their programs and have based curricula decisions on evidence derived from their evaluation studies. In addition, the faculties of some have adopted evidence-based practice as a major focus of students' learning (see, for example, the George Warren Brown School of Social Work of Washington University in St. Louis).

Evidence-based practice is also gaining in popularity because of other external pressures as well. "For most of the profession's history, there were very few internal or external mandates that held practitioners accountable for the efficacy of their professional interventions" (Cournoyer & Powers, 2002, pp. 798-799). Clearly, this is no longer the case. Social workers and the programs they staff are increasingly held to rigorous standards of accountability.

Managed care processes tend to encourage the provision of services that reflect research-based evidence of safety, effectiveness, and efficiency. Consumers and their families individually and collectively have lost much of their "trust" of professionals and increasingly demand accountability. Other constituents (e.g., private and public funding sources, legislatures, boards of directors, and citizens' watch groups) are also demanding greater accountability as indicated by positive outcomes. Social work practitioners and organizations are subject to an increasing number of lawsuits—some of which are based upon provision of unsafe, unproven, or inappropriate services.

Methodological and technological advances also fuel the growth of EBP. The evolution of both single-system and meta-analytic research methods, and the development relatively user-friendly software to maintain, analyze, and analyze data contribute to the ease with which both nomothetic and ideographic research may be undertaken. The continuing, fast-growing base of empirical knowledge about effective biopsychosocial policies, programs, practices, and interventions; and he expansion of online, electronic information resources facilitate access to research-based knowledge.

As a result of these and other factors, the popularity of evidence-based social work in the United States will also grow—albeit probably at a slower rate and to a lesser extent than in our sister professions of medicine, nursing, and psychology. The number of published books, book chapters, practice guidelines, treatment manuals, articles, and reports about EBP in social work will continue to grow as they have in the past several years.

A keyword search of the Social Work Abstracts (SWABS) electronic bibliographic database using the terms "evidence-based" or "evidence based" produced nearly 70 citations. Three citations appeared in 1998, 4 in 1999, 8 in 2000, 8 in 2001, 10 in 2002, 13 in 2003, and 19 through June 2004. A similar keyword search of the Social Services Abstracts (SSA) database yielded 191 English language journal articles. Three citations appeared in 1998, 8 in 1999, 23 in 2000, 29 in 2001, 24 in 2002, 59 in 2003, and 23 through August 2004. A keyword search of Bowker's Global Books-in-Print online database, the United States Library of Congress online catalog, and the World Wide Web for recent books related to EBP in social work yielded 19 books (Barrett & Ollendick, 2004; Bilson, 2004; Briggs & Rzepnicki, 2004; Corcoran, 2000, 2003; Cournoyer, 2004; CWLA, 2003; Dulmus & Sowers, 2004; Gibbs, 2003; Glicken, 2004; Hilarski, 2005; Macdonald, 2001; Newman, 2004; Roberts & Yeager, 2004; Rosen & Proctor, 2003; Smith, 2005; Thyer & Kazi, 2004; Vincent, 2000; Wodarski & Dziegielewski, 2002). The publication of books by and for social workers about evidence-based practice has quadrupled during the period from 2000 to 2004.

Although the majority of books and book chapters thus far produced have focused on the "what" and "how" of EBP, we anticipate a significant growth in the number of books that incorporate systematic reviews and meta-analyses of practice-relevant research studies for specific social problems and populations. Some of these may include summaries of practices in sufficient detail that they may adopted for use in replication studies or actually applied in service to clients. Evidence-based practice guidelines and treatment manuals will also be published in increasing numbers. Many will be available as books or book chapters in print and electronic format, and others will be freely accessible via the World Wide Web. For example, the United States Agency for Healthcare Research and Quality (AHRQ) has established the National Guideline Clearinghouse (NGC) at http://www.guidelines.gov to facilitate professionals' access to and evaluation of guidelines that meet a certain standard of quality. Although most are geared toward healthcare practices, several would support social workers in their service as well (e.g., Substance Abuse Treatment for Persons with Child Abuse and Neglect Issues; HIV Infection: Detection, Counseling, and Referral; Elderly Suicide).

In the field of mental health, psychiatry and psychology have taken the lead in the development and dissemination of practice guidelines. Many are available through the website of the American Psychiatric Association at http://www.psych.org and some are available through the American Psychological Association's website at http://www.apa. org. Although the National Association of Social Workers (NASW) publishes policy statements (see, for example, those abstracted on the "Policy Statements Abstracts" page at http://www.socialworkers.org/resources/abstracts/default.asp), some standards for practice, and several "clinical indicators" (see, for example, the "Practice" page at http://www. socialworkers.org/practice/default.asp), a search of the NASW website in December 2004 did not produce any practice guidelines derived from systematic reviews of the research literature. However, the number of published practice guidelines and manuals that directly or indirectly apply to social work will undoubtedly continue to increase at a substantial rate (see, for example, Allness & Knoedler, 1998; Barlow, 2001; Barrett & Ollendick, 2004; Budney & Higgins, 1998; Carroll, 1998; Corcoran, 2003; Foa, Keane, & Friedman, 2000; Henggeler, Borduin, Schoenwald, Rowland, & Cunningham, 1998; LeCroy, 1994; Meichenbaum, 1995; Mercer & Woody, 1999; Miller, 1995; Roberts & Yeager, 2004; Saunders, Berliner, & Hanson, 2001; Van Hasselt & Hersen, 1996; Van Hasselt & Hersen, 1998; White, 1999a, 1999b).

The growing number of practice guidelines and treatment manuals based upon systematic reviews of the research may advance the quality of care to consumers—if widely disseminated, easily accessed, and prepared in practitioner-friendly fashion,. However, in addition to evidence-based practice guidelines and manuals, we will also see an increase in those unsupported by research. Social workers and other helping professionals that are unfamiliar with the knowledge base and do not read critically, may unwittingly adopt guidelines and manuals that lack evidentiary support and are, essentially, based upon the opinions of their authors.

Practice Relevant Research

There will be continued growth in the number of both primary and meta-analytic research studies that relate to the efficacy and effectiveness of various policies, programs, practices, and interventions—including some that evaluate the effectiveness of evidence-based practice itself. Most of these practice-relevant research studies will be conducted and published by researchers and practitioners in medicine, psychology, nursing, sociology, and allied professions. We can also expect an increase in such research by social workers. Encouraged by the efforts of the Society for Social Work Research and Practice (SWRR); the Institute for the Advancement of Social Work Research (IASWR); the National Institute of Mental Health (NIMH); the editors, boards, and contributors to journals such as *Social Work Research, Research on Social Work Practice*, and the new *Journal of Evidence-Based Social Work*, and those of several social work research centers. The proposed National Center for Social Work Research Act (H.R. 844) would contribute substantially as well. However, its passage in the near future appears unlikely.

In general, the rate of growth and the overall production of practice-relevant research by social workers will continue to be modest in comparison to those of other disciplines and professions. Despite the fact that the United States has at least 600,000 college-educated, employed social workers, only a tiny percentage conduct and publish research studies. Although schools and departments of social workers graduate approximately 30,000 social work students each year, only 300 or so receive doctoral degrees. Doctoral-level social workers—trained in research methods—could conduct and publish practice-relevant research studies. However, relatively few social work dissertations involve research of the effectiveness of policies and practices. An index search of the Social Work Abstracts (SWABS) electronic database identified 2556 social work dissertations completed during the period from November 1977 through May 2004. A scan of the titles revealed only a small number that involved the effectiveness or efficacy of policies, programs, practices, or interventions. The overwhelming majority of social work dissertation studies could be considered sociological or anthropological in nature—often involving surveys of or interviews with members of various special population groups. Based upon the titles, relatively few social work dissertations directly contribute to the knowledge based needed to support evidence-based practice.

The situation is similar in our social work journals. In an examination of 1849 articles published in 13 social work journals during the period from 1993 to the middle of 1997, the reviewers found that less that half (47%) could be classified as research articles. Of those, approximately 85% involved explanatory or descriptive research. Some 126 articles (about 15 percent of the 863 research articles or slightly less than 7% of all 1849 articles) involved studies of interventions in relation to outcomes. Unfortunately, only 42% of the 126 intervention studies were described with sufficient specificity to allow replication (Rosen, Proctor, & Staudt, 1999).

Consistent with its traditions, the profession of social work in the future will continue to make modest contributions to the knowledge based needed for effective practice. Social workers who consume research-based knowledge will rely primarily on findings from studies conducted by other professionals.

Access to Research Literature

The information and technology explosion will continue to extend both the amount of research literature available to social workers and the ease by which it may be accessed. The number of online, electronic bibliographic databases with full-text accessibility will expand and the cost for access will decrease. In addition to the large fee-based bibliographic databases currently available, free services will emerge to aid those helping professionals and organizations interested in improving the quality and effectiveness of their policies, programs, and practices. Most of these will be interdisciplinary in nature and dominated by health and allied health professions (see, for example, MEDLINE/PubMed at http://www.pubmed.gov; the National Library of Medicine at http://www.nlm.nih.gov; the Substance Abuse and Mental Health Services Administration's [SAMSHA] Mental Health Information Center at http://www.mentalhealth.samhsa.gov and the National Clearinghouse for Alcohol and Drug Information [NCADI} at http://ncadi.samhsa.gov;

the National Health Service [NHS] Centre for Reviews and Dissemination [DRD] at http://www.york.ac.uk/inst/crd and the Cochrane Library at http://www.thecochranelibrary.com). However, the number of specialized online, electronic bibliographic services useful for evidence-based social work will also grow (see, for example, the Campbell Collaboration [C2] Library with its Social, Psychological, Educational & Criminological Trials Register [C2-SPECTR] and C2 Reviews of Interventions, and Policy Evaluations [C2-RIPE]) at http://www.campbellcollaboration.org, the Electronic Library for Social Care [eLSC] at http://www.elsc.org.uk, and Be Evidence-Based at http://www.be-evidence-based.com).

We also anticipate the development of social work notification systems through which policy makers, adminstrators, and practitioners receive electronic updates about research studies that pertain to their particular areas of interest. Healthcare professionals have long been able to receive timely notification of current research via electronic newsletters (see, for example, the various medical specialty newsletters available through www.medscape.com; PsychiatryMatters NewsWatch via http://www.psychiatrymatters.md; the Psych-Watch Newsletter at http://www.psychwatch.com; the NCADI Update via http://ncadi.samhsa.gov/promos/ncadiupdate). Several professional journals currently email interested readers tables of contents of forthcoming issues (see, for example, the table of contents electronic alert system available through NASW Press at http://ninetta.naswpressonline.org and Sage Publication's at http://online.sagepub.com). Increasingly, social workers will be able to access online, electronic bibliographic information and indeed the full-text of practice-relevant research articles, books, and book chapters. Furthermore, the search and retrieval processes will become ever more user-friendly.

Applying Research to Practice

The continuing explosion in and growing ease of access to the research literature and evidence-based practice guidelines or treatment manuals, growing constituent demands for effective practices, and increased efforts by some educators (Mullen, 2004b; Rosen, 1996) and some schools and departments of social work to teach skills needed to implement EBP (Howard, McMillen, & Pollio, 2003) will modestly reduce the substantial gap between the actual practices of social workers and the research-based evidence of what works. We hope that social workers—individually and collectively through journal clubs, study groups, and practice research networks—will avail themselves of these information resources and incorporate program and practice evaluation processes in efforts to improve the quality of service to clients. However, we do not anticipate a dramatic reversal in previous patterns. Survey studies of social workers' use of the professional literature in general and research studies in particular support the conclusion that only a small percentage of social workers regularly read scholarly publications and apply research findings research in service. "Social work practitioners are unlikely to have the time, inclination, support, or resources to either read research or integrate it into their day-to-day practice" (Holosko & Leslie, 1998, pp. 436-447). For some time to come, relatively few social workers in the United States will access, understand, critically analyze, and apply practice-relevant knowledge in their service to clients in need.

CONCLUSION

Since its origins during the late 1800's, social work has been characterized by internal conflict and polarization. We social workers have disagreed among ourselves about almost every conceivable issue—including our primary mission and goals, and the means by which they should be pursued. It is hardly surprising that many social workers—perhaps especially those who serve as educators in schools and departments of social work—disagree about the value of evidence-based practice and the assumptions upon which it is based. The current and historical evidence suggests that conflict and polarization about EBP—and many other issues—will continue for the foreseeable future.

Despite continued challenges to its legitimacy, evidence-based practice in social work will evolve conceptually and empirically to incorporate greater attention to the particular needs, values, and preferences of particular individuals and specific population groups. The popularity of evidence-based social work among social workers will also grow—albeit probably at a slower rate and to a lesser extent than in our sister professions of medicine, nursing, and psychology. In general, we anticipate modest progress toward idealized aspirations of an emerging generation of social workers who are, in essence, scholarly, research-minded professionals who routinely access, review, understand, and analyze the practice-relevant research literature; apply research findings to their practice; and evaluate the process and outcomes of their services through time-series or single-system designs (Mullen & Bacon, 2004).

References

Allness, D. J., & Knoedler, W. H. (1998). *The PACT model of community-based treatment for persons with severe and persistent mental illnesses: A manual for PACT start-up.* Arlington, VA: National Alliance for the Mentally Ill.

Barlow, D. H. (Ed.). (2001). *Clinical handbook of psychological disorders: A step-by-step treatment manual* (3rd ed.). New York: Guilford.

Barrett, P. M., & Ollendick, T. H. (Eds.). (2004). *Handbook of interventions that work with children and adolescents: Prevention and treatment.* Hoboken, NJ: John Wiley.

Bilson, A. (Ed.). (2004). *Evidence-based practice and social work.* London: Whiting & Birch.

Briggs, H. E., & Rzepnicki, T. L. (Eds.). (2004). *Using evidence in social work practice: Behavioral perspectives.* Chicago: Lyceum Books.

Budney, A. J., & Higgins, S. T. (1998). *Manual 2: A community reinforcement approach: Treating cocaine addition*: National Institute on Drug Abuse, U.S. Department of Health and Human Services, National Institutes of Health.

Carroll, K. M. (1998). *Manual 1: A cognitive-behavioral approach: Treating cocaine addition*: National Institute on Drug Abuse, U.S. Department of Health and Human Services, National Institutes of Health.

Corcoran, J. (2000). *Evidence-based social work practice with families: A lifespan approach.* New York: Springer.

Corcoran, J. (2003). *Clinical applications of evidence-based family interventions.* New York: Oxford University Press.

Cournoyer, B. R. (2004). *The evidence-based social work skills book.* Boston: Allyn & Bacon.

Cournoyer, B. R., & Powers, G. T. (2002). Evidence-based social work: The quiet revolution continues. In A. R. Roberts & G. J. Greene (Eds.), *Social workers' desk reference* (pp. 798-807). New
York: Oxford University Press.

CSWE. (2001). *Educational policies and accreditation standards.* Retrieved January 23, 2002, from
http://www.cswe.org/epas.htm

CWLA. (2003). *Child Welfare League of America: Best practice guidelines for behavior management.*
Washington, DC: Child Welfare League of America.

Dulmus, C. N., & Sowers, K. M. (Eds.). (2004). *Kids and violence: The invisible school experience.*
Binghamton, NY: Haworth Social Work Practice Press.

Entwistle, V. A., Sheldon, T. A., Sowden, A. J., & Watt, I. A. (1998). Evidence-informed patient
choice. *International Journal of Technology Assessment in Health Care, 14,* 212-215.

Foa, E. B., Keane, T. M., & Friedman, M. J. (Eds.). (2000). *Effective treatments for PTSD: Practice
guidelines from the International Society for Traumatic Stress Studies.* New York: Guilford Press.

Gambrill, E. (1999). Evidence-based practice: An alternative to authority-based practice. *Families
in Society, 80*(4), 341-350.

Gambrill, E. (2001). Social work: An authority-based profession. *Research on Social Work Practice,
11*(2), 166-176.

Gibbs, L. E. (2003). *Evidence-based practice for the helping professions: A practical guide with integrated multimedia.* Pacific Grove, CA: Brooks/Cole-Thomson Learning.

Gilgun, J. F. (2005). The four cornerstones of evidence-based practice in social work. *Research on
Social Work Practice, 15,* 52-61.

Glicken, M. D. (2004). *Improving the effectiveness of the helping professions: An evidence-based practice
approach*: Sage Publications.

Henggeler, S. W., Borduin, C. M., Schoenwald, S. K., Rowland, M. D., & Cunningham, P. B.
(1998). *Multisystemic treatment of antisocial behavior in children and adolescents.* New York: Guilford.

Hilarski, C. (Ed.). (2005). *Addiction, assessment, and treatment with adolescents, adults, and families.*
Binghamton, NY: Haworth Social Work Practice Press.

Holosko, M. J., & Leslie, D. (1998). Obstacles to conducting empirically based practice. In J. S.
Wodarski & B. A. Thyer (Eds.), *Handbook of empirical social work practice: Social problems and
practice issues* (Vol. 2, pp. 433-451). New York: John Wiley & Sons.

Howard, M. O., McMillen, C. J., & Pollio, D. F. (2003). Teaching evidence-based practice: Toward
a new paradigm for social work education. *Research on Social Work Practice, 13*(2), 234-259.

Joint Initiative of Mental Health Professional Organizations. (2000). *Mental health ill of rights: Principles for the provision of mental health and substance abuse treatment services.* Retrieved December
30, 2004, from http://www.apa.org/pubinfo/rights/rights.html

LeCroy, C. W. (Ed.). (1994). *Handbook of child and adolescent treatment manuals.* New York: Free
Press.

Macdonald, G. M. (2001). *Effective interventions for child abuse and neglect: An evidence-based approach to planning and evaluating interventions.* New York: John Wiley & Sons.

McNeece, C. A., & Thyer, B. A. (2004). Evidence-based practice and social work. *Journal of Evidence-Based Social Work, 1*(1), 7-25.

Meichenbaum, D. (1995). *A clinical handbook/practical therapist manual for assessing and treating
post-traumatic stress disorder (PTSD).* Waterloo, Ontario, Canada: Institute Press.

Mercer, D. E., & Woody, G. E. (1999). *Manual 3: An individual drug counseling approach to treat
cocaine addiction: The Collaborative Cocaine Treatment Study model*: National Institute on Drug

Abuse, U.S. Department of Health and Human Services, National Institutes of Health.

Miller, W. R. (1995). *Motivational enhancement therapy manual: A clinical research guide for therapists treating individuals with alcohol abuse and dependence.* Washington, DC: U.S. Government Printing Office.

Mullen, E. J. (2002). *Evidence-based knowledge: Designs for enhancing practitioners use of research findings (a bottom up approach).* Retrieved December 27, 2004, from http://www.uta.fi/laitokset/sospol/eval2002/EvidenceF2002.PDF#search='evidencebased%20and%20social%20work'

Mullen, E. J. (2004a). Evidence-based social work—theory & practice: Historical and reflective perspective. In E. J. Mullen (Ed.), *Evidence-based practice in a social work context—the United States case* (pp. 1-13). Helsinki, Finland: National Research and Development Centre for Welfare and Health (STAKES).

Mullen, E. J. (2004b). Facilitating practitioner use of evidence-based practice. In A. R. Roberts & K. R. Yeager (Eds.), *Evidence-based practice manual: Research and outcome measures in health and human services* (pp. 205-210). New York: Oxford University Press.

Mullen, E. J., & Bacon, W. (2004). Implementation of practice guidelines and evidence-based treatment. In A. R. Roberts & K. R. Yeager (Eds.), *Evidence-based practice manual: Research and outcome measures in health and human services* (pp. 210-218). New York: Oxford University Press.

Myers, L. L., & Thyer, B. A. (1997). Should social work clients have the right to effective treatment? *Social Work, 42*(3), 288-299.

NASW. (1999). *Code of ethics of the National Association of Social Workers.* Washington, D.C.: National Association of Social Workers.

Newman, T. (2004). *Evidence-based social work: A guide for the perplexed.* London: Russell House.

Roberts, A. R., & Yeager, K. R. (Eds.). (2004). *Evidence-based practice manual: Research and outcome measures in health and human services.* New York: Oxford University Press.

Rosen, A. (1996). The scientific practitioner revisited: Some obstacles and prerequisites for fuller implementation in practice. *Social Work Research, 20,* 105-111.

Rosen, A., & Proctor, E. K. (Eds.). (2003). *Developing practice guidelines for social work intervention: Issues, methods, and research agenda.* New York: Columbia University Press.

Rosen, A., Proctor, E. K., & Staudt, M. M. (1999). Social work research and the quest for effective practice. *Social Work Research, 23*(1), 4-14.

Saunders, B. E., Berliner, L., & Hanson, R. F. (2001). *Guidelines for the psychosocial treatment of intrafamilial child physical and sexual abuse (Final Draft Report: July 30, 2001).* Retrieved July 23, 2002, from http://www.musc.edu/cvc/OVCGuidelinesFinalDraft7-30-01.PDF

Smith, D. (Ed.). (2005). *Social work and evidence-based practice.* London, UK: Jessica Kingsley.

Thyer, B. A., & Kazi, M. A. F. (Eds.). (2004). *International perspectives on evidence-based practice in social work.* Basingstoke: Venture Press.

Van Hasselt, V. B., & Hersen, M. (Eds.). (1996). *Sourcebook of psychological treatment manuals for adult disorders.* New York: Plenum.

Van Hasselt, V. B., & Hersen, M. (Eds.). (1998). *Handbook of psychological treatment protocols for children and adolescents.* Mahwah, N.J.: Erlbaum.

Vincent, J. P. (2000). *Domestic violence: Guidelines for research-informed practice.* London: Jessica Kingsley.

White, J. R. (1999a). *Overcoming generalized anxiety disorder: Client manual: A relaxation, cognitive restructuring, and exposure-based protocol for the treatment of GAD.* Oakland, CA: New Harbinger.

White, J. R. (1999b). *Overcoming generalized anxiety disorder: Therapist protocol.* Oakland, CA: New

Harbinger.

Wodarski, J. S., & Dziegielewski, S. F. (Eds.). (2002). *Human behavior and the social environment: Integrating theory and evidence-based practice.* New York: Springer.

Author's Note

Address correspondence to: Barry R. Cournoyer, D.S.W., L.C.S.W., Professor, Indiana University School of Social Work, 902 West New York Street, Indianapolis, Indiana 46202-5156. e-mail: bcourno@iupui.edu.

THE FUTURE OF STRENGTHS-BASED SOCIAL WORK

Charles A. Rapp
Dennis Saleebey
W. Patrick Sullivan

Abstract: *The future of strengths based social work is both promising and precarious. In this article we seek to capture this uncertain state by sketching the evolution of the strengths approach and offering a brief evaluation of its status today. There are any number of approaches to both theory and practice at present that profess to be strengths-based. It is imperative that we develop stable and concrete criteria for determining whether a given perspective or framework is, in fact, funded by strengths principles and practices. We offer six standards for making such a judgment. We also examine the future of the strengths model. Of course, writing on the future tempts one to make predictions. We have eschewed such folly. Instead, we offer four tasks that we believe would bolster the development of strengths-based social work in the future.*

Keywords: future, strengths, social work

BACKGROUND

It remains an object of some curiosity, our culture's fascination and near obsession with aberrations, problems, pathologies, deficits—the "evil" and the bizarre beguile us. Perhaps it was ever so, but contemporary culture and the helping and ministering professions have developed a language fairly bursting with pessimistic, off-putting, and somewhat disparaging terms to describe those human conditions that we choose to define as out of the norm (even though we are fascinated by them), beyond the realm of the "normal," good, and upstanding. We characterize many groups of "others" (read: not us) with a lexicon that frightens, limits, and in some ways is a perjury of someone's life. A swelling conglomerate of institutions and agencies, professions and disciplines, businesses and services including medicine, psychiatry, big Pharma, the insurance industry, and not the least, the mass media, turn handsome profits by assuring us that we are, in some critical way flawed, victims of toxic childhood experiences or warped by flawed decisions or contaminated relationships.

We can only escape a dread future by turning to that ever expanding phalanx of practitioners, both degreed and ersatz—the variety of gurus, swamis, ministers, and the genuine and counterfeit therapists standing ready to attend to our miseries. Add to that the continuing penchant toward "medicalizing" and "pathologizing" almost every pattern, habit, trait, and inclination of human behavior and you have an enthralling mix of diagnoses, labels, and identities at the ready --all broadcasting our abnormalities, disorders, weaknesses, fallibilities, and deficits (Kaminer, 1993; Peele, 1995; Peele & Brodsky, 1991; Reiff, 1991, Walker III, 1996). But important, too, has been the developing realization that our focus on aberrations and problems has not yielded much in the way of social

Charles A. Rapp is Professor and Dennis Saleebey is Professor Emeritus, School of Social Welfare, The University of Kansas, Lawrence, Kansas. W. Patrick Sullivan is Professor, School of Social Work, Indiana University, Indianapolis.

betterment, or the lessening of the incidence and prevalence of various disorders (Hillman & Ventura, 1992). Likewise, there is a growing body of evidence and thought that the favored theme of many theories of disorder and mental illness-- *childhood troubles of various kinds are fateful for the development of pathology in adulthood*—is not very powerful or convincing (Lewis, 1997; Kagan, 1998). The lingua franca of the heightened allure with pathology is found in the Diagnostic and Statistical Manual IV TR of the American Psychiatric Association (2000).

HISTORY & SOCIAL WORK TRADITIONS

The lines between the modern-day strengths perspective and certain fashions, philosophies, movements, and appreciations of the past in American culture are faint but nonetheless real. Elements of strengths thinking can be traced back to the ideals of democracy, American idealism, the romance of the frontier, transcendentalism, the social gospel, and the persistent beat of positive thinking in American society. In this culture, strains of optimism, hope, positive expectations, the promise of tomorrow, and the possibility of remaking of the self have flourished in one form or another. They have been manifest in philosophies, religions, nostrums and panaceas peddled by a variety of gurus, shamans, evangelists, physicians, philosophers and politicians. These were, in some ways, reactions against the increasing secularization, industrialization, and commercialization of American culture. But it is important to reiterate that they also sought to find the best in human capacity and desire, both individually and collectively.

Intimations of the strengths orientation in the early years of social work include: the settlement house movement and the writings of Jane Addams and others; the views of Virginia Robinson, Bertha Capen Reynolds, the functional school of social work, the development of social group work, and, somewhat later, Ruth Smalley and Herbert Bisno. The words of Jane Addams reflected the thinking of many in this new profession of social work in the early 1900s:

> "We are gradually requiring of the educator that he [sic] shall free the powers of each man and connect him with the rest of life. We ask this not merely because it is the man's right to be thus connected but because we have become convinced that the social order cannot afford to get along without *his special contribution* [my emphasis]." (1902, p. 178)

More recent contributions to, and intimations of the strengths perspective flow from the expanding empowerment literature in social work. Paulo Freire, Barbara Simon, Barbara Solomon, and Anthony Maluccio and, more currently, the work of Lorraine Guiterrez and Judith A. B. Lee, multicultural and feminist critiques and frameworks have provided lessons and directions for the emergent strengths approach. From these varied points of view, we can extract some central ideas: 1) the necessity of a critical consciousness, what Paulo Freire called conscientization—the developing awareness of the sources of oppression, and the intentions and methods of the oppressors; 2) developing a sense of individual and collective efficacy and agency, moving toward liberation; 3) encouraging dialogue between those who would be freer and those who would assist in their liberation—so that people can "think, see, talk, and act for themselves" (Lee, 1994); 4) assuring equity, enhancing collective responsibility, and providing connections to social resources so that all can move toward individual development and greater contributions to the social order (Gutie'rrez, DeLois, & GlenMaye,1995; Lee, 1994; Freire, 1996).

WHAT IS STRENGTHS-BASED PRACTICE?

Strengths-based approaches have been criticized as being poorly defined (Staudt, Howard & Drake, 2001) and not really new or different then many other traditional approaches (McMillen, Morris & Sherraden, 2004). Since the strengths model has gained currency, many people are claiming they are "doing strengths". Sometimes that seems to mean "being nice to people" or having a small section at the bottom of an assessment form calling for a listing of strengths. A recent article described an intervention emphasizing "skills training and client input" as a strengths intervention (Bjorkman, Hansson & Sandlund, 2002). Others lay claim to a strengths approach because they attribute a client's problems to environmental causes (Tice & Perkins, 2002). These over-simplifications could emanate from either poor specification by the model developers or by a limited understanding of the approach.

The following is our attempt to identify the six hallmarks of strengths-based practice. Four diverse practice approaches that we view as strengths-based are used to demonstrate the six criteria. The four strengths-based approaches are: strengths case management (Rapp, 1998), solution-focused therapy (Miller, Hubble & Duncan, 1996), individual placement and support model of supported employment (IPS) (Becker & Drake, 2003), and the asset-building model of community development (Kretzmann and McKnight, 1993).

1. *It is goal oriented.* Clients are invited to set the goals they would like to achieve in their lives. Often, social workers help clients to define the goal. Common examples are clients who are so depressed and crushed that they claim not to have any goals or have no idea what they may be; or the family who can only frame their situation as a surfeit of serious problems. Methods for developing goals and visions include use of the "Miracle Question" in solution-focused therapy; framing client's behavior as a series of small (or large) achievements in strengths case management; and competitive job acquisition and retention in IPS. In asset-based community development, the first area of concentration is "agenda setting". The central dependent variable in strengths-based work is client-set goal attainment.

2. *Systematic assessment of strengths.* A strengths-based approach has a systematic set of protocols for assessing and documenting strengths and avoids assessment of problems, deficits or pathology. Methods include assets mapping in community development; strengths assessment in multiple life domains in case management; and the vocational profile in IPS. In solution-focused therapy, assessment is focused on what already works, searching for exceptions to the problems, and identifying coping strategies already in the client's repertoire. . The emphasis is often on the current situation although the past may be mined for talents, assets, resources that were extant at one time but may have been lost or forgotten.

3. *The environment is seen as rich in resources.* An emphasis in each of the four

practices is that the natural community is the primary source of people, opportunities, supports, and resources. In IPS, the work is done directly with employers; strengths-based case management places a primacy on the identification and use of natural resources; solution-focused therapy requires consideration of whether the intervention plan builds on the support system's strengths and resources. In asset-based community organization the work begins with what is present in the community--the assets, resources and capacities of the residents, local associations, and groups, and not with what is absent or what is problematic or what is missing. A central notion is that the path to goal attainment is the matching of client desires, strengths, and environment resources.

4. *Explicit methods are used for using client and environmental strengths for goal attainment.* In solution-focused therapy, the protocol requires client-goal setting first with the identification of relevant strengths (e.g. what works now, what can be imagined as working, exploring exceptions to the problems) to be anchored by the goal. In strengths case management, Rapp (1998) describes how the strengths assessment is used to help clients set goals, generate resource options, set short-term goals and tasks, and guide assignment of roles and responsibilities. In IPS, the individual employment plan grows straight from the vocational profile.

5. *The relationship is hope-inducing.* In strengths-based work, the importance of the relationship is explicitly focused on increasing the hopefulness of the client. The relationship is accepting, purposeful, and empathetic. As an empowering relationship it also should: 1) increase the client's perceptions of their abilities; 2) increase the client's options and perception of options; 3) increase the opportunities and confidence of the client to choose and act on those choices"(Rapp, 1998, pg 64). [where does the quote start?] In strengths-based case management, the relationship is viewed as one of the six core principles. Becker and Drake (2003) start their description of IPS methods with a section on the relationship. In community development, the dynamic of change is the building, rebuilding, and recasting of relationships between local residents, local institutions, and local groups.

6. *The provision of meaningful choices is central and clients have the authority to choose.* In the four strengths-based approaches, each stage of the process from goal setting, resources to be acquired, the pace of the work together, assignment of responsibility, etc. emphasize the worker's role in extending the list of choices, clarifying choices, and giving the clients the confidence and authority to direct the process. In IPS, the goals, type of job, type of employer, specific approach to the employer, and how fast to proceed are based on a mutual generation of alternatives and client selection. The same is true in strengths-based case management across all life domains not just employment. In solution-focused therapy, clients are perceived as the experts on their own lives and are urged to generate possible solutions and alternative paths.

WHERE ARE WE NOW?

Over the last two decades or so, a number of areas of research, conceptual development and practice have reflected some of the ideas and approaches reminiscent of the strengths model.

The development of strengths-based interventions has occurred in two ways. The first concerns the use of strengths-based case management that grew directly from the work at the University of Kansas in the early 1980's. Since the first application of the strengths approach (by that name) with case management in mental health (Rapp & Chamberlain, 1985; Modricin, Rapp & Chamberlain, 1983), case management practice applications have grown rapidly. These include people in poverty (Jones & Bricker-Jenkins, 2003), physical and sexual abuse (Anderson, 2001; Walsh, 1998) and older adults (Fast & Chapin, 2002). Of particular importance is the work led by Sheldon Siegal and Richard Rapp from Wright State University is using strengths case management with people who have substance abuse problems. They have developed practices and found promising results through experimental testing.

Second, growing out of a discontent with problem, deficit and pathology–oriented models that have long dominated social work and other helping professions, independent efforts to design strengths-based approaches have emerged. This would include the afore-mentioned approaches of asset-based community development (Kretzmann & McKnight, 1993), solution-focused therapy (Miller, Hubble & Duncan, 1996), and the individual placement and support model of supported employment (Becker & Drake, 2003). In adult mental health, newer program models, like supported education (Mowbray, Brown, Furlong-Norman & Saydan, 2002), and supported housing (Ridgway & Rapp, 1997) are being developed. In youth services, positive youth development and resiliency approaches (Bernard, 2002) offer a significant alternative to traditional approaches. Below are some approaches to theory and practice that reflect strengths model thinking and doing.

Resilience. In the fields of developmental psychology and developmental psychopathology in particular, the research has increasingly shown (and this was surprising to early investigators in this field) that many more children than ever imagined rebound from adverse and difficult life circumstances so that, in adulthood, you would not necessarily be able to distinguish between them and their cohorts (Benard, 2004). This is not to say that they do not suffer, that they do not have problems stemming from their difficult past. They do. But it is to say that many of them make conscious life decisions and choices that allow them to walk the path to reasonably effective functioning in their daily lives (Masten, 2001). McLaughlin and Talbert (2003) suggest inner strengths develop and surface as these children and youth confront hardships but are also given a hand by caring adults and teachers, and a context in which they are both safe and challenged to learn and develop.

Health and Wellness. Much of modern medicine seems to be a war against symptoms, pain, discomfort, and the meaning of illness for a given person. More importantly, precious little attention is given to wellness, healing and wholeness. Luckily, there is a rising interest in the possibility of wellness and the transformative potentials of illness (Dossey, 2003). People do seem to have the capacity for healing, even in the midst of crisis. Given half a chance, the body and mind together are, at heart, proactive life-enhancers.

Hope. The interest in the transformative and guiding powers of hope and positive expectations has grown enormously in recent years. Hopefulness, even if only a "positive illusion", is now seen by many as central to successful practice (therapy, counseling, etc,) of all kinds. Hans Strupp (1999) argues that the therapist-client relationship is central to all successful approaches to therapy, and successful ones, among other things, foster hope. There is an abiding sense among strengths-based practitioners that spurring hope is the central dynamic in helping clients change their lives for the better.

Positive psychology. The work of Martin Seligman, Beatrice Wright, Shane J. Lopez, C. R. Snyder and others is dedicated to the proposition that helping others is most productively done by creating a positive, optimistic, and collaborative therapeutic relationship, seeking out the strengths and constructive resources within the client and the environment, and mobilizing those in assisting the individual, family, or community achieve their goals and accomplish their intentions.

Health realization/community empowerment. The results of the work of Roger Mills, and Jack Pransky (1998), building on some of the ideas of Syd Banks, in helping to resurrect dispirited, demoralized and economically distressed communities is nothing short of miraculous. The basic idea seems simple enough—too simple, perhaps--but it has a power that has been amply documented in many communities. This lengthy quote by Roger Mills (1998) says it plainly but compellingly.

> "The residents started to realize that what was keeping them down in life was their thoughts. See, they'd bought the con game. They'd bought the lie. They'd bought the rap that they're supposed to be poor and not be able to do any better—because they're Black, because they dropped out of school, because they started having children when they were thirteen, because they're in public housing and on welfare….They bought into a set of beliefs—but it's just a thought. *It's just a thought!* Everything is created and maintained via thought. That's the simplicity of it. And all they did was let go of that way of thinking, because they started to see it as beliefs as beliefs programmed like a computer, as opposed to reality….If you put a crack in someone's "normal" way of thinking what comes up in its place is common sense." (Pransky, pp. 258-259)

It is clear from this short review of approaches to helping sharing similar appreciations regarding the capacities and resources within and around clients that there is a growing interest in focusing essentially on strengths rather than deficits and problems in assisting clients in creating a better life for themselves, their significant others, and their communities.

SHAPING THE FUTURE

As we sit here today, its hard to envision that strengths-based social work will ever be the dominant mode of practice. The culture in which we are imbedded is overwhelmingly shaded in the perspective and language of problem, deficit, and pathology. There often seems to be a powerful "conspiracy of understanding" between clients and their helpers that maintains the oppression under which they live and "victim" status they adopt.

This pessimistic assessment must be tempered, however, by the recognition of how far strengths-based approaches have come in the last twenty years. This includes application in a wide-range of fields of practice and in diverse methods form case management to social policy (Chapin, 1995; Rapp, Pettus & Goscha, 2004), and a beginning base of research with promising results. The future will be influenced by how well we are able to address the following.

Gaining Conceptual and Practice Clarity.

One task is to develop a clearer definition of strengths-based practice. Earlier in this article, we tried to define the six core ingredients but many questions remain. How many of these elements are required before the label of strengths-based practice is used? If a practice has three or four of the elements, for example, does it qualify? Should intervention only using one or two core ingredients be described as having "some strengths features"? Can (and should) practice be viewed on a continuum from pathology / problem approaches to purely strengths- based approaches? Much of the clarity we seek is about the precise relationship, in any given case or context, between struggles, challenges, problems, on the one hand, and strengths, competencies and resources, on the other. Such clarity depends importantly on accumulating the clinical wisdom of practitioners, the views of clients, and, as we see below, marshaling programs of inquiry and research.

Building an Empirical Base

It is significant that there has been growth in research on strengths-based approaches and that much of it is promising. Statistically significant differences favoring strengths-based case management include: increasing social support (Macias, Farley, Jackson & Kinney, 1997); lessening the severity of symptoms (Barry, Zeber, Blow & Valenstein, 2003); and more positive employment outcomes (Siegel et al, 1996; Modrcin, Rapp & Poertner, 1988). R. Rapp (2002) found that strengths-based case management increased retention in treatment of substance abusers and thereby decreased drug use and criminal justice involvement, and enhanced employment functioning. Other approaches generally viewed as strengths-based have also found positive results--community development (Mills, 1995; Bernard, 2000), solution-focused therapy (Miller, Duncan & Kebble, 1997), and individual placement and support model of employment services (Becker & Drake, 2003). Having said this, the research is sometimes flawed and far from conclusive, generally suffering from small subject populations, poor descriptions of the independent variable, and varied dependent measures. Other concerns include the confounding of treatment modality and treatment intensity in several studies, and inadequate description of the services received in the control conditions (Staudt, Howard & Drake, 2001).

While the early studies of strengths-based approaches are somewhat promising, mounting programs of research is badly needed. In intervention research, we need to better conceptualize the dependent variable. Is individual client goal attainment, although most compatible with the model's conception, sufficient evidence? How are goals of different magnitude and order analyzed as a collective? Given the model's intent, should measures of hope and self-confidence be used as well as measures such as hospitalization, employment, reduction of substance use etc. Is there a core set of measures relevant to most tests of strengths-based approaches?

Concerning the independent variable, researchers need to be explicit about the elements of strengths-based practice being employed and systematically monitor the fidelity of implementation. A promising fidelity measure for strengths case management is currently being developed by Rick Goscha and associates at the University of Kansas.

There is also ample room for inquiry more amenable to qualitative research approaches. For example, we know very little about how clients and workers generate options or by what processes clients choose between options. Since hope is such a complex phenomenon (Ridgway, 2004), what are the hope-inducing processes that are used and how are they experienced by clients?

The implementation of evidence-based practices in mental health and human services is poor. In mental health, most clients with severe and persistent mental illness do not receive services based on evidence-based practice (Lehman, Steinwachs, Dixon, Postrado, et al 1998).

The difficulty in diffusing innovations suggests research directed at the problem. What strategies are most effective? What agency conditions are necessary for high fidelity strengths-based practice implementation? What is their necessary attitude or structure or training or supervision?

Imbuing MSW and PhD Curricula.

Clearly there would have to be changes in the standard practice and research curricula at all levels of social work education if the strengths perspective is to gain a foothold in the thinking and doing of educators and would-be practitioners. This requires a coordinated effort in the development and dissemination of educational materials that would encourage the inclusion of strengths model thinking and practices in the standard curricula in practice, policy, research and human behavior. A key here would be helping educators to incorporate such knowledge within the curriculum they already teach. There are increasing numbers of textbooks in human behavior and social work practice that do have the strengths perspective as an important part of their conceptual frameworks (for example, Krogsrud-Miley et al., 2004). Generally, most textbooks incorporate the strengths approach as one of many approaches (ecological, solution-focused, empowerment, etc,.) to social work practice and its theoretical and conceptual foundations (e.g., Compton & Galloway, 2005) but few have the strengths model as the base of their conceptual scaffolding.

The key, however, is to assure that educators have been exposed, in practice and their education, at professional conferences and workshops, and in the professional literature to the strengths perspective. This requires, among other things, that there is a substantial core of researchers and practitioners, academicians and administrators who are conversant with, and teach, do research and practice guided by strengths concepts, principle and methods. The Council on Social Work Education includes in its most current Educational Policy and Accreditation Standards (2001) the following statement regarding the content of foundation social work practice classes, "Social work practice content is anchored in the purposes of the social work profession and focuses on strengths, capacities, and resources of client systems in relation to their broader environments." (p. 11)

Creating an Institute for Strengths-based
Social Work Practice, Teaching, and Inquiry

The purposes of a strengths institute would be manifold. What follows is a brief description and forecast of some of them. The overall purpose of this institute would be to foster the continuing conceptual and practical development of the principles and practices of the strengths perspective. The institute would sponsor and carry out research on the effectiveness of the strengths model with a variety of different consumer populations. Part of such inquiry would be based on a comparative effectiveness model with other theories and methods of practice. Such an institute would investigate and develop the further expansion, on the basis of conceptual advances and these inquiries, of the use of the strengths perspective with groups, families, and communities.

Such an institute would issue reports of these developments for publication in journals, for use by agencies and practitioners, and for dissemination to other organizations involved in strengths-based and related approaches to research and practice (e.g., resilience, positive psychology). The institute would also dedicate itself to the continuing articulation of research and inquiry actually conducted on the basis of strengths principles.

The institute would offer workshops, seminars, consultation, and classes on various aspects of the strengths-based practice for students, practitioners, administrators, and faculty. Seminars and workshops on the design of practice curricula using the strengths perspective for faculty in BSW, MSW, and Ph.D. programs in social work, and related professions and disciplines would be offered. In addition, the institute could prepare and offer monographs on the development and articulation of the strengths model in classroom curricula, field placements, and faculty development.

Among other things, an institute could provide a variety of materials—monographs, tracts, videos, articles, etc.—to schools, agencies, practitioners, administrators, researchers—who want to become more knowledgeable about the strengths model and how to employ and apply its principles and practices.

Finally, an institute would be essential in the development of annual conferences (local, national, and international) designed to promote, extend, revise, and evaluate the strengths approach, and in sharing actual practices in a array of fields—from child welfare to aging, from juvenile justice to mental health.

CONCLUSION

In our view, perhaps clouded a bit by assumptions and biases, the future of the strengths approach to case management and, perhaps clinical practice as well, seems, if not robust, at least promising. Of course, its growth and development depends, as it must, on a number of factors including further conceptual and practical development, a more robust program of inquiry and evaluation, and increasing acceptance in the practice and pedagogical communities. Naturally, these are interdependent. Given our experience with the strengths-based approach, we see its worth, the positive impact it has on clients, practitioners, and students. Given these, we can only feel hopeful.

References

Addams, J. (1902*). Democracy and social ethics*. NY: Macmillan & Co.

American Psychiatric Association. (2000). *Diagnostic and statistical manual of mental disorders IV TR (Text revision)*. Washington, DC: APA.

Anderson, K. (2001). *Resistance and resilience in survivors of incest*. Lawrence, KS: School of Social Welfare, University of Kansas. Doctoral dissertation.

Barry, K.L., Zeber, J.E., Blow, F.C., & Valenstein, M. (2003). Effect of strengths model versus assertive community treatment model on participant outcomes and utilization: two-year follow-up. *Psychiatric Rehabilitation Journal 26*(3), 268-277.

Becker, D.R. & Drake, R.E. (2003). *A Working Life for People with Severe Mental Illness*. New York: Oxford.

Benard, B. (2004). *Resiliency: What we have learned*. San Francisco: WestEd.

Bernard, B. (2002). Turnaround people and places: Moving from risk to resistance. In D. Saleebey (ed.). *The Strengths Perspective in Social Work Practice (3rd edition)*. Boston: Allyn and Bacon, pp 213-227.

Bjorkaman, T., Hasson, L. & Sandlund, M. (2002). Outcome of case management based on the strengths model compared to standard care. *Social Psychiatry and Psychiatric Epidemiology, 37*, 147-152.

Chapin, R.K. (1995). Social Policy Development: The Strengths Perspective. *Social Work, 40*(4), 506-514.

Compton, B. R., Galaway, B. & Cournoyer, B. R. (2005). *Social work processes*. 7th Ed.Pacific Grove, CA: Brooks/Cole.

Council on Social Work Education (2001). *Educational policy and accreditation standards*. Alexandria, VA: CSWE.

Dossey, L. (2003). *Healing beyond the body: Medicine and the infinite reach of the mind*. Boston: Shambala.

Fast, B. & Chapin, R. (2002). The strengths model with older adults: Critical practice components. In D. Saleebey (ed.). *The Strengths Perspective in Social Work Practice*. Boston: Allyn and Bacon. 143-162.

Freire, P. (1996). *The pedagogy of hope: Reliving pedagogy of the oppressed*. NY: Continuum.

Gutie'rrez, L., DeLois, K., & GlenMaye, L. (1995). Understanding empowerment practice: Building on practitioner based knowledge. *Families in Society*, 76, 534-542.

Hillman, J., & Ventura, M. (1992). *We've had a hundred years of psychotherapy and the world is getting worse*. San Francisco: Harper.

Jones, J.C., & Bricker-Jenkins, M. (2003). Creating Strengths-Based Alliance to End Poverty. In D. Saleebey (ed.). *The Strengths Perspective in Social Work Practice (3rd edition)*. Boston: Allyn and Bacon.

Kagan, J. (1998). *Three seductive ideas*. Cambridge, MA: Harvard University Press.

Kaminer, W. (1993). *I'm dysfunctional, you're dysfunctional: The recovery movement and other self-help fashions*. NY: Vintage Books.

Kretzmann, J. P., & McKnight, J. L. (1993). *Building communities from the inside out: A path toward finding and mobilizing a community's assets*. Evanston, IL: Center for Urban Affairs and Policy Innovations, Northwestern University.

Krogsrud-Miley, K., O'Melia, M., & Dubois, B. (2004).*Generalist social work practice: An empowering approach*. 4th. Ed. Boston: Allyn&Bacon.

Lee, J. A. B. (1994). *The empowerment approach to social work practice.* NY: Columbia University Press.

Lehman, A.F., Steinwachs, D.M., Dixon, L.B., Postrado, L. et al (1998). Patterns of usual care for schizophrenia: Initial results from the Schizophrenia Patient Outcomes Research Team (PORT) Client Survey. *Schizophrenia Bulletin24*(1), 11-23.

Lewis, M. (1997). *Altering fate: Why the past does not predict the future.* NY: Guilford.

Macias, D., Farley, O.W., Jackson, R., & Kinney, R. (1997). Case management in the context of capitation financing: An evaluation of the strengths model. *Administration and Policy in Mental Health, 24*(6), 535-543.

Masten, A. (2001) Ordinary magic: resilience processes in development. *American Psychologist,*56, 227-238.

McLaughlin, M., & Talbert, J. (2001.) *Professional communities and the work of high school teaching.* Chicago: University of Chicago Press.

McMillen, J.C., Morris , & Sherraden, M. (2004). Ending social work's grudge match: Problems versus strengths. *Families in Society, 85*(2), 1-9.

Miller, S.D., Hobble, M.A., & Duncan, B.L. (1996). Handbook of Solution-Focused Brief Therapy. San Francisco: Jossey-Bass.

Mills, R. (1995). *Realizing mental health.* NY: Sulzburger & Graham,

Modrcin, M., Rapp, C.A., & Poertner, J. (1988). The evaluation of case management services with the chronically mentally ill. *Evaluation and Program Planning, 11*, 307 314.

Mowbray, C.T., Brown, K. ., Furlong-Norman, K. & Soydan, A.S. (eds). (2002). Supported Education and Psychiatric Rehabilitation. Linthium, Md.: International Association of Psychosocial Rehabilitation Services.

Peele, S. (1995). *Diseasing of America.* San Francisco: Jossey-Bass.

Peele, S., & Brodsky, A. (1991) *The truth about addiction and recovery.* NY: Simon & Schuster.

Pransky, J. (1998). *Modello: A story of hope for the inner-city and beyond.* Cabot, VT: NorthEast Health Realization Institute Publications.

Rapp, C.A. (1998). *The Strengths Model: Case Management with People Suffering from Severe and Persistent Mental Illness.* New York: Oxford.

Rapp, C.A., & Chamberlain, R. (1985). Case managers services to the chronically mentally ill. *Social Work, 30*(5), 417-422.

Rapp, C.A., Pettus, C., & Goscha, R. (2004). *Strengths-based social policy.* Lawrence, Kansas: The University of Kansas School of Social Welfare.

Rapp, R.C. (2002). Strengths-Based Case Management: Enhancing Treatment for Persons with Substance Abuse Problems. In D. Saleebey (ed.). *The Strengths Perspective in Social Work Practice (3rd Edition).* Boston: Allyn and Bacon.

Reiff, D. (1991). Victims all. *Harper's Magazine.* October, 49-56.

Ridgway, P. (2004). *Hope and Mental Health Recovery: Con-constructing New Paradigm Knowledge.* Unpublished dissertation. Lawrence, Kansas: The University of Kansas School of Social Welfare.

Ridgway, P., & Rapp, C.A. (1997). *The Active Ingredients of Effective Supported Housing: A Research Synthesis.* Lawrence, Kansas: The University of Kansas School of Social Welfare.

Siegal, H. A., Fisher, J.A., Rapp, R.C., Keliher, C.W., Wagner, J.H., O;Brien, W.F., &Cole, P.A. (1996). Enhancing substance abuse treatment with case management: Its impact on employment. *Journal of Substance Abuse Treatment, 13*(2), 93-98.

Staudt, M., Howard, M.O., & Drake, B. (2001). The operationzlization, implementation and effectiveness of the strengths perspective: A review of empirical studies. *Journal of Social Service Research, 27*(3), 1-21.

Strupp, H. H. (1999). Essential characteristics of helpful therapists. *Psychotherapy*, 36, 141-142.

Tice, Carolyn J. & Perkins, Kathleen. (2002). *The Faces of Social Policy—A Strengths Perspective.* Brooks/Cole, Thomson Learning.

Walker III, S. (1996). *A dose of sanity: Mind, medicine and misdiagnosis.* NY: John Wiley & Sons.

Walsh, F. (1998). *Strengthening family resilience.* NY: Guilford.

Author's Note

Address correspondence to: Charles A. Rapp, Ph.D., Professor, The University of Kansas, School of Social Welfare, Lawrence, Kansas 66044

TECHNOLOGY CONVERGENCE AND SOCIAL WORK:
WHEN CASE MANAGEMENT MEETS GEOGRAPHIC INFORMATION

Robert Vernon

Abstract: *Two information management technologies, case management systems and geographic information systems may merge. This will foster better service planning and delivery to people in need. This may also result in continued agency mergers and mission revisions.*

Keywords: services, planning, geographic information system, case management system, convergence, future

INTRODUCTION

Fifteen years ago, David Macarov (1991) wrote a courageous book predicting future trends in social work practice. In it, he provided speculative forecasts about how technology would influence and direct social work practice. Macarov suggested that the uses of computers for research, agency management, case management, policy planning , and direct services to clients would increase, resulting in time saving and increased job effectiveness. Increased worker surveillance, shifting power relationships between and within agencies, recording and records practices, and practice issues such as confidentiality concerns might also result. Macarov's forecasts have been remarkably accurate. Technology is indeed shaping the many faces of practice. Computers are now common fixtures on worker's desks. Case management systems (CMS) are proliferating and supplanting paper records. Geographic Information Systems (GIS) are beginning to emerge as assists for practice (Vernon, 2003). The web is being used more and more to retrieve and circulate information (Vernon and Lynch, 2000).

Let's explore how two types of information management systems may merge within the next decade. Specifically, case management systems and geographic information systems may evolve, converge, and become pivotal in how social service organizations operate.

TWO EMERGING TECHNOLOGIES

One of the most important technologies to emerge within the past decade has been case management systems. These programs – there are many – automate data entry and tasks and compile case record information throughout the agency. They have become common within the industry. This makes service provision, tracking, billing and evaluation *within the agency* far easier than in times past. Case histories and records, once entered, can help keep track of what has been done and what yet needs to be accomplished. At the organizational level, CMS can produce aggregate summaries that are extremely useful for personnel evaluation, service planning, reports to funders, and many other managerial tasks.

Yet at this time, CMS systems are idiosyncratic and unique to each agency. Some have been custom built and nursed along for decades. Others are proprietary, and written in

Robert Vernon is Associate Professor, School of Social Work, Indiana University, Indianapolis.
Copyright © 2005 *Advances in Social Work* Vol. 6 No. 1 (Spring 2005), 91-96

"closed code" so they cannot be modified by the end user. Still others are generic and "out of the box". Different computing platforms abound. Some still run on DOS, others on Unix, Linux, Windows, MacOS, and heaven only knows what else. Moreover, the investment in a CMS system is considerable. In addition to purchasing the software the agency must build the technology infrastructure within the organization and train personnel to use it. As a result, the industry has many agencies that have invested in "legacy" systems that vary considerably, and agency directors are unlikely to reinvest in new systems when the older ones work.

These CMS systems cannot communicate with each other. While legacy systems have been hard-won through extensive investments, these hold little collaboration and integration abilities *between agencies.* As a result, coordination of services between agencies cannot be facilitated by most case information management systems. "Wraparound" interventions are not supported. Clients must go through the same vetting process for every new agency they must access. They must tell their stories again and again in order to be considered for services, a "revolving door" experience that is demeaning and discouraging. This contributes to the often fragmentary, frustrating and spotty nature of service delivery to the people who need them the most. Thus, while services to clients *within* the agency may be well managed with good oversight, a repetitive, disjointed and disappointing maze awaits both providers and consumers when efforts to coordinate services between agencies are attempted. Frontline workers often provide what is readily available as opposed to what is needed. Opportunities for effective interventions are lost because the constellation of services and eligibility requirements within the community remain opaque to clients, workers and providers.

Enter the web. The idea of making CMS compatible across agencies is beginning to emerge within the industry (Kunkel and Yowell, 2001). While incompatible systems cannot readily communicate with one another owing to major platform, age and technical differences, almost all can be connected to the Internet. If one can program the agency's CMS system to access the web through what are termed "last mile programming efforts," then the potential for communication between agencies becomes substantially enhanced.

Pioneering efforts to accomplish this have been underway in Indiana for about five years, culminating in the Central Indiana Community Network (CICN).[1] Developed by Bitwise Solutions, Inc., this system is similar to historic urban community prototypes described by Hile and others (1997) but more complex by an order of magnitude. Similar to post-TANF welfare-to-work computer support systems (La Prad and Sand, 1997) the network provides the ability to collect, update, collaborate, and share social service and workforce development data in a secure environment that is accessed through a common, easy to use, world wide web-style user interface. The CICN project leverages the best of today's web browser-based technology. Moreover, the CICN system is scalable, meaning that tiny agencies can participate just as easily as huge service organizations. A basic CMS package is included for agencies that do not have them. Its interface can be easily mastered within a few hours, making the employee training investment modest. Finally, the CICN system has an "open architecture."

CICN promises unified inter-agency consumer service planning and delivery. Families in need will have electronically coordinated access to a comprehensive array of services:

emergency assistance, quality affordable child care, remedial education, health care, substance abuse treatment, basic social services, assessments, case management, legal counseling, mental health services, domestic violence assistance, housing assistance, work based employer centered job training, transportation assistance, job readiness placement and retention services, recreational and cultural activities, and nutrition programs. Nothing of this scale has ever been attempted in the human service infrastructure of Central Indiana, or anywhere else to this author's knowledge.

Of critical importance, once entered into a CICN networked agency, the clients need not endlessly repeat their stories. The revolving door of continually having to reapply to each new agency for help will finally open. Clients only need to be vetted once.

A second technology is also maturing: Geographic Information Systems (GIS).

GIS systems are becoming commonplace. We find them popping up in many places, such as when the cashier in a store asks us for our zipcode so the merchant can track its market or when we hit the web for driving directions to East Overshoe. GIS technology makes it possible to render precise geographical maps of myriad factors from multiple databases. In essence, GIS software makes it possible to graphically link *where things are* with *what things are* (ESRI, 2002). While many applications in urban planning have been developed over the last two decades, social workers are beginning to discover how powerful this medium can be for planning social services (Vernon, 2003). Enter SAVI.

The Social Assets and Vulnerabilities Indicators (SAVI) project, begun in 1994, is a vast web-delivered community information system for Central Indiana. It is one of the largest and most comprehensive systems of its type in the United States. It is publicly accessible through the web (http://www.savi.org) as well as though selected public libraries, service organizations, and government agencies. The system permits the pooling of data from participating public and private providers, and has the ability to create maps from several thousand social indicator variables. Sponsored by The Polis Center at Indiana University Purdue University Indianapolis (IUPUI), SAVI allows the visitor to specifically create and tailor GIS maps for very specialized purposes. The system can dramatically enable a visitor to discover if public transportation is available for pregnant Hispanic teens within a specific township towards locating a health clinic and hiring bilingual outreach workers. An evaluator or researcher wanting to establish baseline data for a county employment initiative can do so with relative ease. A funder can discern where, exactly, a new HIV clinic or WIC program should be located.

All chosen variables – one can enter as many as desired—can be layered and color-coded, making it possible to create very complex maps with multiple facets and dimensions that can be easily interpreted. Layers can be switched on and off or reordered. SAVI offers fast mapping, profiles for different communities within its eleven county area, comparison and trend abilities, and supports individualized user accounts. The sources for data in SAVI—there are about forty—are provided, making it possible to determine how reliable the GIS map and its resulting information may be. (Vernon, 2003) Moreover, SAVI also has an open architecture, and is capable of bringing in data via web services from servers that are external to the host system. (Sharon Kandris, SAVI Project Manager, personal communication, January 4, 2005).

Let us make the assumption that systems such as CICN and SAVI will become widely diffused and adopted in many communities over the next few years. This seems plausible: As the usefulness for these systems become apparent – better case resolution and better service planning – more and more communities will want to use them.

What may happen if these two different types of information management systems merge? Given that on the horizon we have the ability for agencies to pool client information through programs such as CICN and also the ability to graphically trace emerging trends and characteristics for populations at risk through programs such as SAVI, a beguiling possibility emerges: What if these two information technologies converge? This seems likely in the near future: Open computing architectures foster convergence.

CONVERGENCE

Both SAVI and CICN have open architectures. The great advantage to this is that anyone can design programs that can be relatively easily combined together, resulting in technological convergence into a hybrid. Technology convergence has been with us since Paleolithic hunters learned to haft stone points onto wooden sticks. It is still with us as anyone who owns a combination cell phone – PDA-camera-MP3 player can attest. In computing, architectures are often intentionally designed for convergence (Audin, 2004).

Why should case management and geographic information systems converge in the first place? Several factors may drive these two technologies into a single hybrid. While CMS systems promise immediate benefits to workers and consumers, the ability to generate service utilization reports is a valuable planning tool for agency administrators. A GIS-enhanced ability will allow leaders to gain a far more fine-grained and exquisitely detailed understanding of service needs that will be invaluable for planning service delivery.

This potential will not be lost on funders. Both public funders such as states and third-party payers value efficiency in cost-benefit planning. A merged community-level CMS-GIS ability will make fiscal decisions far easier than the current state of the art. Economically, the ability to deliver comprehensive wrap around services will become cheaper. The advantages of potential savings and need for smaller investments in social services will certainly be an incentive to develop and adopt community-wide CMS-GIS systems. As a prediction, state legislatures may clamor for merged systems in order to maximize service allocations. Insurance firms, given rising health care costs, will certainly be interested in maximizing services in a more efficient manor. In short, funders will drive convergence.

A second, subtler factor may also drive CMS-GIS convergence: Evidence-based practice. This movement has been ongoing for several years and we are beginning to see it become prominent in social work practice and education (Cournoyer, 2004; Gambrill, 1999; Howard., McMillen, and Pollio, 2003). Presuming the success of this paradigm, current and future agency leaders will want to have evidence-based information to ground their decisions. Funders and managers will be able to discretely analyze accurate service delivery and geographic patters with ease. They may come to rely on CMS-GIS systems as the authoritative source for informed decision-making. A combined CMS-GIS system will provide evidence.

A third factor is risk management. Many sectors within the social services are influenced by litigation that arises from malpractice problems and events. The incorporation of technology into practice brings a new dimension. The development process for the CICN project is a case in point. The project's steering committee lost one full year of time because of the need to resolve how the system could be made HIPAA compliant. Distance-based interventions across state lines as well raise liability issues concerning licensure and liability. At present, the National Association of Social Workers and Association of Social Work Boards are developing guidelines and practice standards for technology.[2] A CMS-GIS system offers demonstrable accountability. Worker actions, client outcomes, and community demographics, when combined, will yield risk-perspectives that make risk management planning easier for both the service and insurance industries.

While other factors may certainly enable convergence, the political economics, educational initiatives, and liability concerns may force the convergence of these two types of information systems.

WHAT MAY RESULT?

Consider what the resulting industry may look like. All participating agencies will now share common databases that clearly and easily map service delivery and needs. Funders will have the ability to readily discern and evaluate the merits of grants and requests. Administrators, socialized into requiring evidence, will have the ability to provide it. Liability issues should become more easily resolved.

I think that two trends will emerge: Greater coherence in agency missions and mergers between agencies. If the dominant agencies in an area—those with the capital to adopt a community-wide CMS-GIS—are all sharing the same data, then the discrete mission of each one will become more publicly visible. The enhancement of service coordination will make mission salient: Agencies will want to revise missions to better conform to community characteristics and needs because these will become better understood. Collaterally, smaller agencies that do not participate may have to conform and revise missions as well in order to cooperatively contract with the better-resourced agencies.

Coupled with this will be more mergers between agencies. A CMS-GIS system will readily uncover service duplications in the community, perhaps with clarity on an order of magnitude more that what is presently possible. Agencies that are providing similar, compatible services will find that merging forces may be fiscally more advantageous. This is nothing new: Agencies have been doing this for some time because of dwindling human services funds. Community-level CMS-GIS systems will make mergers more feasible because they will provide grounded data that will facilitate merger consideration.

At the risk of being wrong, I predict that within five to ten years, networks of agencies will be sharing client information that is coupled with localized and highly sophisticated geographic information. This converged and synthesized hybrid information technology will yield extremely powerful tools for helping people in a far more efficient and fiscally responsible ways. I hope I am at least as accurate as David Macarov was.

Footnotes:

1. Information about the CICN project and a slide demonstration if the system is available at http://www.cicn.org. The writer has been a member of the Steering Committee for the CICN project since 2000, and is the principle investigator for the project's evaluation.

2. The writer is a member of this taskforce. The resulting standards should become available in late 2005.

References:

Audin, G. (2004). Architectures for convergence. *Business Communications Review,34*, 4-5.

Hile, M. (1997). The history and function of the Target Cities management information systems: An introduction to the special issue. *Journal of Technology in Human Services,* 14(3-4).

Cournoyer, B. (2004). *The Evidence-Based Social Work Skills Book.* Boston, MA: Allyn-Bacon.

Howard, M., McMillen, C., and Pollio, D. (2003). Teaching evidence-based practice: Toward a new paradigm for social work education. *Research on Social Work Practice. 13,* 234-259.

Gambrill, E. (1999). Evidence-based practice: An alternative to authority-based practice. *Families in Society: The Journal of Contemporary Human Services, 80*(4) 341-350.

Kunkel, B. and Yowell, T. (2001) e-tools and organization transformation techniques for collaborative case management. *Journal of Technology in Human Services, 18*(1/2).

La Prad, J. and Sand, S. (1999) *Integration of welfare and workforce development systems in the Midwest: Analysis of implementation.* Ann Arbor, MI: Corporation for a Skilled Workforce.

Macarov, D. (1991). *Certain change: Social work practice in the future.* Silver Springs, MD: NASW Press.

Vernon, R. and Lynch, D. (2000) *Social work and the web.* Pacific Grove, CA: Brooks-Cole.

Vernon, R. (2003) Web-based support for program planning and research. *Journal of Technology in Human Services,* 22(2), 81-87.

Author's Note

Address correspondence to: Robert Vernon, Associate Professor, School of Social Work, Indiana University, 902 West New York Street, ES 4113, Indianapolis, Indiana 46202-5156. e-mail: rvernon@iupui.edu.

THE FUTURE OF SPIRITUALITY IN SOCIAL WORK:
THE FARTHER REACHES OF HUMAN NURTURE

Edward R. Canda

Abstract: *This essay discusses the development of the social work profession in relation to the subject of spirituality and proposes future possibilities and recommendations for innovation. It presents historical trends within four phases leading to the present and beyond. Current trends indicate rapidly increasing quantities of publications and other professional activities about spirituality within a pattern of an ever farther reaching integrative approach that encompasses diverse religious and nonreligious perspectives, academic disciplines, international collabora- tions, and humanity's relationship with the Earth.*

Keywords: Spirituality, religion, diversity, transpersonal, history, future

INTRODUCTION

In many religious traditions, telling about the future involves two functions that may or may not be combined: prognostication and prophecy. From Greek root words, prognosti- cation literally means 'to know before'; a prognosticator predicts what *will* be. Also from Greek, prophecy literally means 'to speak before'; a prophet proclaims what *should* be. These kinds of foretelling set out the organization of this essay.

Regarding prognostication, this essay will present currently emerging trends based on evidence from the social work literature and my experience with the topic during the past 2 decades. Regarding prophecy, this essay will offer recommendations for future work that expands on current trends. Prophecy arises from deeply felt moral, value, and ethical commitments. In both prediction and proclamation, the 'foreteller's' own vantage point and biases influence what is said. So in order to avoid the pretense of objective or absolute truth, this essay is written in the 'first person' style of I, me, and my. Use of this style is not meant to imply that my view should set the standard for future work on spirituality in social work. Rather, it emphasizes the limits of my view and invites others to join in dialogue and critique.

In 1969, Abraham Maslow published a groundbreaking essay called "The Farther Reaches of Human Nature." In that essay, he reviewed major trends in the field of psychol- ogy's understanding of human nature, identified the limits, and proposed an expansion of view toward the highest human possibilities of creativity and consciousness—beyond the egocentric to the transpersonal. Much of what I will say in this article is informed by a transpersonal perspective on social work (Canda & Smith, 2001; Robbins, Chatterjee, & Canda, 1998). The subtitle of my essay is a play on the words of Maslow's essay, since I explore the farther reaches of the social work profession's commitment to promote nur- ture, well-being, and justice for all people. As the essay proceeds to these 'farther reaches,' it may seem indeed more and more 'far-out' if not 'on the fringe'. However, it is necessary

Edward R. Canda is Professor & Director of the Ph.D. Program in Social Work, University of Kansas, School of Social Welfare, Lawrence, Kansas 66044-3184.

for future looking innovators to take this risk. Otherwise, the profession remains confined to what is taken for granted in the present.

PROGNOSTICATION

In order to set a context for emerging directions of work, it is helpful to consider where our profession has come from in its relationship with topics of spirituality and religion. Canda and Furman (1999) and Canda (2002a) have suggested a concise and simplified historical perspective. They suggest that our profession in the United States has moved through three broad overlapping phases and is in the midst of a fourth. The following discussion adapts and expands their view of these phases. This historical review is meant only as a helpful heuristic framework; it is an oversimplification of a complex and dynamic worldwide process. One of the most glaring limitations of this review is that it starts from a USA based professional social work outlook.

In phase one, *sectarian origins*, (colonial period through early twentieth century), many congregational and community based philanthropic activities, the settlement house movement, the Charity Organization Society, the Social Gospel movement, and social welfare institutions and policies that led toward the development of professional social work were strongly influenced by religious sectarian views, especially Christian and Jewish, as well as some nonsectarian humanistic spiritual ideologies (Cnaan, 1999). In addition, Indigenous, African American, and French or Spanish colonial influenced Catholic helping and healing traditions existed prior to, outside of, along with, and sometimes within the prior mentioned predominantly Northern European-American social welfare developments (Canda & Furman, 1999; Martin & Martin, 2002; Van Hook, Hugen, & Aguilar, 2001).

In phase two, *professionalization and secularization* (1920s to 1970s), social work solidified as a profession. Social work and social welfare education, practice, institutions, and policy became increasingly secularized in the mainstream due to concerns about separation of church and state, inappropriate religious proselytization and judgmentalism as well as optimism about scientific and humanist alternative approaches to human behavior and social problems. Social work education over time increasingly neglected the subjects of spirituality and religion. National curriculum guidelines of the Council on Social Work Education (CSWE) deleted references to these subjects in the 1970s and 1980s. However, religiously based social services, tacit religious ideologies, and community based religious helping traditions continued. Ideas from Asian religions and philosophies began to enter social work literature (e.g. Brandon, 1976). In addition, humanistic and other nonsectarian spiritual perspectives grew within social work, such as humanistic psychology, existentialism, and 12 Step programs (Robbins, Chatterjee, & Canda, 1998). Some authors called for attention to religion and spirituality, but these generally did not gain wide acceptance (e.g. Spencer, 1956; Towle, 1965).

In phase three, *resurgence of interest in spirituality* (1980s to mid 1990s), religiously based social services and ideas increased in diversity and were discussed more in the social work literature, such as Buddhism, Christianity, Confucianism, Hinduism, Judaism, Shamanism, Spiritism, and Taoism (Canda, Nakashima, Burgess, Russel, & Barfield, 2003). Nonsectarian spiritual perspectives such as existentialism, Gandhian social activism, and transpersonal theory increased.

One of the most significant innovations during this time was conceptualization of spirituality for social work purposes that addressed the holistic body-mind-spirit-relational qualities of human beings, encompassed diverse religious and nonreligious spiritual perspectives in a respectful way, and provided guidelines for dealing with spirituality consistent with professional values and ethics (e.g. Canda, 1988; Joseph, 1987; Loewenberg, 1988; Sheridan, Wilmer, & Atchison, 1994; Siporin, 1985). This approach overcame the concerns of many educators and practitioners that social workers might fall into religiously based biases, exclusivism, judgmentalism, discrimination, and oppression when dealing with spirituality in practice, policy, and education. It provided the beginnings of an orientation for social workers and clients of diverse religious and nonreligious perspectives to cooperate while honoring their own various religious and nonreligious commitments. It also emphasized that addressing spirituality is consistent with the historical foundations of our profession, the enduring person-environment social work vantage point, the reality of increasing diversification in the United States, and the professional mission of promoting dignity, respect, and well-being for all people.

Another significant innovation during this time was the establishment of professional networks and organizations that encouraged information sharing, collaboration and synergy among scholars and practitioners committed to an inclusive approach to spiritual diversity. For example, the Society for Spirituality and Social Work began with informal networking in 1986 and was founded as an organization in 1990. This organization also connected with Christian, Jewish, and other professional religious and nonsectarian spiritual networks and organizations. (See links for this Society and other groups dealing with spiritual diversity in social work at www.socwel.ku.edu/canda, retrieved on February 13, 2005.)

I believe that the establishment of an inclusive approach to spiritual diversity founded in professional values and ethics is a major reason why work on spirituality in our profession has been able to increase rapidly in quantity and quality during the next phase. This trend in social work was parallel to and fueled by similar trends in religious studies, anthropology, medicine, nursing, psychology, pastoral care, and other disciplines. It was also stimulated by increasing interests in spirituality (not always inclusive in nature) within the larger popular culture and political discourse.

The fourth phase brings us to the present. The main distinguishing characteristic of this phase is *transcending boundaries*, that is, boundaries between spiritual perspectives, academic disciplines, nations, governmental and religious institutions, and between humans and nature. Differences and distinctions remain important; but they are embraced by more encompassing perspectives and farther reaching connecting activities. This is similar to what Wilber refers to as the emergence of an integral or holistic mode of consciousness and culture (Robbins, Chatterjee, & Canda, 1998; Wilber, 1998). I will discuss this phase and its emerging trends in more detail than the previous phases in order to establish a basis for predictions and recommendations about the future. The main trends of phase four are summarized in Table 1.

I mark transition to the fourth phase at the mid 1990s because the Council on Social Work Education's curriculum guidelines returned attention to belief systems, religion, and spirituality in 1995 (Canda & Furman, 1999). Since the mid 1990s, the numbers of publications (including textbooks), courses, conferences, and symposia escalated more quickly (Russel, 1998 and personal communication). Some of the textbooks have created for the first time coherent general frameworks of values, knowledge, and skills for practice with spiritually diverse groups (Bullis, 1996; Canda & Furman, 1999; Ellor, Netting, & Thibault, 1999). All the previous trends of dealing with an increasing range of both religious and nonreligious approaches to spirituality grew, including for example deep

TABLE 1. Trends in the Fourth Phase (mid 1990s-present): Transcending Boundaries

1.	Rate of research and publication increased significantly.
2.	General and context-specific concepts of spirituality and religion refined.
3.	Curriculum guidelines, courses, and textbooks about spirituality widely established.
4.	Frameworks for spiritually sensitive practice formulated.
5.	Range of spiritual diversity significantly expanded.
6.	Postmodern perspectives on spirituality increased.
7.	Faith-based governmental social policy initiatives formalized.
8.	Interdisciplinary collaborations and networks established.
9.	International collaborations, networking, and global perspective rapidly increased.
10.	Whole Earth perspective introduced.

ecological, range of context specific understandings have been explored (e.g. Canda, 1997; Canda & Furman, 1999; Canda & Smith, 2001; Canda, Nakashima, Burgess, Russel, & Barfield, 2003; Hodge, 2000 & 2002a; Martin & Martin, 2002; Nelson-Becker, 2003; Praglin, 2004; Van Hook, Hugen, & Aguilar, 2001).

> During this fourth phase, there has been increased influence from post-modern perspectives on spirituality in social work, such as feminist, social constructionist, deep ecological, post-colonial, and transpersonal (Cowley, 1996; Meinert, Pardeck, & Murphy, 1998). These postmodern perspectives have challenged social work to extend its inclusive approach to spirituality to all people and nations, with special attention to the oppressed and marginalized, to all beings on the planet, and to the Earth itself as a living being deserving of honor and respect. Social workers are being challenged to address links between environmental destruction, poverty, disproportionate wealth of national elites and so-called developed countries, and oppression of women and people of color (e.g. Besthorn & Canda, 2002; Coates, 2003).

Interdisciplinary collaborations and formal networks increased, such as the Center on Religion, the Professions, and the Public, established in 2003 (see http://rpp.missouri.edu, retrieved February 13, 2005). Indeed, most current scholarly writing on spirituality in social work draws heavily on empirical and conceptual work of other disciplines. In the social policy arena, the controversial Charitable Choice provisions of the Clinton administrations and the faith-based initiatives of the Bush administrations have been stimulating more governmental funding of and collaborations with religious specific congregations, social service agencies, and community groups (Cnaan, 1999; Gibelman & Gelman, 2003; Tirrito & Cascio, 2003; Wineburg, 2001).

Finally, an extremely important distinguishing feature of this phase is the internationalization of work on spirituality in social work (e.g. Banerjee, 1997; Canda, 2002a; Canda &

Canda, 1996; Furman, Benson, Grimwood, & Canda, 2004; Nash & Stewart, 2002; Patel, Naik, & Humphries, 1997; Rice, 2002; Zahl, 2003). The first international conference of the Society for Spirituality and Social Work occurred in 2000. The Canadian Association for Spirituality and Social Work was established in 2002 (see http://people.stu.ca/~cnssw/, retrieved February 15, 2005). International symposia on spirituality, social work, and related fields expanded at the Inter-University Center in Dubrovnik, Croatia. Networks on spirituality and social work have begun development in South Korea. In 2004, the web based Spirituality and Social Work Resource Center, with a transdisciplinary, international, and interfaith approach to spirituality, social work, and health was established. (This center can be reached via www.socwel.ku.edu/canda, retrieved February 13, 2005.)

Regarding these international developments on spirituality in social work, a clarification is important. All societies in every country have developed social work and social welfare approaches rooted in spirituality long before the formation of professional social work in the United States and elsewhere. For example, the Confucian tradition elaborated philosophy and ideology of social welfare beginning at least 2500 years ago in China. Confucian inspired community based and governmental based social welfare systems existed for many centuries in East Asia (Canda, 2002b; Chung, 2001). What is distinctive in this fourth phase is that professional social workers in various countries are developing various religion-specific, country-specific, and inclusive approaches to spirituality in conjunction with international collaborations.

The topic of spirituality in social work has achieved sufficient acceptance in phase four to appear in mainstream and specialized journals, social work courses, conferences, and textbooks. Therefore, students, practitioners, researchers, and educators can pursue the topic with far less risk of ostracism than in the past. Faculty and agency supervisors can no longer claim legitimately that there is insufficient knowledge or guidance in our field to address spirituality ethically and competently. Because there are now more than 800 publications within social work on related topics, and many hundreds in related fields, there is a solid foundation of theory, empirical knowledge, and practice wisdom on which to build. There are networks and organizations that reach throughout social work and across disciplines with the United States and around the world so that tremendous mutual learning and synergy can occur, as long as these interactions are guided by values of mutual respect, equity, and collaboration.

All of this is not to imply that the social work profession generally has advanced very far in understanding, appreciation, and skill regarding spiritual diversity. Many social workers in the United States and the United Kingdom are not likely very aware of these trends. Regional and national surveys have indicated that most respondents have not received professional education about spirituality although most do appear to be addressing it in practice somehow (e.g. Canda & Furman, 1999; Furman, Benson, Grimwood, & Canda, 2004; Sheridan, 2004). I still occasionally hear from students, practitioners, and researchers that their teachers, supervisors, or colleagues say that there is not much work done on this topic or that they should not consider it. There are allegations and counter-claims that social work systematically oppresses conservative Christian students and points of view (see Hodge, 2002b and letters to the editor in Social Work April 2003). My impression from conversations with colleagues in many other countries is that there has been even less attention paid to spirituality in contemporary professional social work outside North America. This impression is supported by articles about spirituality and social work in the United Kingdom, Norway, Australia, and South Korea (Canda & Canda, 1996; Furman, Benson, Grimwood, & Canda, 2004; Rice, 2002; Zahl, 2003). Although our profession has established a solid foundation in this field of interest, there is much more to build (Canda, 1998; 2002a; 2003).

Most importantly, we have established ways to reconnect with our roots in spiritual insights while honoring the particularities of religious and nonreligious spiritual perspectives, the commonalities among individuals' and communities' spiritualities, and the usefulness of cooperation within and between peoples throughout the world who identify with diverse spiritual perspectives or who claim no spiritual interests. This developmental transformation is a breakthrough of spiritual insight and action. It is a paradigm shift that transcends rigid boundaries and polarized views. It has gone beyond arguments that social workers should address spirituality from a 'one spiritual way is the only right way' or that social workers should not deal with spirituality because it is irrelevant or dangerous.

It is highly likely that these trends of the fourth phase will continue and increase, assuming that human life is not suddenly and seriously decimated by nuclear war, a meteor strike, or some other calamity. The question is how should the profession of social work engage with these trends. This is the province of prophecy.

PROPHECY

I believe that there is an extremely important general developmental process that enfolds the various trends of the fourth phase. Creative thinking and acting about spirituality in social work is catalyzing our profession to grow beyond egocentric, ethnocentric, nationalistic, humanocentric and other divisive and parochial views. It is not surprising that professional social work in the United States would have been biased toward Eurocentric, patriarchal, nation-centered, Judeo-Christian and human privileged perspectives during most of the 20th century because that was the conditioning cultural context. As Coates (2003) pointed out, professional social work formed within a modernist set of world view assumptions. However, it is remarkable and praiseworthy that the profession kept moving in the direction of inclusion, caring and justice from its inception—moving into wider and deeper understandings of human diversity and ideals of well-being for all people.

On a practical level, the development of American social work to include and transcend bounded perspectives is shaped by a larger worldwide transformation of consciousness, culture, and technology. Given that virtually all people and all parts of the world are now actually or potentially in contact, through political and economic institutions, mass communications, movement of populations, and the internet, social work in any country can no longer rest on parochial views. For better *and* worse, globalization is happening. This includes the interconnection of social workers, social welfare organizations, informal community support systems, and spiritual perspectives around the world. As social workers outside the USA are also influenced by these world trends, they too are reaching out in expanded worldview and collaborations.

This developmental process is not just a reaction to social environmental pressures. Many social workers, including founders such as Jane Addams, had and continue to have creative and proactive spiritual visions of welfare and justice. We keep challenging ourselves to expand our understanding, compassion, and justice activism to ever widening circles of at-one-time unacknowledged and marginalized groups. This is a spiritual growth process toward a professional consciousness and culture of inclusion that appreciates diversity while including and transcending the spiritual insights of particular individuals, groups, communities, and religions. This developmental process helps us to respect spiritual beliefs and experiences in particular contexts. It also helps us to communicate, collaborate, and cohabitate in a mutually beneficial way. As the profession conveys expanded consciousness to students, it challenges them to expand their personal views toward spiritually sensitive and culturally competent ways of doing social work (Canda & Furman, 1999; Raines, 2004; Rey, 1997).

However, continued development toward greater inclusion within the profession in general or within the movement toward spiritual sensitivity is not automatic or guaranteed. This future will be a matter of decision, action, and perseverance along each moment of the present. All the trends of phase four need to continue for a long time if spirituality is to become pervasively understood and addressed in social work around the world. Dangers of religiously and ideologically based intolerance, divisiveness, and competition for privilege can derail or corrupt any of these trends.

However, if these trends continue at the present rate, I expect that there will be well-established movements of appreciation for spiritual diversity in social work on every continent within 20 years and that these will be interconnected thoroughly. I believe this development is crucial to meet the challenges of counter trends in the USA and around the world of imperialism, genocide, sexism, religious persecution, environmental racism, homophobia, and other forms of alienation and oppression (Coates, 2003).

CONCLUSION: EVEN FARTHER REACHES

Perusal of the extensive bibliography on spiritual diversity in social work shows some gaps and limitations of current scholarship that should be addressed (Canda, Nakashima, Burgess, Russel & Barfield, 2003). We should expand research about the range of spiritual perspectives within the USA and around the world. For example, there is still little published on Asian originated religions, First Nations religions, Islam, ecophilosophy, and transpersonal perspectives. Wicca, Neo-paganism, and alternative or new religious movements are barely addressed. Even within the spiritual perspectives considered so far in social work literature, greater depth and breadth of knowledge is needed, especially through ethnographic and participatory action research methods that give rich and detailed accounts of people's experience of spirituality in their own terms and contexts.

More information and guidance are needed with regard to spiritually sensitive practice with specific cultural groups and in particular national contexts. Much more work on international and cross-cultural perspectives for social action and social development is crucial. Work on specific fields of social work practice needs much more expansion both through new studies by social workers and by drawing on rapidly increasing studies in other disciplines. For example, the adult mental health field has had most attention so far, but even that has not yet used much of the current work on spirituality in psychology of religions, transpersonal psychotherapy, and the consumer driven mental health recovery movement. Fields of gerontology, addictions, hospice, and health are good examples of re-cent rapid growth. But there is very little regarding school social work, agency administra-tion, community organizing, macro social development, social policy, and international social work. There has been very little published in social work about issues of gender, disability, and sexual orientation connected to spirituality. There is very little published on addressing spirituality with children in social work.

Generally, we need to know more about what social workers actually do in practice (at all system levels and in all fields), what works well, and what spiritually focused helping approaches we could learn from helping professionals and community based religious helpers and healers beyond social work. Most studies of how social workers address spiri-tuality in practice have been concentrated on clinicians through surveys, small-scale an-ecdotal reflections, and relatively brief interviews. While we need more of these, we also need greater attention to mezzo and macro levels of practice. We should engage in more direct observational and field studies with prolonged engagement for greater depth and realistic portrayal, mixed methods studies to join breadth and depth perspectives, and quasi-experimental and experimental designs to examine efficacy. We need to utilize more transpersonal research methods geared to the exploration of consciousness, alternative and complementary healing modalities, and spiritual qualities of group dynamics in collective action for justice (e.g. Braud & Anderson, 1998). And we can reach vision for inquiry, education, and practice even farther.

One of the most far-reaching visions of spirituality in social work is that shared by deep ecologists and ecofeminists. They call for an expansion of social work's person-environ-ment perspective and social justice action to encompass all people, beings, ecosystems, and the entire Earth. However, even these do not go far enough-- they have not gone beyond concern with the Earth.

Some readers might be thinking that Earth wide consciousness and concern is already going far if not too far for social work. But I believe that our profession has quite a way to go if we are to catch up to the activities of national and international space agencies, military operations, communication technology companies, and new private entrepre-neurial space tourism companies. Human beings have already traveled beyond the Earth's atmosphere, walked on the moon, orbited surveillance and communication satellites, worked toward orbiting military weapons, lived together in a space station, landed rovers on Mars, and sent probes beyond the solar system. There are long range plans to colonize other planets. Perhaps social workers could encourage ecologically sustainable models of human interactions both within and beyond the Earth. We could advocate for distri-bution of resulting benefits in an equitable manner across nations and socio-economic classes; genuine respect for any sentient beings we may encounter; and appreciation for the human-Earth-cosmos interconnection wherever we are. Granted there are urgent and seemingly overwhelming needs for more conventional feet-on-the-ground social work in every country. All I am suggesting is that we should keep our minds open, stay alert for ever expanding arenas to advance well-being and justice, and do what we can. Otherwise, at some point, we are likely to be very badly surprised.

Another far-reaching vision about spirituality in social work goes to the transpersonal and nonphysical qualities of reality: subjectivity, consciousness, spirit, immanent sacredness and transcendent divinity. For example, various transpersonal theories and religious traditions explore altered or expanded states and flows of consciousness (as in trance, prayer, meditation, hypnotism). They posit nonphysical aspects of humans, other beings, and the universe as a whole, such as souls; plant and animal spirits; spirits of mountains, waters, lands, skies, stars, and underworlds; angels, ancestors, ghosts, and deceased saints and sages; life force energies (such as kundalini or ch'i); cosmic principles (such as Tao); and the ultimate nature of reality itself (such as God, Buddha Nature, Brahman, Tao, unitary consciousness). Some nonphysical entities are considered to be intrinsically good and helpful. Others are considered to be mischievous, ambiguous, or outright evil.

I do not believe that it is the proper domain of professional social work to proselytize particular metaphysical beliefs. However, given that most people in the world believe in nonphysical spiritual qualities and that some clients believe them to be crucially involved in their lives and goals, we should further explore their role, if relevant to clients, in helping or hindering individuals and communities. We need to become more familiar with such issues as differential assessment of spiritual crises from psychopathology; the way people experience the presence of God, angels, and helping spirits in recovery and resilience; how beliefs and experiences regarding harmful, imbalanced, or evil spiritual forces affect them; and how beliefs of communities about divine will, fate, cosmic evolution, and eschatology may shape views of personal situation, social policy and social justice. Social work may contribute to people's experiences of well-being in relation with their own souls, the spirits around them, and Ultimate Reality itself, however they understand these spiritual phenomena.

As the farther reaches of human nurture extend, we are likely to discover more amazing possibilities for spirituality in social work. If we pursue the trends of the fourth phase, perhaps spirituality will no longer be viewed just as a special interest, but rather as the true heart of helping. Then we will have made a significant leap into a fifth phase or beyond.

References

Banerjee, M. M. (1997). Strengths despite constraints: Memoirs of research in a slum in Calcutta. *Reflections: Narratives of Professional Helping, 3*(3), 36-45.

Besthorn, F. H. & Canda, E. R. (2002). Revisioning environment: Deep ecology for social work education. *Journal of Teaching in Social Work, 22*(1/2), 79-101.

Brandon, D. (1976). *Zen in the art of helping.* New York: Delta/Seymour Lawrence.

Braud, W. & Anderson, R. (1998). *Transpersonal research methods for the social sciences.* Thousand Oaks, CA: Sage.

Bullis, R. K. (1996). *Spirituality in social work practice.* Washington, DC: Taylor & Francis.

Canda, E. R. (1988). Conceptualizing spirituality for social work: Insights from diverse perspectives. *Social Thought, 14*(1), 30-46.

Canda, E. R. (1997). Spirituality. In R. L. Edwards (Ed.-in-Chief). *Encyclopedia of social work* (19th ed., Suppl., pp. 299-309). Washington, DC: NASW Press.

Canda, E. R. (1998). Afterword: Linking spirituality and social work: Five themes for innovation. In E. R. Canda (Ed.). *Spirituality in social work: New directions.* (pp. 97-106). New York: Haworth Press.

Canda, E. R. (2002a). A world wide view on spirituality and social work: Reflections from the USA experience and suggestions for internationalization. *Currents: New Scholarship in the Human Services* [on-line serial]. Available: http://fsw.ucalgary.ca/currents/articles/articles/Canda1/canda_main.htm

Canda, E. R. (2002b). Toward spiritually sensitive social work scholarship: Insights from classical Confucianism. *Electronic Journal of Social Work,* 1(1), article 2 [on-line serial]. Available: www.ejsw.net/IssueView1.asp

Canda, E. R. (2003). Heed your calling and follow it far: Suggestions for authors who write about spirituality or other innovations for social work. *Families in Society, 84*(1), 80-85.

Canda, E. R. & Canda, H. J. (1996). Korean spiritual philosophies of human service: Current state and prospects. *Social Development Issues, 18*(3), 53-70.

Canda, E. R. & Furman, L. D. (1999). *Spiritual diversity in social work practice: The heart of helping.* New York: Free Press.

Canda, E. R., Nakashima, M., Burgess, V. L., Russel, R., & Barfield, S. T. (2003). *Spiritual diversity and social work: A comprehensive bibliography with annotations* (second ed.). Alexandria, VA: Council on Social Work Education.

Canda, E. R. & Smith, E. D. (Eds.). (2001). *Transpersonal perspectives on spirituality in social work.* New York: Haworth Press.

Chung, D. K. (2001). Confucianism. In M. Van Hook, B. Hugen, & M. Aguilar (Eds.), *Spirituality within religious traditions in social work practice* (pp. 73-97). Pacific Grove, CA: Brooks/Cole.

Cnaan, R. A. (with Wineburg, R. J. & Boddie, S. C.). (1999). *The newer deal: Social work and religion in partnership.* New York: Columbia University Press.

Coates, J. (2003). *Ecology and social work: Toward a new paradigm.* Black Point, Nova Scotia, Canada: Fernwood Publishing.

Cowley, A. (1996). Transpersonal social work. In F. J. Turner (Ed.)., *Social work treatment: Interlocking theoretical approaches* (4th ed., pp. 663-698). New York: Free Press.

Ellor, J. W., Netting, F. E., & Thibault, J. M. (1999). *Religious and spiritual aspects of human service practice.* Columbia, SC: University of South Carolina.

Furman, L. D., Benson, P. W., Grimwood, C., & Canda, E. R. (2004). Religion and spirituality in social work education and direct practice at the millennium: A survey of UK social workers. *British Journal of Social Work, 34,* 767-792.

Gibelman M. & Gelman, S. R. (2003). The promise of faith-based social services: Perception versus reality. *Social Thought: Journal of Religion in the Human Services, 22*(1), 5-23.

Hodge, D. R. (2000). Spirituality: Towards a theoretical framework. *Social Thought, 19*(4), 1-20.

Hodge, D. R. (2002a). Conceptualizing spirituality in social work: How the metaphysical beliefs of social workers may foster bias toward theistic consumers. *Social Thought, 21*(1), 39-61.

Hodge, D. R. (2002b). Does social work oppress Evangelical Christians? A "New Class" analysis of society and social work. *Social Work, 47*(4), 401-414.

Joseph, M. V. (1987). The religious and spiritual aspects of social work practice: A neglected dimension of social work. *Social Thought, 13*(1), 12-23.

Loewenberg, F. M. (1988). *Religion and social work practice in contemporary American society.* New York: Columbia University Press.

Martin, E. P. & Martin, M. M. (2002). *Spirituality and the Black helping tradition in social work.* Washington, DC: NASW Press.

Maslow, A. H. (1969). The farther reaches of human nature. *Journal of Transpersonal Psychology, 1*(1), 1-9.

Meinert, R. G., Pardeck, J. T., & Murphy, J. W. (Eds.). (1998). *Postmodernism, religion and the future of social work.* New York: Haworth Press.

Nash, M. & Stewart, B. (Eds.)., (2002). *Spirituality and social care: Contributing to personal and community well-being.* London: Jessica Kingsley Publishers.

Nelson-Becker, H. B. (2003). Practical philosophies: Interpretations of religion and spirituality by African American and European American elders. *Journal of Religious Gerontology, 14*(2/3), 85-99.

Patel, N., Naik, D., & Humphreys, B (Eds.). (1997). *Visions of reality: Religion and ethnicity in social work.* London: Central Council for Education and Training in Social Work.

Praglin, L. J. (2004). Spirituality, religion, and social work: An effort towards interdisciplinary conversation. *Journal of Religion & Spirituality in Social Work: Social Thought, 23*(4), 67-84.

Raines, J. C. (2004). Emotional themes in cross-faith encounters among MSW students: A qualitative exploration. *Journal of Religion & Spirituality in Social Work: Social Thought, 23*(3), 109-125.

Rey, L. D. (1997). Religion as invisible culture: Knowing about and knowing with. *Journal of Family Social Work, 2*(2), 159-177.

Rice, S. (2002). Magic happens: Revisiting the spirituality and social work debate. *Australian Social Work, 55*(4), 303-312.

Robbins, S. P., Chatterjee, P., & Canda, E. R. (1998). *Contemporary human behavior theory: A critical perspective for social work.* Boston: Allyn and Bacon.

Russel, R. (1998). Spirituality and religion in graduate social work education. In E. R. Canda (Ed.), *Spirituality in social work: New directions* (pp. 15-29). New York: Haworth Press.

Sheridan, M. J., Wilmer, C. M., & Atcheson, L. (1994). Inclusion of content on religion and spirituality in the social work curriculum: A study of faculty views. *Journal of Social Work Education, 30*(3), 363-376.

Sheridan, M. J. (2004). Predicting the use of spiritually-derived interventions in social work practice: A survey of practitioners. *Journal of Religion and Spirituality in Social Work: Social Thought, 23*(4), 5-25.

Siporin, M. (1985). Current social work perspectives on clinical practice. *Clinical Social Work Journal, 13*(3), 198-217.

Spencer, S. (1956). Religion and social work. *Social Work, 1*(3), 19-26.

Tirrito, T. & Cascio, T. (Eds.)., (2003). *Religious organizations in community services.* New York: Springer Publishing Company.

Towle, C. (1965). *Common human needs* (rev. ed.). Washington, DC: NASW Press.

Van Hook, M., Hugen, B., & Aguilar, M. (Eds.). (2001). *Spirituality within religious traditions in social work practice.* Pacific Grove, CA: Brooks/Cole.

Wilber, K. (1998). *The marriage of sense and soul: integrating science and religion.* New York: Broadway Books.

Wineburg, B. (2001). *A limited partnership: The politics of religion, welfare, and social service.* New York: Columbia University Press.

Zahl, M. A. (2003). Spirituality and social work: A Norwegian reflection. *Social Thought: Journal of Religion in the Social Services, 22*(1), 77-90.

Author's Note

Address correspondence to: Edward R. Canda, Ph.D., Professor & Director of the Ph.D. Program in Social Work, University of Kansas, School of Social Welfare, Twente Hall, 1545 Lilac Lane, Lawrence, Kansas 66044-3184. e-mail: edc@ku.edu.

SOCIAL WORK PRACTICE AND PEOPLE WITH DISABILITIES: OUR FUTURE SELVES

Lisa S. Patchner

Abstract: *During the past fifty years a revolution in how we recognize, advocate, medically treat, and interact with people with disabilities has taken place within contemporary society. From historical civil rights legislation to greater access to society's rights and benefits, to technological advances and population longevity, people with disabilities are integrating themselves into society. As we begin to explore the twenty-first century new concerns regarding the cost of chronic care and society's desire to fund these costs are beginning to emerge. The desire to qualify the cost of care by functional longevity has begun to emerge in both private and public service delivery systems. As professional social workers continue to expand their sociopolitical influence, they will be challenged to uphold the rights of self-determination that people with disabilities have striven to attain.*

Keywords: Disability, Consumer Driven Care, Health, Quality of Life Measurement, Person Centered Planning

INTRODUCTION

Social work professionals have historically approached disability from a medical perspective where the definition of the problem was the physical, or behavioral impairment of the individual (Condeluci, 1995; Mackelprang, 2002). People with disabilities were treated by professional experts where the desired outcome was a cure. The affect of this approach to disability was to equate the cure as desirable and a failed attempt as a reason to discard or maintain the individual with disability. In essence, people with disabilities were oppressed by this societal medical perspective (Gilson & DePoy, 2002; Mackelprang, 2002).

In recent decades, as social service delivery systems matured, professional social workers utilized a social service/rehabilitation perspective when providing intervention to people with disabilities (Condeluci, 1995). This perspective views the individual with disabilities as having a lack of adaptability to the surrounding environment and views the experts as those providing the intervention. This perspective has been viewed as patronizing the person with disabilities by allowing little decision-making and control to the individual being helped (Condeluci, 1995). In the 1970's the independent living perspective began where the person with disabilities was viewed as a self-determining and independent person. The desired outcomes to this perspective were to challenge the existing status quo and empower the individual to define their own needs without the dependence on professionals and family (Condeluci, 1995). The independent living movement encouraged the development of federally funded Centers for Independent Living and passage of civil rights social policy and laws, such as The Americans with Disability Act (Mackelprang, 2002).

Lisa S. Patchner is Associate Professor, School of Social Work, Ball State University, Muncie, IN 47306.

Within the past decade, access to technology and advanced medical interventions allowed people with disabilities to share with the rest of the U. S. population in longevity. Approaches to disability services began to embrace self-determination and self-directed care in order to maximize the functional ability of the individual. What has gradually emerged is a constructionist approach to disability, where the disability is viewed as interacting within a dysfunctional environment and that targeted interventions could address this interaction (Gilson & DePoy, 2002). Technological advances have raised concerns over costs and the quality of life at what price? New disease prevention and management approaches have been implemented primarily by private, public health and social service delivery systems in an effort to improve the overall health of populations with disabilities, thereby reducing costs.

According to the 2000 U. S. Census, 19.3 % of the noninstitutionalized U. S. population have some form of physical or mental disability (U. S. Census Bureau, 2003). In 2002, according to the National Health Interview Survey, 12.2 % of the noninstitutionalized U. S. population had some form of limitation in usual activities due to chronic conditions (U. S. Dept. of Health and Human Services, 2004a). With life expectancy for the year 2001 at 77.2 years (U.S. Dept. of Health and Human Services, 2004b) and with 41.9 % of those 65 years and older experiencing a disability (U. S. Census Bureau, 2003) we can expect a greater number of social work consumers manifesting some form of disability.

This article will highlight several traditional social work practice areas and their recent applications with people with disabilities. It will also address several new challenging areas of practice and their future applications. Reflecting on the numbers of individuals with functional disabilities as we enter the 21st century, social work professionals will be working, not only for the person with disabilities, but also for themselves and their family members. Disability exists among all cultural, economic, religious and racial groupings and due to its' heterogeneity, will require many different approaches and practice applications.

CASE MANAGEMENT

Case management, although used frequently by social workers in health and social services delivery, has deep practice applications within several professions, specifically social work, nursing and later, in the for-profit health and service delivery industries (Patchner, 2004). Today, multiple terms are used to denote case management functions, such as: care management, utilization management, coordinated care, structured care, financial case management, disease management, service coordination, health care navigation and managed care. Many new applications of case management have emerged as a result of cost containment and disease prevention and chronic care management within private as well as public health care delivery systems (Carneal & D'Andrea, 2001; Patchner, 2002; Patchner, 2004; Smith, 1995).

Historically, case management strategies have fluctuated between consumer-driven to provider-driven approaches depending upon the current sociopolitical climate. There has been ongoing concern among social work professionals, whether case managers can function as client advocates and system agents simultaneously, and whether the desires and needs of people with disabilities and the provider delivery system are consistent (Austin, 1996; Rose & Moore, 1995).

As western society becomes more sophisticated in delivering technology and information to all members of the population who have access to revolutionary advances, greater empowerment of the average individual has resulted (Maddox, 1991). People with disabilities and their families have been especially empowered and informed by the technology revolution. This allows them unprecedented access to more resources within modern society. As people with disabilities integrate more fully into their rightful place within the mainstream of society, will traditional social work case management be obsolete?

As the profession of social work endeavors to address issues of diversity and oppression in serving people with disabilities, attention to the changing role of the consumer in self-determining their needs and services needs to occur. Recent initiatives such as person centered planning and client directed treatment have facilitated consumers and their families in designing personalized service and treatment plans. Additionally, legislation and public policy are attempting to address the injustice and inequality that has been experienced by people with disabilities (The National Council on Disability, 2004).

Increasingly, people with disabilities and their families are acting as their own case managers as the contemporary delivery system has failed to understand and respond to the changing and complex needs of multiple consumers. Disability advocates have continued to advocate for the use of voucher systems whereby the consumer, and not the professional, would select from a menu of community based services that they believe are needed (Eidelman, 2004; Sheehan, 2004; Wehmeyer, 2004). Currently, many states are experimenting with Medicaid waiver arrangements where the consumer, with the assistance of family and friends if warranted, chooses an approved case management organization to arrange for services they deem as necessary for independent living. Beginning in 2001 the federal government initiated the New Freedom Initiative which provided grant money to states to improve community-integration services and remove barriers to community living by encouraging people with disabilities and their families to plan for their specific care needs (U. S. Dept. of Health and Human Services, 2003).

Social work professionals will modify their case management strategies as the sociopolitical landscape changes. People with disabilities will have better defined roles in the self management of their care.

PERSON CENTERED PLANNING

People with disabilities and their families have long complained about navigating the disability service delivery system (National Council on Disability, 2004; Partnership for Solutions, 2002). A strategy that has been successfully used to ease service navigation is person centered planning. Person centered planning can be described as a systematic personalized information gathering process that focuses on the capabilities of the individual and has been used extensively with people with disabilities and their families over the past several decades. Originally developed by Karen Green-McGowan and Mary Kovaks for the Canadian National Institute on Mental Retardation, it quickly spread to the United States where it has been used most recently by both state and local agencies to assist persons with disabilities and their families in planning for the future (O'Brien & O'Brien,

2000a). It is an excellent application of consumer driven service delivery that involves group work, advocacy and case management.

The sharing of information between the person with disability, family, friends, care takers, teachers and others occurs in a supportive team setting. Components of the planning process include a personal profile, visions for the future, action plans and always a continuous modification of the visions and the action plans. Person centered planning attempts to empower the person with disability by exploring resources, recognizing lifestyle issues and the person's abilities while promoting accountability. It also allows the team to recognize that everyone on the team is both a part of the problem as well as part of the solution.

Although person centered planning appears seemingly simple in design and application, O'Brien & O'Brien (2000b) have indicated that politics, related to control, can creep into the process. This is especially evident as the role of the provider can change based on the realistic desires of the person with disabilities. People with disabilities can realistically articulate their vision for the future based on a menu of services and providers that they select from. As with a free market economy, people with disabilities can be empowered to support services and service providers that they desire and favor. For professionals involved with the person centered planning process it is important to remember that the process is a means to assist the person with disabilities to realize their wants and desires within larger systems that provide both opportunities and limitations. In order for person centered planning to empower people with disabilities, the focus must always be on the individual consumer and not the provider (Smull, 1996).

Due to our strong belief in self determination, social work professionals will act as consumer advocates in promoting person centered planning within their organizations.

CONSUMER DRIVEN SERVICE DELIVERY

Terms such as consumer directed care, client controlled care, consumer case management and consumer driven service delivery are similar in meaning and all focus on the empowerment of people with disabilities to take control of their lives. The specific term consumer driven has been used by economists to describe the consumer as the demander of services, as conversely provider driven services is used to describe the supply of services available within the American health and welfare system.

Economic supply and demand is important whenever we apply them to the public market place which is artificially controlled by government regulation and spending unlike the private market system which strives to operate with the least amount of government intervention. In fact, the private market system strives to provide services that the consumer demands in order to make a profit. Within the new federalism and privatization of social welfare services the demand sided approach to service acquisition and delivery can affect which organizations will be utilized by people with disabilities (Tilly & Weiner, 2001; Herzlinger, 2004).

Research on consumer driven service delivery has indicated that consumers who are able to cognitively participate in decision making are generally pleased with the approach. However, seniors and those with cognitive disabilities were less inclined to like this approach. What has been recommended, is a systematic prospective study of this approach by both private and public funded health and welfare providers (Cuellar, Tilly, & Wiener, 2000; Tilly & Weiner, 2001; Herzlinger, 2004; Stone, 2004).

We can also anticipate that the evolution of technology will allow consumers greater access to information and providers. Fitch (2004) recently proposed a model for client control of case information that has the potential to improve access and quality of services. However, we do not have a clear strategy on how to equalize services to those who are unable to logistically or cognitively access providers of care.

Social work professionals will qualify their applications of consumer driven service delivery based on the needs of the individual. Although greater numbers of people with disabilities will embrace consumer driven service delivery, some consumers because of cognitive difficulties will require the assistance of family, friends or professionals to receive appropriate care.

MANAGED HEALTH CARE

Early experimentation by the U. S. Dept. of Health and Human Services Health Care Financing Administration (HCFA) with consumer driven health delivery to people with disabilities was conducted in the 1980's and 1990's. With Medicare and Medicaid waivers the social health maintenance organizations (SHMO's) used a social case management model, and attempted to control costs while expand chronic care services through careful case management and coordination of services (Harrington & Newcomer, 1991; Leutz, Greenlick & Capitman, 1994). Findings from those demonstrations were mixed. Harrington and Newcomer (1991) reported that the demonstrations increased overall costs while Leutz, Greenlick and Capitman (1994) found that the SHMO's demonstrated that chronic care services can be integrated with acute care at manageable overall costs. As suggested by Leutz and other pioneers of the SHMO models, the linkages made during these early demonstrations, between integrating acute and chronic care needs, have had positive influences on current health delivery paradigms. A second round of SHMO's involving six demonstrations models, authorized by HCFA, was initiated in 1996. According to Goben (1997) the newer SHMO's were considered more of a medical model where a preventive health focus and a risk-adjusted payment system was utilized.

During the 1990's as Medicaid expenditures rose, states began to turn to the private managed care systems to provide solutions for publicly funded populations through the use of federal Medicaid waivers. Through the 1915(b) and 1115 waivers, there are now managed care systems funded under Medicaid in all states. The 1915(b) waivers are restricted to specific populations or geographical locations. The 1115 waivers came into active use after the defeat of the Clinton health care reform initiatives. These research and demonstration waivers are usually statewide and are mandatory for enrollment. The 1115 waivers also allow for expansion of coverage to individuals who would not otherwise be covered under Medicaid (HCFA, 1996). Even though the privatized managed care numbers have dropped in recent years, and the Medicare managed care enrollment is slowly increasing, the Medicaid managed care numbers have steadily increased (Centers for Medicare and Medicaid Services, 2004 & 2005; Gorin, 2003). For the year 2003, according to the Centers for Medicare and Medicaid Services (2004), 59.1% of the Medicaid population, were enrolled in managed care. The Medicaid population is considered an at-risk population due to the large numbers of enrolled persons with disabilities who can present with complex psychosocial needs.

What has emerged is a health care industry that is largely owned by private investors and which includes public subsidy through Medicaid and Medicare. Earlier managed care plans, which were not-for-profit, considered cost containment as an unexpected benefit rather than the central purpose, with profits invested in improvement in health care delivery. The newer generation of managed care which are for-profit and commercially influenced, invest profits in another realm, that of the investor. What has resulted is continuous debate regarding increasing Medicaid costs, while improving quality of care in order to prevent further costly disease and disability. As Goben (1997) asserts, containing costs is not the same as improving the efficiency of health care delivery. Increasing efficiency and effectiveness improves quality of health care, while containing costs without innovations in delivery leads to no improvement in health care services.

There continues to exist many unanswered questions regarding enrollment of people with disabilities into managed care systems which are accustomed to a healthy commercially employed population. Keigher (1995) reports that besides decreasing access and benefits as a response to budget cuts, state governments have increasingly enrolled Medicaid populations into managed care arrangements as a primary strategy for limiting escalating Medicaid costs. By controlling access and benefits in order to decrease inappropriate waste of health resources, while at the same time employing public health strategies for disease prevention, states hope for greater overall efficiency and effectiveness in health delivery. Some states under their Medicaid waiver arrangements have designed new public health strategies that contain linkages with community based providers and social service agencies so that individuals with disabilities have greater access to services at the local level (Centers for Medicare and Medicaid Services, 2004; Minkoff, 2000).

Due to fiscal concerns, social work professionals will need to advocate for people with disabilities to ensure that health and welfare care is not rationed and that there are appropriate channels to address appeals when denied services.

DISEASE PREVENTION AND MANAGEMENT

As accountability for health care costs increase, interest groups, policy makers, and health delivery systems will strive for additional control over health and welfare outcomes among those served. In order to improve these outcomes, the traditional "supply sided" approach to services has begun to evolve into a "demand sided" approach where strengthened consumer relations would be sought through more self-determination and decision making on the part of the individual (Goldsmith, Goran & Nackel, 1995). Health and welfare service delivery systems will focus increasingly on promoting wellness, empowering the individual, providing for a continuum of care approach, accountability, appropriate level of care standards, and improved integrated delivery systems (Institute of Medicine 2004, Partnership for Solutions, 2002; Black, 1997).

In 1989, the U. S. Congress passed the Patients Outcome Research Act which stressed biopsychosocial measurement of health outcomes with the goal of measuring and ultimately preventing further disease and disability. Over the past decade numerous health outcomes have been collected by the U. S. Department of Health and Human Services on Medicare and Medicaid populations. One such measure is the Minimum Data Set (MDS) which measures the medical and functional status of all nursing home residents in Medicare and Medicaid funded facilities (Patchner & Patchner, 2004). Health Plan Employer Data Information Set (HEDIS) health measurements are routinely collected by both publicly and privately owned health insurance systems for evaluation of quality, service access, patient satisfaction, membership, utilization, finance and health plan management Stiles, Rahl, Bernstein, Halman, Harrison & Standiford, 2000). The National Academies (2004), (which includes the National Academy of Sciences, the National Academy of Engineering, the Institute of Medicine and the National Research Council), have called for a serious review and application of recent recommendations outlined in their publication: *Insuring America's Health: Principles and Recommendations*. This report calls for an integrated disease prevention and management approach to health care delivery with evidence-based research to examine health outcomes (Institute of Medicine, 2004).

A concern that arises is the validity of the health outcomes that are measured. With the complex maize of health delivery systems and the different mechanisms for data collection there is concern regarding the effectiveness of outcome studies. This is especially worrisome for those with chronic conditions including people with disabilities (Partnership for Solutions, 2002). A recent randomized national study conducted during May of 2001 found that U. S. patients with chronic conditions get insufficient care (The Robert Wood Johnson Foundation, 2005b). In yet another study conducted by RAND Health, it was also found that patients with chronic conditions get insufficient care (The Robert Wood Johnson Foundation, 2005a). In a recent article published by Maramaldi, Berkman & Barusch, (2005) the validity of patient-based assessments of health related quality of life when applied to cultural minority groups was questioned.

Social work professionals can anticipate collecting health outcome data on their consumers. With respect to people with disabilities, outcome data will be sought in order to manage chronic disease and disability and the costs associated with these conditions.

QUALITY OF ADJUSTED LIFE YEARS

Interest in quality of life has been driven in recent decades due to longevity and the costs associated with health care delivery as we age and develop chronic diseases and disabilities. Quality of Adjusted Life Years (QALY's) measurements are a mechanism to quantify the quality of a person's life. As defined by the Centers for Disease Control and Prevention:

QALY's are estimates of person-years lived at particular levels of health. They are mostly used in cost-effectiveness analyses and clinical trials involving health conditions that consider the quality as well as the length of life. Quality is typically measured on a scale of 0.0 (death) to 1.0 (perfect health) by assigning various weights to potential health states (CDC, 2003, p. 5)

QALY's were originally designed by economists, using complex micro-economic models that theoretically quantify the benefits vs. the costs of disease and medical intervention. Today there are multiple means of assessment that are used to gauge quality of life. Some familiar forms are patient based assessments (PBA's), health-related quality of life (HRQL) questionnaires and the SF-36 health survey which has been rigorously tested for construct validity and is currently used with QALY measurements (Nichol, Sengupta & Globe, 2001; Maramaldi, Berkman & Barusch, 2005).

Studies funded through the National Institutes of Health, the World Health Organization and the World Bank have utilized QALY's to gauge the overall health of a population and what medical treatments and interventions benefits populations the most for the money spent (CDC, 2003; Homedes, 2000). Both governments and private companies are interested in the health status of their populations, the health impact of utilitarian systems of care upon a population and how to gauge costs related to care. However, it is important to recognize that there are ethical criticisms in using QALY's.

Some of these criticisms deal with the inability of any micro-economic model to accurately reflect the quality of life (Sacristan, 2003; Duru, G., Auray, J. P., Beresniak, A., Lamure, M. Paine, A. & Nicoloyannis, N., 2002). QALY measurements are especially worrisome when applied to people with disabilities because they involve some subjective value judgments regarding human functional status (Homedes, 2000). The use of QALY's in health care decisions could compromise both individual patient autonomy and the clinical judgment of health and welfare providers (La Puma & Lawlor, 1990; Homedes, 2000). As we apply QALY's within the larger health delivery market we can expect the judicial system to become involved when there is conflict regarding the health rights of the individual. It is important for us to note, that the judicial system in the United States leans toward a utilitarian form of justice when interpreting the Constitution (Longest, 2002). As consumer advocates, social workers will attempt to modify health delivery decisions to the desires and needs of the individual with the disability.

Social work professionals will become increasingly familiar with QALY applications as both the private and public sectors attempt to quantify and measure all service delivery in an attempt to project costs, increase efficiency and increase effectiveness. It is possible that future social workers will be asked to justify the costs of our services associated with the meaningful longevity of the individual consumer or population with disabilities.

FUTURE PRACTICES IMPLICATIONS AND TRENDS

As we enter the 21st century we can anticipate many changes to our traditional disability service delivery system and the services we provide. Individual autonomy and the civil rights of the person with disabilities will compete with larger utilitarian systems of care. Policy makers will struggle between the utilitarian vs. the egalitarian forms of justice as they attempt to meet the needs of people with disabilities.

Traditional case management services will evolve into consumer driven case management where a partnering between the consumer and the professional will occur by use of person centered planning or some related approach. Since the consumer will have greater control, we will be placing the interests of the person first and the needs of the organization that we work for second. As we place the consumer's interest above organizational interests, we can envision our existing disability service delivery system modifying into something less structured and more responsive to consumer needs. Some people with disabilities and their families will want to manage their own health and welfare service acquisition. For those who are unable to navigate service acquisition, social work professionals will be employed by people with disabilities under contractual arrangements made by the consumer or their family. These contractual arrangements may involve a voucher payment system set up by a privatized managed care entity under contract with a public funder. We can expect that our professional services will be measured by both the health outcomes of the consumer and the satisfaction of the consumer with our services. Our employer may also have contractual arrangements with privatized managed care entities to assist in local community based disease prevention and health management activities. Social workers will be challenged to be good consumers as well as contributors toward evidence based research. A strong ethical understanding of the implications and flaws of measuring the human condition will be essential because we may be asked to measure the quality of life or to quantify what is meant by a meaningful life. Since functional disability will become more prominent as longevity increases, many persons with disabilities that we serve could be our friends, family members or our very selves.

CONCLUSION

Current scientific and technological advances will continue to enrich and extend the lives of those with disabilities. Yet society has many unanswered questions on how best to proceed with caring for large populations who have multiple needs.

Future health and welfare policy for individuals with disabilities will undoubtedly be influenced by numerous inputs of information from the managed care industry, quality assurance initiatives, government entities, funded research, interest groups, medical providers, unions, employers, and consumer advocacy groups (Church, 1997). As these multiple groups attempt to influence future health and welfare policies, future strategies will have to recognize these stakeholders and integrate their multiple ideas into a cost effective and coherent system of care that improves the functional health of people with disabilities.

It is easy for policy makers to look at the larger population and describe it in utilitarian demographic terms, without addressing the many individual faces with unique needs that we, as social workers, are called to advocate for. Social work professionals must remain informed regarding evolving policy and consumer perceptions, as well as, newly emerging research developments so that they can provide services that address the needs of their constituents within a human rights context.

We, as a profession, will serve well by recognizing the dignity, self-determination and worth of every unique individual, regardless of health status and functionality. Only then can we implant the human rights context into the larger disability service delivery process.

References

Austin, C. D. (1996). Case management practice with the elderly. In M. J. Holosko and M. D. Feit (Eds.) *Social work practice with the elderly*, (2nd ed.). Toronto, Ontario: Canadian Scholars' Press.

Black, J. T. (May 5, 1997). The revolution in health care: Trends and implications. *Public Health Social Work Institute Presentation*. Pittsburgh, PA: The University of Pittsburgh.

Carneal, G. & D'Andrea, G. (2001). Defining the parameters of case management in a managed care setting. *Managed Care Quarterly*, 9(1), 55-60.

Centers for Disease Control and Prevention. (2003). Special focus: Health-related Quality of life, part I. *Chronic Disease Notes & Reports, 16*(1), winter 2003.

Centers for Medicare and Medicaid Services (2004). *Medicaid statistics and data.* Baltimore, MD: Centers for Medicare and Medicaid Services.

Centers for Medicare and Medicaid Services (2005). *Medicare health plans.* Baltimore, MD: Centers for Medicare and Medicaid Services.

Church, G. J. (1997). Backlash against HMO's: Doctors, patients, unions, legislators Are fed up and say they won't take it anymore. *Time, 149*(15), 32-36.

Condeluci, A. (1995). *Interdependence: The route to community,* (2nd ed.).Winter Park, FL: GR Press, Inc.

Cuellar, A. E., Tilly, J. & Wiener, J. M. (2000). *Consumer-Directed Home and Community Services Programs in Five Countries: Policy Issues for Older People and Government.* Washington, D. C.: The Urban Institute.

Dura, G., Auray, J., Beresniak, A., Lamure, M., Paine, A. & Nicoloyannis, N. (2002). Limitations of the methods used for calculating quality-adjusted life-year values. *Pharmacoeconomics, 20*(7), 463-73.

Eidelman, S. (2004). Advocacy of the future and the future of advocacy. *The ARC Insight, 3*(2004), 4-5.

Fitch, D. (2004). Client-controlled case information: A general system theory perspective. *Social Work, (49)*3, 497-505.

Gilson, F. G., & DePoy, E. (2002). Theoretical approaches to disability content in social work education. *Journal of Social Work Education, 38*(1), 153-165.

Goben, R. (1997). Social HMOs: The second phase. *Case Review, 3*(1), 39-40.

Goldsmith, J. C., Goran, M. J., & Nackel, J. G. (1995). Managed care comes of age. *Healthcare Forum Journal, 38*(5), 14-24.

Gorin, S. H. (2003). The unraveling of managed care: Recent trends and implications. *Health and Social Work, 28*(3), 241-246.

Harrington, C., & Newcomer, R. J. (1991). Social health maintenance organizations' service use and costs, 1985-89. *Health Care Financing Review, 12*(3), 37-52.

Health Care Financing Administration. (1996). *Managed care in Medicare and Medicaid.* Washington, D. C.: HCFA Press Office.

Herzlinger, R. (2004). *Consumer-Driven Health Care: Taming the Health Care Cost Monster.* New York, NY: The Manhattan Institute.

Homedes, N. (2000). *The DisabilityAadjusted Life Year (DALY) Definition, Measurement and Potential Use.* Washington, D.C.: World Bank HCO Working Papers.

Institute of Medicine. (2004). *Insuring America's Health: Principles and Recommendations.* Washington, D. C.: Institute of Medicine.

Keigher, S. M. (1995). Managed care's silent seduction of America and the new politics of choice. *Health and Social Work, 20*(2), 146-151.

La Puma, J. & Lawlor, E. (1990). Quality-adjusted life-years. Ethical implications for Physicians and policymakers. *The Journal of the American Medical Association, 263*(21).

Leutz, W. N., Greenlick, M. R., & Capitman, J. A. (1994). Integrating acute and long-term care. *Health Affairs, 13*(4), 58-74.

Longest, B. B. (2002). Health Policymaking in the United States, (3rd ed.). Ann Arbor, MI: AUPHA Press/Health Administration Press.

Mackelprang, R. W. (2002). Social work practice with persons of disability. In S. F. Gilson (Ed.). *In-*

tegrating disability content in social work education: A curriculum resource. Alexandria, VA: Council on Social Work Education.

Maddox, G. L. (1991). Aging and well-being. *The Futurist, 27*, 557-564.

Maramaldi, P., Berkman, B. & Barusch, A. (2005). Assessment and the ubiquity Of culture: Threats to validity in measures of health-related quality of life. *Health and Social Work, 30*(1), 27-36.

Minkoff, K. (2000). An integrated model for the management of co-occurring Psychiatric and substance disorders in managed-care systems. *Dis Manage Health Outcomes, 8*(5), 251-257.

The National Academies. (2004). *Officials Should Target 20 Key Areas to Transform Health Care System.* Washington, D. C.: The National Academy of Sciences.

National Council on Disability. (2004). *Consumer-directed health care: How well does it work?* Washington, D. C.: National Council on Disability.

Nichol, M., Sengupta, N. & Globe, D. (2001). Evaluating quality-adjusted life years: Estimation of the health utility index (HUI2) from the SF-36. *Medical Decision Making, 21*(2), 105-112.

O'Brien, C. L., & O'Brien, J. (2000a). *The Origins of Person Centered Planning: A Community of Practice Perspective.* Syracuse, NY: Center on Human Policy, Syracuse University.

O'Brien, C. L., & O'Brien, J. (2000b). *The Politics of Person Centered Planning.* Syracuse, NY: Center on Human Policy, Syracuse University.

Partnership for Solutions. (2002). *Chronic conditions: Making the case for ongoing Care.* Baltimore, MD: Johns Hopkins University.

Patchner, L. S. (2002). In the belly of the beast: A case study of social work in a Managed care organization. *Advances in Social Work, 3*(1), 16-32.

Patchner, L. S. (2004). Health services. In A. L. Sallee (Ed.). *Social work and social Welfare: An introduction.* Peosta, Iowa: Eddie Bowers Publishing, Inc.

Patchner, L. S. & Patchner, M. A. (2004). Social work practice in nursing homes. In M. J. Holosko & M. D. Feit (Eds.) *Social Work Practice with the Elderly*, (3rd ed.). Toronto, Canada: Canadian Scholars' Press.

Patients Outcome Research Act of 1989, S. 702, 101st Congress (1989).

The Robert Wood Johnson Foundation. (2005a). *A Portrait of the Chronically Ill in America.* Princeton, NJ: The Robert Wood Johnson Foundation.

The Robert Wood Johnson Foundation. (2005b). *U. S. Patients Get Insufficient Care.* Princeton, NJ: The Robert Wood Johnson Foundation.

Rose, S. M., & Moore, V. L. (1995). Case management. In R. L. Edwards (Ed.) *Encyclopedia of Social Work*, (19th ed.). Washington, D. C.: National Association of Social Workers Press.

Sacristan, P. (2003). Problems and solutions in calculating quality-adjusted life years (QALYs). *Health Quality Life Outcomes, 1*(1), 80.

Sheehan, L. (2004). Creativity and innovation. *The ARC Insight, 2*(2004), 2-3.

Smith, D. S. (1995). Standards of practice for case management: The importance of practice standards. *The Journal of Care Management, 1*(3), 6-16.

Smull, M. W. (1996). *Person Centered Planning, Should We do it with Everyone?* College Park, MD: Support Development Associates.

Stiles, R. A., Bahl B., Bernstein, S. J., Halman, L. J., Harrison, R. V., and Standiford, C. (2000). Improving HEDIS measurement: Linking managed care organization and health system ambulatory care data. *Quality Managed Health Care, 8*(2), 40-48.

Stone, R. E. (2004). *Consumer-Driven Health Care: Choosing vs. Using.* Nashville, TN: American Healthways.

Tilly, J. & Wiener, J. M. (2001). *Consumer-Directed Home and Community Services: Policy Issues.* Washington, D. C.: The Urban Institute.

U. S. Census Bureau. (2003). *Disability status: 2000.* Washington, D. C.: U. S. Dept. of Commerce.

U. S. Department of Health and Human Services. (2003). *New freedom initiative progress report released: HHS announces steps to facilitate state programs to foster community integration.* Washington, D. C.: U. S. Department of Health and Human Services.

U. S. Department of Health and Human Services. (2004a). *Disabilities/limitations.* Hyattsville, MD: National Center for Health Statistics.

U. S. Department of Health and Human Services. (2004b). *Life expectancy.* Hyattsville, MD: National Center for Health Statistics.

Wehmeyer, M. L. (2004). Self-determination and the empowerment of people with disabilities. *American Rehabilitation,* (Autumn 2004), Washington, D. C.: U. S. Government Printing Office.

Author's Note

Address correspondence to: Lisa S. Patchner, DrPH, ACSW, Associate Professor, Ball State University, Muncie, IN 47306. e-mail: lpatchner@bsu.edu.

THE FUTURE OF SOCIAL WORK IN AGING:
"EVERYTHING OLD IS NEW AGAIN"

Nancy P. Kropf
Margaret Adamek

Abstract: *With the aging of the baby boom generation, the number of older adults in the US will increase substantially. Using a biopsychosocial framework, this article presents cutting-edge issues of older adulthood and considers emerging roles of social workers with older adults and their families. Research, education, and policy perspectives that will advance social work knowledge, skills and resources in aging are proposed. Social work as a profession is challenged to lead the way in making "everything old new again."*

Keywords: Future of aging, social work with older adults, geriatric social work

INTRODUCTION

By now, the "gerontologizing" of the population is well documented as estimates indicate that one in every five people will be over age 65 in 2030 (U.S. Bureau of the Census, 2000). Even more profound is the expected increase in the oldest segment of the population. Between 1900 – 2000, individuals 85 years and above increased over 43 times! (U.S. DHHS, 2001). By 2050 there will be over one million centenarians living in the U.S. (Aaron, 2005).

In spite of the magnitude of these age-related shifts, the profession of social work has been slow to respond. Several decades ago, Elaine Brody (1970), a pioneer in social work and aging, admonished the profession for the lack of responsiveness to gerontological issues. By some accounts, aging continues to remain a low career priority among social workers compared to other fields of practice (Rosen, Zlotnik & Singer, 2002; Scharlach, Damron-Rodriguez, Robinson & Feldman, 2000). This situation is unfortunate, as a lifespan approach and a person-in-environment perspective-- important frameworks for understanding both normative and problematic aspects of aging --are hallmarks of our profession.

Using a biopsychosocial framework, this article highlights important health, mental health and social issues in late life and anticipates future roles of social workers working with older adults and their families. Borrowing from a seasoned phrase, "everything old is new again," the impending demographic changes will demand that the field of gerontological social work consider new paradigms encompassing broader conceptualizations of aging, new curriculum strategies, new practice models, and new policy directions. Given this imperative, the conclusion explores issues on the horizon for education, practice, policy, and research in social work and aging.

Nancy Kroft is Professor, School of Social Work, University of Georgia, Athens 30602. Margaret Adamek is Professor, School of Social Work, Indiana University, Indianapolis 46202.
Copyright © 2005 *Advances in Social Work* Vol. 6 No. 1 (Spring 2005), 121-131

PHYSICAL AND MENTAL HEALTH ISSUES

While the majority of adults age 65 and over are functionally independent, there are subgroups of the older population with significant physical health challenges. The greatest needs are among those 85 and older who more often have major health restrictions and require help with the activities of daily living (ADLs) and instrumental activities of daily living (IADLs) (McInnis-Dittrich, 2002; Quadagno, 1999). The oldest-old are the fastest growing segment of the older population. At least 80% of older adults have at least one chronic condition, and 50% have at least two (CDC, 2004a). The CDC (2004a) estimates that 12 million older adults living in the community have chronic conditions that limit their activities. Findings from the National Health Interview Survey reveal that the most common chronic conditions of older adults are arthritis, hypertension, and heart disease (Desai, Zhang, & Hennessy, 1999). Preventive interventions are gaining ground as a means to lessen the negative consequences of these and other chronic conditions (CDC, 2004a). Nevertheless, technological advances in the health care arena have contributed to more and more people living longer, often with complex physical and mental health conditions. The Centers for Disease Control & Prevention (2004a) recognizes that the aging of the population will "trigger a huge demand for health care and social services." Social workers will be challenged to remain abreast of changes in patient care "stimulated by technological advances in biomedicine and pharmacology" (Berkman & Harootyan, 2003, pp.2-3). Social workers with geriatric expertise will be especially valued in health care settings (Berkman & Harootyan, 2003).

One of the most difficult practice situations faced by health care social workers concerns the difficult ethical issues surrounding end-of-life care (Csikai & Bass, 2000). The growing complexity of illness at the end of life has contributed to a burgeoning literature on end-of-life care (e.g., Berzoff & Silverman, 2004; deVries, 1999; Emanuel, 2004). The *NASW Standards on Palliative and End-of-Life Care* (NASW, 2004) provide guidance for social workers in facilitating communication among older adults, family members, and health care professionals with decision-making around such issues as the use of life-prolonging medical technologies. The ethical dilemmas associated with end-of-life care go beyond practice issues to unresolved political and social controversies over issues such as assisted suicide, adherence to advanced directives, untimely referrals to hospice care, and unrelieved pain of dying persons (Roff, 2001). As more people live longer and face advanced illness, social workers will increasingly need a clear understanding of bioethics and end-of-life care issues. Much work is needed to enhance social workers' preparation to work with dying patients and their families (Christ & Sormanti, 1999), particularly considering the growth in hospice social work and the fact that over 80% of hospice patients are 65 and over (Waldrop, 2005). Nakashima (2002) calls for the profession to envision social work with older adults at the end of life going beyond coping and adaptation to embracing psychosocial and spiritual well-being.

Social workers must be aware that spirituality is a significant resource for many older adults in addressing a variety of late life challenges (Nelson-Becker, 1999). Many argue that spirituality is integral to mental health in late life (e.g., Kanitsaki, 2002; Kimble, 2002; MacKinlay, 2002; McNamara, 2002). Ortiz and Langer (2002) offer a brief inventory of spiritual questions that social workers can include in a biopsychosocial assessment with older adults to help ascertain the role of spirituality and spiritual resources in their lives. While it is critical to take into account the impact of older adults' individual spiritual beliefs on their aging experience, it is equally important for social workers to be proactive in engaging in the broader social discourse about aging—a discourse that persistently projects older adulthood as a life stage that is about decline, disability, and depression.

Pervasive negative stereotypes of late life buttress the view that it is normal for older adults to be depressed. Such culturally acceptable notions hamper efforts to effectively identify and treat depression in late life. As many as one in five older adults experience mental health problems that are *not* associated with normal aging (USDHHS, 1999). The most common mental health diagnoses among older adults are anxiety and depression. The highest rates of depression are found in nursing homes where up to half of residents exhibit depressive symptoms (Adamek, 2003). While many barriers exist to identifying and treating geriatric depression, Adamek (2003) presents a social work agenda for combating late life depression—an agenda that emphasizes the collaborative, holistic, social-environmental perspective that social work can offer.

The strong link between depression and suicide among older adults suggests an urgent need for improved and more widespread measures to prevent, assess for, and treat geriatric depression. It is estimated that suicidal behavior among older adults is associated with depression in approximately 90% of cases (USDHHS, 1999). The *Surgeon General's Call to Action to Prevent Suicide* (USPHS, 1999) identifies adults 65 and over as a group with particularly high risk of suicide. Over 5,000 older adults in the US commit suicide every year, making them the age group with the highest suicide rate (CDC, 2004b). "Suicide in later life represents a significant public health challenge that will rapidly grow during the early decades of the 21st century" (Pearson, Caine, Lindesay, Conwell, & Clark, 1999, p. 203). Haas and Hendin (1983) project a two-fold increase in elderly suicides by 2030.

Social workers' training and skill in conducting psychosocial assessments make them ideal candidates for assisting in identification of older adults at risk for depression and suicide. Social workers can play a key role in educating health care providers, older adults, and family members about the connections among physical illness, depression, and suicide in late life (Adamek & Yoder-Slater, 2005). Given that firearms are the most common method of suicide used by older adults in the U.S., Adamek & Yoder-Slater (2005) further call for social workers to support efforts to assess for firearm availability and to advocate for policies to limit firearm access.

While the issues mentioned thus far focus on the "problems" in late life, social workers must remain cognizant that future cohorts of older adults will have longer life expectancies, and will be better educated, healthier, more active, and have greater resources at their disposal. Creativity, energy, and enthusiasm will be paramount for any social worker who sets out to partner with aging baby boomers that are looking forward to many productive years of life. Freedman (1999) asserts that the "demographic revolution" should be viewed as an opportunity to be seized rather than as a problem to be solved. Referring to baby boomers as "pioneers on the frontier of a new stage of life," Freedman claims that retirement is being reinvented through the emergence of a growing group of older adults who plan to remain productive and pursue activities that make a meaningful contribution to their communities. The social work roles that may come about to support and facilitate new opportunities for retirement-age individuals are yet to be conceptualized, let alone embraced.

Whether working with chronically ill or able-bodied older adults, social workers in the coming years must consider new paradigms of aging that embrace diversity, possibility, and potential---notions typically reserved for younger generations. Neysmith (1999) calls for social workers to let go of the "old gerontology that was focused on age as a major category delimiter" (p. 22). Instead, they call for social workers to become partners in "a transformative agenda" informed by older adults themselves, especially those whose voices are rarely heard:

> ...this breaking apart of the age center of gerontology is a moment of op-
> portunity for envisioning alternatives for what aging can mean in the years
> ahead. What social workers can do is to open up rather than foreclose pos-
> sibilities because social workers are strategically located to witness the ineq-
> uities that affect peoples' lives on a daily basis. (p. 22).

Part of the transition that will be needed in social workers' approach to working with older adults is a willingness to learn about and adopt rapidly advancing technologies with the potential to enhance well-being in late life. Charness, Parks, and Sabel (2001) describe some of the technological advances that will enhance older adults' communication opportunities in the future. Computer-based technologies for advancing home care for older adults include interactive websites, electronic monitoring devices, "virtual house calls," sensors to detect movements and prevent falls, electronic health records, Global Information Systems (GIS), and online support groups (Kropf & Grigsby, 1999; Spry Foundation, n.d.). Social workers who are more comfortable with human interactions and face-to-face communication may need to step outside of their comfort zone and expand their technological knowledge and skills to the extent that such innovations offer promise to enhance practice with older adults. Given core social work values such as self-determination and respect for individual human worth and dignity, social workers can make a contribution to policy and practice decisions about adopting and even designing technological tools to enhance well-being in late life.

SOCIAL RELATIONSHIPS

Increased life expectancies, combined with social role changes, will continue to impact family forms and relationships. A major change has been in the length of marriages, which have increased as a result of extended life spans. Some couples report happy and stable relationships that are able to adapt to the changing life conditions of the partners (Bachand & Caron, 2001). However, mid- and late-life divorces are also increasing as the stresses of aging, including economic, social, and health changes, challenge these relationships (McDaniel & Coleman, 2003). Widowhood is another late life experience that face many older adults, especially older women. By age 85, 79% of all women are widowed (U.S. Bureau of the Census, 2002). Interventions that assist widows through grief and loss provide information to facilitate role adjustment and establish criteria for risk situations in this process as appropriate and necessary (Raveis, 1999).

Families increasingly face the prospect of caregiving for an older family member. Caregivers of older family members often require multiple types of support from social workers such as assessing the need for long term care, dealing with stress, and accessing community resources. As the population ages, some families will have multiple generations of older members who may require care. For example, a centenarian may have grandchildren who are in their sixties, and also in need of support and assistance. In coming years, social workers will be challenged by serving greater numbers of families with multiple generations in later life.

Besides being care recipients, older adults often serve as care providers to younger generations. With community-based care on the rise, more parents of adults with mental health and developmental disabilities maintain their care provider roles into later life (Bigby, Ozanne & Gordon, 2002; Botsford & Rule, 2004). In addition, the rates of grandparents who raise grandchildren have increased dramatically. Current estimates of these "custodial grandparents" indicate that about 5—6% of children live in households with grandparents, with about 10% of grandparents having responsibility to raise children (Pebley & Rudkin, 1999). Clearly, the number of older adults who serve as caregivers within their families and communities is growing. As social workers, we can contribute to expanding the conceptualization of "late life caregiving" to include appreciation for the varied care provider roles of older adults.

As people age, their peer relationships may be based more upon proximity to others than earlier in life. Programs that provide an opportunity for social connection with others and that focus on enhancing the emotional well-being of older adults are vitally important. An example of a novel approach is an intergenerational program where high school students teach nursing home residents computer skills. For both populations there are rewards; the residents learn skills and establish relationships, while the students experience positive interactions with older adults in an area of shared interest [c.f. http://www.seniorconnects.org/]. Even older adults who are quite frail can learn how to use computers to stay connected through email, access information on the internet, and play games (Namazi & McClintic, 2003). In addition to providing health and social programs, senior centers have become primary places for a variety of self-enrichment classes including helping older adults learn new technology applications (Turner, 2004).

Other social issues have to do with the composition of the older population as it becomes increasingly diverse. Projections indicate that the percentage of non-Hispanic Whites will decrease from about 83% in 2003 to about 61% of the older population in 2050. During this same time period, the two groups that will increase most dramatically are Hispanics (from 6% to 18%) and African Americans (from 8% to 12%) (Federal Interagency Forum on Aging Related Statistics, 2004). As the older population becomes more diverse, cultural and language issues related to programs and services will gain significance in community-based and long term care settings.

Another form of diversity in late life relates to sexual orientation. While sexuality in older adults is often an avoided issue, sexual orientation and gender identity issues in late life are often omitted in both the gay/lesbian and gerontology literature (Barranti & Cohen, 2000; Humphreys & Quam, 1998). The current cohort of older adults who are gay, lesbian, bisexual or transgendered lived much of their adult life during a time when it was unsafe to openly identify as GLBT (Morrow, 2001). While oppression and intolerance towards people who are GLBT continues, younger cohorts are more open about their sexual and gender identity and more demanding (rightfully!) of responsive social services.

GLBT-specific support groups, living arrangements, retirement planning and other options will be part of the future of aging.

Many other issues fall under the umbrella of social work with older adults including Alzheimers and other forms of dementia, guardianship, elder mistreatment, HIV/AIDS, caregiving, sexuality, assisted living, long-term care, fall prevention, polypharmacy, resistance to care, and home health. A key component to social workers' future success in working with older adults and their families who encounter challenges in late life is the ability to work effectively as members of interdisciplinary teams (Naleppa, 2003). Social work roles with a range of health, mental health, and social issues are carefully considered in two recent edited volumes that provide much needed direction for social work with older adults and their families (Berkman, 2005; Berkman & Harootyan, 2003).

AGENDA SETTING FOR THE FUTURE

Clearly, the older population is rapidly both growing and changing. Every seven seconds, another Baby Boomer turns 50 which translates to about 12,000 each day (Alliance for Aging Research, http://www.agingresearch.org/aging_stats.cfm). We have scarcely begun to consider how the impending demographic changes will impact daily life in the coming years. Although social work practitioners should be at the forefront of service provision to older adults, intensified efforts are needed to expand our knowledge about older clients and their families.

On the occasion of its 25th anniversary, the National Institute on Aging published an agenda which outlines specific priorities in aging research (National Institute on Aging, 2000). The major research initiatives included improving the health and quality of life of older adults, understanding healthy aging, reducing health disparities within the older population, and increasing resources to further high-quality research in aging. As this agenda indicates, future research in aging needs to identify risk situations in later life. However, research on protective and buffering factors is also needed to add to the knowledge of aging successfully.

Within social work, there have also been efforts to establish a research agenda on aging. Using a Delphi technique, Burnette, Morrow-Howell, and Chen (2003) surveyed expert panels of social work researchers and practitioners. The item that received the highest degree of consensus for future social work research with older adults was developing and testing psychosocial interventions across specific populations and conditions. Other items that received high consensus include evaluation of long term care policies, studies on living arrangements and transitions, evaluation of various service delivery issues, understanding caregivers and evaluating services to families, studying mental health issues of late life, and recruiting and training a professional workforce in aging.

In order to adequately prepare graduates for practice with an older population, schools of social work need to consider ways to recruit and educate students for work with older clients and families (Kropf, 2002, 2003). Evidence suggests that exposure to gerontological content and quality of contact with older adults can positively influence students' career choices to work in aging (Carmel, Cwikel & Galinsky, 1992; Cummings, Galambos & DeCoster, 2003). As programs consider ways to recruit students into gerontology, one important issue is how to provide students with the opportunity to work with older adults across a variety of settings and contexts.

A few strategies seem particularly worthwhile in helping students understand the range of exciting careers with older adults. One is to include service learning opportunities as a required component of the curriculum (e.g., Kropf & Tracey, 2002). Service learning, a teaching technique that has students work in teams to work on real issues within the community, integrates academics with experiential learning. In order to assist programs to establish service learning projects, the Association for Gerontology in Higher Education (AGHE) has developed a compendium of resources to establish service learning projects with older adults (AGHE, 1998-2004).

Another logical place for students to have experiences working with older adults is through their internships. The John A. Hartford Foundation, in partnership with the New York Academy of Medicine, established the Practicum Partnership Program to develop aging-rich internships at six social work programs (e.g., Bures, Toseland & Fortune, 2002; Ivry & Hadden, 2002). Students in these internships have worked with older adults in community – partnership agencies across a continuum of care. In this way, students gain exposure to those older adults who are in frail health, as well as those who have more functional health status. The John A. Hartford Foundation has provided over $25 million to support other initiatives to build capacity in social work and aging including faculty development programs, curriculum transformation institutes and grants, and doctoral student support (O'Sullivan, 2004; Robbins & Rieder, 2002). These and other programs stemming from the Hartford Geriatric Social Work Initiative are described at www.gswi. org. Other organizations, such as the Association for Gerontology Education – Social Work (AGE – SW) and the Aging Section of NASW also provide opportunities for developing networks within aging and social work.

Another resource to build capacity in geriatric social work is the Institute for Geriatric Social Work (IGSW), established at Boston University in 2003 with funding from the Atlantic Philanthropies. The IGSW offers grants and training to upgrade the skills and knowledge of practicing social workers and is "dedicated to advancing social work practice with older adults" (www.bu.edu/igsw). In addition to its primary education and training mission, the GSWI also supports policy and research initiatives related to social work practice with older adults.

In the area of policy, two high budget priorities are Medicare and Social Security. Predictions estimate that in 2005, Social Security will account for 21% of federal expenditures, with Medicare coming second at 13% of federal expenses (Newhouse, 2004). Since about one-third of the federal budget is being spent on these two programs, it is not surprising that several possible changes are proposed. Any changes to privatize, limit access to programs, or shift responsibility need to be carefully analyzed. While many myths abound about the wealth of the older population, certain segments (especially older women of color) are particularly vulnerable economically (Ozawa, 1995). Therefore, any changes in income or health care costs can be potentially devastating to the overall well-being of these segments.

As this manuscript is being prepared, work is being completed for the fifth White House Conference on Aging (WHCoA) scheduled for October 2005 (see http://www.

whcoa.gov). This event will focus on developing policy for the first wave of the baby boom generation. Past WHCoAs have provided the impetus for such important legislation as Medicare and the Older Americans Act. Priority issues will be health and well-being, income and economic security, civic engagement of older adults in the labor force, volunteerism, and lifelong learning, among many other issues. Social workers much seek a place at the table as these important policy issues are addressed.

CONCLUSION

As we look to the future of social work in aging, we are wise to recall Elaine Brody's (1970) admonishment to our profession. Considering the enormity of the coming "age wave" (Dychtwald & Flower, 1990), we have no choice but to include aging in our research, practice, and educational agendas. Some advancement has been made including a raised awareness of the need to know more about aging within social work, partnerships with private foundations that are in the position to infuse resources to make substantive changes, and a realization that aging is not a period primarily of disability and dependence. As the profession based upon a person-and-environment perspective, social work is in a unique position to inform the aging arena and can take the lead with many new and exciting initiatives. A social work perspective will be vital to making "everything old new again."

References

Aaron, H.J. (2005). The centenarian boom: Providing for retirement in a long-lived America. In H. Cox (Ed.). *Annual editions: Aging.* Dubuque, IA: McGraw-Hill/Dushkin.

Adamek, M. (2003). Late-life depression in nursing home residents: Social work opportunities to prevent, educate, and alleviate. In B. Berkman & L. Harootyan (Eds.). *Social work and health care in an aging society: Education, policy, practice, and research.* NY: Springer.

Adamek, M. & Yoder-Slater, G. (2005). Social work with older adults at risk of suicide. In B. Berkman (Ed.). *Oxford handbook of social work in aging.* NY: Oxford.

Association for Gerontology in Higher Education. (1998-2004). *Intergenerational service learning in gerontology: A compendium.* AGHE & Generations United.

Bachand, L. L. & Caron, S. L. (2001). Ties that bind: A qualitative study of happy long-term marriages. *Contemporary Family Therapy, 23,* 105-121.

Barranti, C. C. R & Cohen, H. L. (2002). Lesbian and gay elders: An invisible minority. In R. L. Schneider, N. P. Kropf & A. Kisor (Eds.). *Gerontological social work* (pp. 302-342). Belmont, CA: Wadsworth.

Berkman, B.(Ed.). (2005). *Oxford handbook of aging and social work.* NY: Oxford.

Berkman, B. & Harootyan, L. (Eds). (2003). *Social work and health care in an aging society: Education, policy, practice, and research.* NY: Springer.

Berzoff, J. & Silverman, P. (Eds.). (2004). *Living with dying: A handbook for end-of-life care practitioners.* NY: Columbia University Press.

Bigby, C., Ozanne, E., & Gordon, M. (2002); Facilitating transition: Elements of successful case management practice for older parents of adults with intellectual disability. *Journal of Gerontological Social Work, 37* (3 /4), 25-43.

Botsford, A. L, & Rule, D. (2004). Evaluation of a group intervention to assist aging parents with permanency planning for an adult offspring with special needs. *Social Work, 49,* 423-431.

Brody, E. (1970). Serving the aged: Educational needs as viewed by practice. *Social Work, 15,* 42-51.

Bures, R. M., Toseland, R. W. & Fortune, A. E. (1992). Strengthening geriatric social work training: Perspectives from the University at Albany. *Journal of Gerontological Social Work, 39, 111*-127.

Burnette, D., Morrow-Howell, N., & Chen, L (2003). Setting priorities for gerontological social work research: A national Delphi study. *The Gerontologist, 43,* 828-838.

Carmel, S., Cwikel, J., & Galinsky, D. (1992). Changes in knowledge, attitudes, and work preferences following courses in gerontology among medical, nursing, and social work students. *Educational Gerontology, 18,* 329-342.

Centers for Disease Control and Prevention. (2004a). *Healthy aging: Preventing disease and improving quality of life among older Americans.* Accessed on the world wide web at: http://www.cdc.gov/nccdphp/aag/aag_aging.htm retrieved on 12/15/2004.

Centers for Disease Control and Prevention, National Center for Injury Prevention and Control (2004b). (producer). Web-based Injury statistics query and reporting system (WISQARS). [online]. (2004). www.cdc.gov/ncipc/wisquars retrieved on 6/30/04 from the world wide web.

Charness, N., Parks, D.C., & Sabel, B.A. (Eds.).(2001). *Communication, technology, and aging: Opportunities and challenges for the future.* NY: Springer.

Christ, G.H. & Sormanti, M. (1999). Advancing social work practice in end-of-life care. *Social Work in Health Care, 30,* 81-99.

Csikai, E. & Bass, K. (2000). Health care social workers' views of ethical issues, practice, and policy in end-of-life care. *Social Work in Health Care, 32,* 1-22.

Cummings, S.M., Galambos, C. & DeCoster, V. A. (2003). Predictors of MSW employment in gerontological practice. *Educational Gerontology, 29,* 295-312.

Desai, M., Zhang, P., & Hennessey, C.H. (1999). Surveillance for morbidity and mortality among older adults—United States, 1995-1996. *Surveillance Summaries, 48,* (SS08), 7-25.

deVries, B. (Ed.). (1999). *End of life issues: Interdisciplinary and multidimensional perspectives.* NY: Springer.

Dychtwald, K. & Flower, J. (1990). *The age wave: How the most important trend of our time can change your future.* NY: Bantam.

Emanuel, L. (2004). *Palliative care.* Philadelphia: Saunders.

Federal Interagency Forum on Aging Related Statistics. (2004). *Older Americans 2004: Key indicators of well-being.* Washington DC: Government Printing Office.

Freedman, M. (1999). *Prime time: How baby boomers will revolutionize retirement and transform America.* Cambridge, MA: PublicAffairs Books.

Haas, A. & Hendin, H. (1983). Suicide among older people: Projection for the future. *Suicide & Life-Threatening Behavior, 13,* 147.

Herdt, G. & deVries, B. (Eds.). (2004). *Gay and lesbian aging: Research and future directions.* NY: Springer.

Humphreys, N. A. & Quan, J. E. (1998). Middle-aged and old gay, lesbian, and bisexual adults. In G. A. Appleby & J. W. Anastas (Eds.). *Not just a passing phase* (pp. 245-268). New York: Columbia.

Ivry, J. & Hadden, B. R. (2002). The Hunter experience: Innovations in the field practicum. *Journal of Gerontological Social Work, 39,* 129-144.

Kanitsaki, O. (2002). Mental health, culture, and spirituality: Implications for the effective psychotherapeutic care of Australia's ageing migrant population. *Journal of Religious Gerontology, 13,*

(3/4), 17-37.

Kimble, M.A. (2002). The defiant power of the human spirit: Mental health in later life. *Journal of Religious Gerontology, 13,* (3/4), 39-47.

Kropf, N. P. (2002). Strategies to increase student interest in aging. *Journal of Gerontological Social Work, 39*(1/2), 57-67.

Kropf, N. P. (2003). Future training and education recommendations for rural gerontological social workers. *Journal of Gerontological Social Work, 41 ,* 287-299.

Kropf, N. P. & Grigsby, R. K. (1999). Telemedicine for older adults. *Home Health Care Services Quarterly, 17*(4), 1 – 11.

Kropf, N. P. & Tracey, M. (2002). Service learning as a transition into foundation field. *Advances in Social Work, 3,* 60-71.

MacKinlay, E. (2002). Mental health and spirituality in later life: Pastoral approaches. *Journal of Religious Gerontology, 13,* (3/4), 129-147.

McDaniel, A. K. & Coleman, M. (2003). Women's experiences of midlife divorce following long-term marriages. *Journal of Divorce and Remarriage, 38,* 103-128.

McInnis-Dittrich, K. (2002). *Social work with elders: A biopsychosocial approach to assessment and intervention.* Boston: Allyn & Bacon.

McNamara, L.J. (2002). Theological perspectives on ageing and mental health. *Journal of Religious Gerontology, 13,* (3/4), 1-16.

Morrow, D. F. (2001). Older gays and lesbians: Surviving a generation of hate and violence. *Journal of Gay and Lesbian Social Services, 13,* 151-169.

Nakashima, M. (2002). A qualitative inquiry into the psychosocial and spiritual well-being of older adults at the end of life. *Social Work Abstracts, 38,* No. 1141.

Naleppa, M. J. (2003). Gerontological social work and case management. In B. Berkman & L. Harootyan (Eds.). *Social work and health care in an aging society: Education, policy, practice, and research.* NY: Springer.

Namazi, K. H. & McClintic, M. (2003). Computer use among elderly persons in long-term care facilities. *Educational Gerontology, 29,* 535-550.

National Association of Social Workers. (NASW).(2004). *NASW standards for palliative and end of life care.* Available online at: http://www.socialworkers.org/practice/bereavement/standards/standards0504New.pdf

National Institute on Aging (2000). *National Institute on Aging strategic plan for fiscal years 2001 – 2005.* (Pub. No. 01-4951).

Nelson-Becker, H. (1999). Spiritual and religious problem-solving in older adults: Mechanisms for managing life challenge. *Social Work Abstracts, 35,* No. 1620.

Newhouse, J. P. (2004). Financing Medicare in the next administration. *The New England Journal of Medicine, 351,* 1714-1716.

Neysmith, S.M. (Ed.).(1999). *Critical issues for future social work practice with aging persons.* NY: Columbia University Press.

Ortiz, L.P. & Langer, N. (2002). Assessment of spirituality and religion in later life: Acknowedging clients' needs and personal resources. *Journal of Gerontological Social Work, 37,* 5-21.

O'Sullivan, J. F. (2004). Overview of the John A. Hartford Social Work Initiatives. Presented at the National Association of Dean's & Directors meeting, October, San Diego.

Ozawa, M. (1995). The economic status of vulnerable older women. *Social Work, 40,* 323-333.

Pearson, J., Caine, E., Lindesay, D., Conwell, Y., & Clark, D. (1999). Studies of suicide in later life:

Methodologic considerations and research directions. *American Journal of Geriatric Psychiatry, 7,* 203-210.

Pebley, A. R. & Rudkin, L. L. (1999). Grandparents caring for grandchildren: What do we know? *Journal of Family Issues, 20,* 218-242.

Quadagno, J. (1999). *Aging and the life course: An introduction to social gerontology.* Boston: McGraw-Hill.

Raveis, V. H. (1999). Facilitating older spouses' adjustment to widowhood: A preventive interventive program. *Social Work in Health Care, 29,* (4), 13-32.

Robbins, L. & Rieder, C. H. (2002). The John A. Hartford Foundation Geriatric Social Work Initiative. In M. J. Mellor & J. Ivry, (Eds.). *Advancing gerontological social work education* (pp. 71-90). NY: Haworth

Roff, S. (2001). Analyzing end-of-life care legislation: A social work perspective. *Social Work in Health Care, 33,* 51-68.

Rosen, A., Zlotnik, J. L., & Singer, T. (2002). Basic gerontological competence for all social workers: The need to "gerontologize" social work education. In M. J. Mellor & J. Ivry, (Eds.). *Advancing gerontological social work education* (pp. 25-36). NY: Haworth.

Scharlach, A., Damron-Rodriquez, J., Robinson, B., & Feldman, R. (2000). Educating social workders for an aging society: A vision for the 21st century. *Journal of Social Work Education, 36,* 521-538.

Spry Foundation. (n.d.). *Computer-based technology and caregiving of older adults: What's new, what's next.* Seattle, WA: Caresource Healthcare Communications, Inc.

Turner, K.W. (2004). Senior citizens centers: What they offer, who participates, and what they gain. *Journal of Gerontological Social Work, 43,* 37-47.

U.S. Bureau of the Census. (2000). Profile of the general demographic characteristics for the United States. http://www.cenusus.gov/Press-release/2001/tables/dp_us_2000.PDF.

U.S. Bureau of the Census. (2002). *Annual demographic supplement to the March 2002 Current Population Survey.* http://factfinder.census.gov.

U.S. Department of Health and Human Services. (1999). *Mental health: A report of the surgeon general-Executive summary.* Rockville, MD: US DHHS.

U.S. Department of Health and Human Services. (2001). *HHS fact sheet: HHS programs and initiatives for an aging America.* http://www.hhs.gov/news.

U.S. Public Health Service. (1999). *US Surgeon General's call to action to prevent suicide.* Washington, DC: US DHHS.

Waldrop, D. (2005). Social work practice in hospice. In B. Berkman (Ed.). *Oxford handbook of aging and social work.* NY: Oxford.

Author's Note

Address correspondence to Nancy Kropf, Professor, School of Social Work, University of Georgia, Tucker Hall, Athens, GA 30602-7016. e-mail: nkropf@uga.edu.

THE FUTURE OF RURAL SOCIAL WORK

Susan A. Murty

Abstract: *Over the years, the extensive literature on rural social work has been consistent in its recommendations for local community-based practice and rural generalist practice. However, rural social work is embedded in the larger social work profession which has been moving in the opposite direction from the one advocated by rural social workers. The gradual processes of centralization and specialization in the profession now make it almost impossible for social workers to use community-based generalist practice approaches in rural areas. In order to ensure a positive future for rural social work, urban and rural social workers must work together to re-introduce a level of community-based generalist practice within regionalized and specialized social and health service systems. A range of alternative approaches to link community-based rural programs with regional programs is presented.*

Keywords: Rural Social Work, Rural Definition, Service Delivery, Regionalization, Community-Based Services, Generalist Practice

BACKGROUND ON RURAL SOCIAL WORK

Rural social work has received the attention of a dedicated group of practitioners in the profession since the early work of Josephine Brown (1933), (Martinez-Brawley, 1981). In the 1970s, an expansion of interest in rural social work produced a "rural social work movement" (Davenport & Davenport, 1995; Ginsberg, 1998a). Since that time, many publications (for ex. Farley, Griffiths, Skidmore, & Thackeray, 1982; Keller & Murray, 1982; Watkins & Watkins, 1984), interest groups, and conferences attest to the success of the upsurge of activity in the field of rural social work (Hickman, 2004). Through the period of the "Farm and Rural Crisis" of the 1980s and more recently as this crisis has continued, innovative programs of rural social work have been mobilized to help farm and rural families and their communities cope with the crisis and to encourage social and economic development to help rural communities survive (Williams, 2001; Rossman & Dvorak, 2001). At the present time rural social and health services and community development programs in rural areas target a variety of issues and populations. In addition to rural agriculture and rural economic and community development (Heartland Center for Leadership Development, 2005; Rural Community Development, 2005), these include rural health (Agency for Health Care Policy and Research, 1991; Evans, 2004), rural mental health (Keller & Murray, 1982; Hann-Morrison, 2003; Evans, 2004), rural substance abuse (Johnson, 1998), rural child welfare (Ray & Murty, 1990), rural domestic violence (Websdale, 1998; Murty & Schechter, 1999; Murty, 2001a), services for the elderly in rural areas (Nelson, 1980; Krout & Coward, 1998; Krout, 1998), services for rural gays and lesbians (Lindhorst, 1997), and services for people living with AIDS (*Human Services in the Rural Environment*, 1989; Rounds, 1998), to name just a few. There are also

Susan Murty is Associate Professor, School of Social Work, University of Iowa, Iowa City, Iowa 52242-1223.
Copyright © 2005 *Advances in Social Work* Vol. 6 No. 1 (Spring 2005), 132-144

organizations focusing on different types of services in rural areas, for example the National Rural Health Association, the National Rural Mental Health Association, and the National Rural Social Work Caucus (see notes). In spite of the diversity of types of services, rural programs share similar concerns in regard to scarce resources, highly dispersed populations, problems of transportation, and lack of trained professionals and specialists (Martinez-Brawley, 1987; Ginsberg, 1998b; Southern Regional Education Board, 1998; HHS Rural Task Force, 2002; NASW, 2002).

Throughout the years, difficulties in defining the rural concept have stimulated much discussion. The inadequacy of the commonly used definitions of rurality has been the basis of much well deserved criticism (Mermelstein & Sundet, 1989; Davenport & Davenport, 1995; York, Denton, & Moran, 1998). Any measure that classifies communities into two dichotomous groups is bound to be inadequate. For example, comparisons of US Census data, between metropolitan areas and non-metropolitan areas, or between urban and rural areas, obscure differences between communities that are more and less rural within each two groups. Many researchers and practitioners agree that urban and rural communities exist on a continuum from the most extremely urban to the most rural communities (Ginsberg, 1998b). Any particular community can be located somewhere between these two extremes. Considerable improvement in the measurement of the rural-to-urban continuum has been achieved in recent years. The term *frontier* has been developed in relation to health service, emergency medical services, and mental health services to indicate extremely low population density areas where service delivery is especially challenging (National Clearinghouse for Frontier Communities, 2004; Frontier Mental Health Services Resource Network, 2005). Another development was the county-based rural-to-urban continuum codes to classify counties on an ordinal continuum of 10 categories (Butler & Beale, 1994). Disadvantages of this county-based classification system remain because within any county, communities can range from very urban to very rural. Especially in the western part of the United States, very large counties may be classified as metropolitan because a large population center is located in one part of the county, while other parts of these large counties may be extremely sparsely populated and should be recognized as having rural characteristics. Recently, RUCA Codes have been developed using census tracts data on population size and commuting patterns to larger communities (Olaveson, Conway, & Shaver, 2004). The RUCA Codes have refined measurement on the rural-to-urban continuum. See notes at the end of this article for resources on defining rurality and for information on the county rural-urban codes, the country frontier definitions, and the new census tract RUCA Codes.

During the decades, as interest in rural social work has persisted and its literature has grown, rural communities have been changing (Wilkinson, 1982; Mermelstein & Sundet, 1998). Some urbanites have been moving to rural areas (Davenport & Davenport, 1998). New types of technology are affecting all rural communities (Enders & Seekins, 1999). Interstate highways, cellular phones, computer access to the Internet, satellite and cable television, increase in automobile transportation, have all lessened the geographical and cultural distance that separates life in rural communities from life in suburbs and population centers. The differences between urban and rural in many regions have gradually become less dramatic than they once were. In addition, new ethnic groups, immigrants and refugees, have been arriving in America´s small towns throughout the country. Many small towns that used to be homogeneous are now experiencing a sudden and unexpected increase in diversity (Snipp, 1996; Johnson, Johnson-Webb, & Farrell, 1999). In spite of these changes, the rural/urban distinction is still relevant. Characteristics of rural communities still distinguish them from the more populated urban and suburban areas. The recommendations in the rural social work literature are still relevant to rural social work today.

RECOMMENDATIONS FROM THE RURAL SOCIAL WORK LITERATURE

The central themes that recur in the rural social work literature over its long history are the importance of local community-based practice and rural generalist practice. Over the years, the extensive literature on rural social work has been consistent in its recommendations for these two related approaches to rural practice. In order to be effective, rural social workers take time to get to know the particular rural community where they work, its assets, its local organizations, its leaders, and informal helping systems (Smith, 1997; Martinez-Brawley, 1987, 1998; Ginsberg, 1998b; NASW, 2002; Menanteau-Horta, 2004; Watkins, 2004). It is necessary to build strong personal relationships with members of the community and local community leaders in order to make good use of the assets which rural communities have to offer (Rolland & Hughes, 2004; Davis & Meyer, 1996). This community-based approach also helps to gradually overcome the initial suspicion which local rural residents tend to have toward outsiders (Murty, 1984). Rural social workers must use high levels of skill and sensitivity to manage unavoidable dual relationships in rural social work to ensure that clients are protected and professional ethics are maintained (Miller, 1998).

Related to the community-based approach for rural social work is the recommendation for generalist practice (Martinez-Brawley, 1987; Davenport & Davenport, 1995; Ginsberg, 1998b; NASW, 2002). Rather than specializing in one particular method of social work practice, or a particular population in need, the rural social worker needs be able to intervene in many ways on behalf of members of the community. This includes the level of social work with individuals and families with a variety of needs, but also includes the levels of work with organizations, the community, and policy (Ray, 2004; Davis & Meyer, 1996). This wide range of intervention skills is focused on the assets and needs of the particular rural communities where the social worker works. In a sense, the rural social worker must be a specialist, but the specialization is not in particular methods of practice or particular levels of intervention. Instead, it is a specialization and in-depth knowledge about particular rural communities. Based on this specialized local knowledge, the rural social worker can provide a wide range of services and interventions in that rural community. In this sense, the rural social worker is both a local specialist and a generalist.

Innovative programs provide services and encourage community development in rural areas using these community-based and generalist practice approaches (Heartland Center for Leadership Development, 2005; Rural Community Development, 2005). These programs are sometimes strikingly different from the typical programs in urban areas. Effective use of rural community volunteers, rural resources, networks, organizations, and local community leadership extends the power of social work where services are spread thin over large rural regions. By building on the local resources and assets of rural communities, social workers have been able to create outstanding programs even where formal services are scarce and under-funded.

THE BARRIERS TO EFFECTIVE RURAL SOCIAL WORK

If the literature is so consistent in its recommendations for rural social work that is generalist and community-based practice, why has it been necessary to repeat the same recommendations from the 1930s to the year 2005? What obstacles have prevented social work from fulfilling the consistent recommendations in the literature (York, Denton, and Moran, 1998; Mermelstein & Sundet, 1998)?

The answer is that rural social work is embedded in the larger social work profession which has been moving in the opposite direction from the one advocated by rural social workers (York, Denton, & Moran, 1998). Instead of becoming more community-based, the profession has become more and more specialized and service progams have developed into separate institutions with separate streams of funding (Martinez-Brawley, 1998). As part of the consolidation which has been affecting rural communities nationally and world-wide for decades (Goldschmidt, 1947; Goldschmidt, 1978), social and health service agencies are growing larger and more centralized, a trend in the opposite direction from community-based generalist practice. The barriers to community-based generalist practice have grown, rather than lessened. Social work programs in general have been moving in the direction of bigger, more efficient, more centralized operations (Martinez-Brawley, 1998). For the most part, social work education has also moved in the direction of training students for specialized types of clinical practice (Mermelstein & Sundet, 1998). Is it any wonder that rural social workers and advocates of rural social work have felt they are shouting into the wind, and that their voices have not been heard (Mermelstein & Sundet, 1998; Martinez-Brawley, 1998)?

A case in point is the dramatic increase of the regionalization of health and human services in rural areas (Lennox & Murty, 1994; Murty, 2001b). The process began with school consolidation that continues today to increase the size of schools and to increase the distance students travel to get to school (Barker & Gump, 1964). Many health and human service programs that used to be administered by counties or local governments, are now administered from offices in large population centers. In the last few decades, the geographical areas which many of these programs serve have grown. It is now common for a community mental health center to serve 4 or more counties, for a juvenile justice program to serve 6 counties, for an Area Agency on Aging to serve up to 20 counties, and for a large teaching hospital to draw patients from surrounding states (for ex., see National Association of Area Agencies on Aging, 1996). Within these programs, specialization has narrowed the scope of work that any particular social worker provides. Rather than rural communities having one social worker who provides a wide range of services, it is now more likely that residents of the small town are expected to travel to population centers to visit a variety of different specialists in their offices. The cost of travel and travel time tends to reduce service use (White, 1986).

An alternative strategy for service delivery is that the rural community may receive services once a month or once a week from travelling "circuit riders." Each "circuit rider" is a specialist from a different urban program and each takes on a narrow scope of work. For example, a special education social worker may be available in a particular rural community twice a week, a community mental health worker may visit once a week, an alcohol counselor may come through twice a month, a juvenile probation officer may come when called, and a specialist in youth development may provide services several times a year. None of these individuals is likely to get to know the particular community well or to develop an understanding of its assets, its community leaders, or the interrelationship of community issues. Moreover, it is rare that these "circuit riders" communicate with each other or even know about the services the others provide.

The gradual processes of centralization and specialization have created a professional climate in which it is almost impossible for social workers to use community-based generalist practice approaches in rural areas (Martinez-Brawley, 1998). Agency job descriptions do not allow a social worker to provide a wide range of generalist services in one single rural community. Categorical funding sources do not allow funding to be used to pay such workers. Programs and policies do not encourage social workers to specialize in knowledge of particular communities; instead they encourage knowledge of specialized treatment approaches, populations in need, or diagnostic groups.

ALTERNATIVE FUTURES FOR RURAL SOCIAL WORK

Based on this analysis, I can foresee two alternative futures for rural social work. In the first, we will witness the gradual disappearance of rural social work as a separate and distinct field of practice. Urban social work will take over more and more rural regions as health and social service regions expand, absorb surrounding rural areas. These programs will provide specialized services from population centers with little or no consideration for the local communities where individuals and families live. Social workers will refer families to formal programs which will become the sources of support for families in need. Community based generalist practice will gradually become an historic anomaly which has no more relevance to current practice, except in a few isolated localities.

The alternative vision of the future is a revival of rural social work. It will be based on changes in the social and health service system to allow and encourage community-based generalist practice. This future will never come to be without the dedicated work of committed social workers and policy makers, because the first alternative will be the result of inaction. The advantages of this approach is that it will build on the ideas and commitment of rural social work practice (Mermelstein & Sundet, 1998), it will encourage innovative programs that reach rural communities and which may well reduce costs by using local informal resources and by intervening early enough to prevent more serious problems that would require expensive interventions. In addition, this alternative will open up the current social and health system to change, as innovative rural programs lead the way to new approaches to social work practice both in urban and rural communities.

It is unlikely that radical changes in the way services are organized, administered, and funded can occur overnight, or even within a decade. Rather than trying to turn the tide of centralization and specialization, it will be more effective to promote changes within current social and health service systems to allow and encourage effective rural social work. Steps can be take that will help to counteract the pressure toward centralization and regionalization that have had such an impact on rural social and health services (O'Looney,

1993). A supportive organizational and policy environment can nurture the kind of social work that benefits rural communities and their residents

In order to bring about this second alternative for the future, I recommend that urban and rural social workers work together on the following initiatives to re-introduce a level of community-based generalist practice within the current social and health service systems:

1. Regional health and social service programs should use the new methods of identifying relatively rural communities using census tracts, zip codes, and rural commuting codes, to identify rural communities within their service areas (See notes at the end of this article.). All service providers in the agency could be trained to identify the particular assets and needs of these rural communities which the agency should be serving, and which up to now have received little consideration for their rural characteristics.

2. Regional service programs should assign workers to particular rural communities within the region and encourage them to use a community-based approach to learn about these communities so that they can use their informal resources and assets. For example, in a teaching hospital, each social worker could become a specialist on particular communities the patients come from. To make this work, time from social workers' busy schedules should be assigned to spend in the community and to get to know local leaders and organizations such as clubs, churches, and volunteer groups (Murty, 2004). Since it will be difficult to justify this allocation of social worker time, the program could begin with a few rural communities where many of the patients live. Data could then be collected to show the improvement in treatment outcome, reduced days of hospitalization because of improved discharge planning, and reduced relapse to hospital treatment. Once the data document the success of the community-based program, it will be easier to advocate for its expansion to the whole region and the hospital will be able to present its new program as a model to other hospitals. Similar approaches could be used by school social workers, hospice social workers, and family counselling, substance abuse programs and community mental health programs, to give just a few examples. Each social worker in any type of regional program would develop expertise in particular communities within the region.

3. Social workers with responsibility for rural communities could collaborate with other social workers who provide completely different services in the same community. The goal would be to establish local rural one-stop multi-service centers in particular rural communities (Norris, 1980; Martinez-Brawley & Delevan,1993; Adams & Kraut,1995; Davis & Meyer, 1996). At a minimum, this would involve co-location of services provided by travelling specialist service providers from population centers. Each of these travelling specialists would use the same local meeting place on their visits to the town. If rent must be paid, the cost could be shared among the programs involved. The initial set of collaborating service providers invited to participate will depend on the community needs, programs active in the

area, and the personalities of the workers. However, the local rural center might host visiting community mental health workers, juvenile justice workers, school social workers, workers from the regional Community Action Programs, social workers from home-nursing programs, social workers from public health programs, workers from county or state TANF and child welfare programs, alcohol and drug treatment and prevention services, and domestic violence and sexual assault programs, as well as workers from the county University Extension Programs, and outreach workers from local and regional programs serving the elderly, people with disabilities, and others. An innovative rural program would include staff from regional programs for economic development, community development, and housing.

Such a multi-service site would encourage a community-based, generalist approach to service provision, even though the visiting service providers would be paid, trained and supervised by different specialized programs. Such a multi-service center's effectiveness would be greatly enhanced if a local community resident were hired to serve as a community liaison to make appointments for local residents with the various service providers, help to connect local people to the services, and do community outreach concerning the services available. The program would be further improved if a time could be scheduled for a team meeting among the service providers using the center so that they could coordinate work with the community and, after appropriate consents for exchange of information, to discuss how to collaborate on with particular families.

Such a plan may sound overly ambitious, but in fact, programs similar to the one proposed, incorporating different groups of co-located service providers, have actually functioned in various areas in the United States and Great Britain and their successes have been documented (Hadley & McGrath, 1985; Martinez Brawley & Delevan, 1991; Adams & Kraut, 1995; Davis & Meyer). Some have been funded by grants, others county governments, and others by state and national policies. The fact that these programs have not been adopted more widely is not due to a lack of effectiveness. Instead the obstacles have been resistance to collaboration among agencies, political and administrative changes, and problems in allocation of funds for costs associated with collaboration, such as the shared community space and staff time for team meetings.

4. Advocacy at regional, state, and federal levels to support procedures, regulations, and policies should allow funding to be allocated and pooled to cover the shared costs of rural community-based practice. According to current policies, most service programs must document that funds are being used only to serve very specific groups of people in need. By establishing funds to support multi-service sites, advocates could provide incentives for regional specialized programs to participate in rural community-based collaboration to provide one-stop multi-service centers. Although such advocacy will run up against resistance from prevailing systems of specialized programs and

from categorical funding streams, this kind of change at the county, state, or national level is not unprecedented. Programs at the county level in Iowa and Pennsylvania and at the state level in Iowa (Martinez Brawley & Delevan, 1991, Adams & Kraut, 1995) have pioneered this type of pooled funding, and programs in Great Britain have also used this approach (Hadley & McGrath, 1985). The success and continued support of these programs will depend on evidence that innovative pilot programs are cost-effective and improve services and outcomes for rural communities. Skilful work with administrators and legislators will be the key to maintaining support for the needed changes in funding allocations and staff and resource assignments. Mobilizing rural community residents and leaders to communicate with administrators and legislators about the importance of multi-service sites to rural communities will help to sustain support for these programs.

5. Regional programs should be reviewed and funding allocated to regional programs should be contingent on the program serving the needs of the rural communities within the region. Evidence that services are provided in rural communities, rather than only in the main office should be required in proposals, regular reviews, and audits. Input should be gathered from residents in their local rural communities rather than at community meetings held in the population center. In addition, formulas for funding should include factors related to the increased cost of delivering services in rural areas, such as the low density of the population, problems of economy of scale, and the challenges of transportation to provide services to rural communities (Martinez-Brawley, 1987; National Association of State Units on Aging, Minority Issues Committee, 1992; Coward, Vogel, Duncan & Uttaro, 1995; Pugh, 2003).

CHALLENGE TO THE SOCIAL WORK PROFESSION

Although a more positive future for rural social work is dependent on the active support and advocacy of rural social workers, their efforts will not be enough. Changes to improve rural social work must occur throughout the profession in programs that serve both urban and rural people. Social workers in regional organizations that serve large geographic areas must begin to focus on the rural communities within the region. The rural social work movement must target social workers in these agencies and programs, and work with them to improve the way regional organizations serve rural communities. By demonstrating the relevance of rural social work to this much larger group of social workers, rural advocates will be able to provide a critical mass concerned about the rural communities and mobilize a larger proportion of social workers on behalf of rural social work. Based on this larger constituency, and using the skills of organizational change, lobbying, and community mobilization which social workers have long used in the history of the profession, it will be possible to bring about the changes recommended for a positive future for rural social work. . In the process, rural social work may be influential in leading the social work profession back toward community-based and generalist approaches that could benefit the profession as a whole.

References

Adams, P., & Kraut, K. (1995). Working with families and communities: The Patch approach. In P. Adams & K. Nelson (Eds.), *Reinventing human services: Community- and family-centered practice* (pp. 87-108). NY: Aldine De Gruyter.

Agency for Health Care Policy and Research. (1991). *Delivering essential health care services in rural areas: An analysis of alternative models* (AHCPR Pub. No. 91-0017). Rockville, MD: Author.

Barker, R. G., & Gump, P. V. (1964). *Big school, small school: High school size and student behavior.* Stanford, CA: Stanford University Press.

Brown, J. C. (1933). *The rural community and social case work.* New York: Family Welfare Association of America.

Butler, M. A., & Beale, C. L. (1994). *Rural-urban continuum codes for metro and nonmetro counties, 1993.* Washington, DC: Economic Research Service, U.S. Dept. of Agriculture.

Coward, R. T., & Lee, G. R. (1985). *The elderly in rural society: Every fourth elder.* NY: Springer.

Coward, R. T., Vogel, W. B., Duncan, E. P., & Uttaro, R. (1995). Should intrastate funding formulae for the Older Americans Act include a rural factor? *The Gerontologist, 35*(1), 24-34.

Davenport, J., & Davenport, J. A. (1998). Rural communities in transition. In L. H. Ginsberg (Ed.), *Social work in rural communities* (3rd. ed., pp. 39-54). Arlington, VA: Council on Social Work Education.

Davenport, J. A. & Davenport, J. (1995). Rural social work overview. In. R. Edwards (Ed.-in-chief), *Encyclopedia of Social Work* (19th ed., Vol. 3, pp. 2076-2085). Washington, DC: NASW Press.

Davis, S., Meyer, S., & Terrasi, M. (1995). The whole village center: A model for promoting client access to services in rural areas. *Human Services in the Rural Environment, 19*(2/3), 25-28.

Enders, A., & Seekins, T. (1999). Telecommunications access for rural Americans with disabilities. *Rural Development Perspectives, 14*(3), 14-21.

Evans, G. D. (2004). Improving behavioural health services in rural America. *Rural Mental Health, 29*(1), 12-16.

Farley, O. W., Griffiths, K. A., Skidmore, R. A., & Thackeray, M. G. (1982). *Rural social work practice.* NY: Free Press.

Frontier Mental Health Services Resource Network.(2005). Western Interstate Commission for Higher Education. Internet site: http://www.wiche.edu/MentalHealth/Frontier/frontier.asp Accessed February 24, 2005.

Ginsberg, L. (1998a). Preface to the third edition. In L. H. Ginsberg (Ed.), *Social work in rural communities* (3rd. ed., pp. v-viii). Arlington, VA: Council on Social Work Education.

Ginsberg, L. (1998b). Introduction: An overview of rural social work. In L. H. Ginsberg (Ed.), *Social work in rural communities* (3rd. ed., pp. 3-22). Arlington, VA: Council on Social Work Education.

Goldschmidt, W. (1947). *As you sow.* NY: Harcourt, Brace and Co.

Goldschmidt, W. (1978). Large-scale farming and the rural social structure. *Rural Sociology, 43*(3), 362-366.

Hadley, R., &McGrath, M. (Eds.) (1985). *Going local: Neighborhood social services* (NCVO Occasional Paper 1). London: Bedford Square.

Hann-Morrison, D. (2003). An alternative approach to rural mental health service delivery: A case study. *Rural Mental Health, 28*(1), 4-7.

Heartland Center for Leadership Development (2005). W. K. Kellogg Collection of Rural Community Development Resources. Internet Site: http://www.unl.edu/kellogg/main.html

Accessed February 24, 2005.

HHS Rural Task Force, USA Department of Health and Human Services. (2002). *One depart-ment serving rural America.* Available at http://ruralhealth.hrsa.gov/PublicReport.htm. Accessed 1/10/2005.

Hickman, S. A. (2004). Rural is real: Supporting professional practice through the Rural Social Work Caucus and the NASW Professional Policy Statement for rural social work. In T. L. Scales & C. L. Streeter (Eds.), *Rural social work: Building and sustaining community assets* (pp. 43-50). Belmont, CA: Brooks/Cole/Thomson Learning.

Human Services in the Rural Environment (HSITRE) (1989). Special Issue on AIDS in Rural America. *Volume 13*(1).

Johnson, H. W. (1998). Rural crime, delinquency, substance abuse and corrctions. . In L.H. Gins-berg, (Ed.), *Social work in rural communities* (3rd.ed.; pp. 249-264). Alexandria, VA: Council on Social Work Education.

Johnson, J., Johnson-Webb, K., & Farrell, W. (1999). A profile of Hispanic newcomers to North Carolina. *Popular Government,* 2-13.

Keller P. A., & Murray, J. D. (1982). Rural mental health: An overview of issues. In P. A. Keller & J. D. Murray (Eds.), *Handbook of community mental health* (pp. 3-19). NY: Human Sciences Press.

Krout, J. A., & Coward, R. T. (1998). Aging in rural environments, In R. T. Coward & J. A. Krout (Eds.), *Aging in rural settings: Life circumstances and distinctive features* (pp. 3-14). NY: Springer.

Krout, J. A. (1998). Services and service delivery in rural environments. In R. T. Coward & J. A. Krout (Eds.), *Aging in rural settings: Life circumstances and distinctive features* (pp. 247-266). NY: Springer.

Lennox, N. D., & Murty, S. A. (1994). Choice, change, and challenge: Managing regional services. In B. Locke & M. Egan (Eds.), *Fulfilling our mission: Rural social work in the 1990s* (Proceedings of the 17th National Institute on Social Work and Human Services in Rural Areas, 1992, pp. 150-159). Morgantown, West Virginia: West Virginia University.

Lindhorst, T. (1997). Lesbians and gay men in the country: Practice implications for rural social workers. In J. D. Smith & R. J. Mancoske (Eds.), *Rural gays and lesbians: Building on the strengths of communities* (pp. 1-11). NY: Haworth Press.

Lusk, M. W., & Mason, D. T. (1992). Development theory for rural practice. *Human Services in the Rural Environment, 16*(1), 5-10.

Martinez-Brawley, E. E. (1981). *Seven decades of rural social work: From country life commission to rural caucus.* NY: Praeger.

Martinez-Brawley, E. E. (1998). Community-oriented practice in rural social work. In L.H. Gins-herg, (Ed.), *Social work in rural communities* (3rd.cd.; pp. 99-113). Alexandria, VA: Council on Social Work Education.

Martinez-Brawley, E, E, (1987). Rural social work. In A. Minahan (Editor-in-Chief), *Encyclopedia of social work* (18th ed.; pp. 521-537). Silver Spring, MD: National Association of Social Work.

Martinez-Brawley, E. E., & Delevan, S. M. (1993). Centralizing management and decentralizing services: An alternative approach. *Administration in Social Work, 17*(1), 81-102.

Menanteau-Horta, D. (2004). Strategies of cooperation and delivery of human services in rural ar-eas: Sharing community assets. In T. L. Scales & C. L. Streeter (Eds.), *Rural social work: Building and sustaining community assets* (pp. 54-64). Belmont, CA: Thomson- Brooks/Cole.

Miller, P. J. (1998). Dual relationships and rural practice. . In L. H. Ginsberg (Ed.), *Social work in rural communities* (3rd. ed., pp. 55-62). Alexandria, VA: Council on Social Work Education.

Murty, S. A.(2004). Mapping community assets: The key to effective rural social work. In T. L. Scales & C. L. Streeter (Eds.), *Rural social work: Building and sustaining community assets* (pp. 278-289). Belmont, CA: Brooks/Cole/Thomson Learning.

Murty, S. A. (2001a). No safe place to hide: Rural family violence. In S. Loue & B. E. Quill (Eds.), *Handbook of rural health* (pp. 277-293). NY: Kluwer Academic.

Murty, S. (2001b). Regionalization and rural service delivery. In R. Moore (Ed.), *The hidden America: Social problems in rural America in the 21st Century* (pp. 199-216). Cranbury, NJ: Associated University Presses.

Murty, S. A. (1984). Developing the trust of a rural community. *Human Services in the Rural Environment, 9*(2), 15-20.

Murty, S., & Schechter, S. (1999). *Reaching rural communities: A national assessment of rural domestic violence service needs.* This report reports the results of the research funded by the Administration for Children and Families, Department of Health and Human Services, Grant No. 90EVO152/01.

National Association of Area Agencies on Aging. (1996). *National directory for eldercare information and referral: 1996-1997 directory of State and Area Agencies on Aging.* Washington, DC: Author.

National Association of Social Workers (NASW) (2002). NASW Professional Policy Statement on Rural Social Work. In *Social work speaks.* Washington, DC: Author.

National Association of State Units on Aging, Minority Issues Committee. (1992). *Description of current and proposed intrastate funding formulas.* Author.

National Clearinghouse for Frontier Communities. (2005) Frontier Education Center. Internet Site: http://www.frontierus.org/index.htm?p=1&pid=6003.

Accessed February 24, 2005.

Nelson, G. (1980). Social services to the urban and rural aged: The experience of Area Agencies on Aging. *The Gerontologist, 20*(2), 200-207.

Norris, J. (1980). Multipurpose centers in a rural county. In H. W. Johnson (Ed.), *Rural human services: A book of readings* (pp. 81-85). Itasca, IL: Peacock Publishers.

Olaveson, J., Conway, P., & Shaver, C. (2004). Defining rural for social work practice and research. In T. L. Scales & C. L. Streeter (Eds.), *Rural social work: Building and sustaining community assets* (pp. 9-20). Belmont, CA: Brooks/Cole/Thomson Learning.

O'Looney, J. (1993). Organizing services in rural communities: Moving toward service integration and flexible specialization. Part 1: Models for organizing service delivery. *Human Services in the Rural Environment, 16*(4), 22-29.

Pugh, R. (2003). Considering the countryside: Is there a case for rural social work? *British Journal of Social Work, 33*, 67-85.

Ray, D. A. (2004). Corndogs, elephant ears, & data: Rural county fair a great place to gather community mental health information. *Rural Mental Health, 29*(1), 17-

Ray, J., & Murty, S. A. (1990). Rural child sexual abuse prevention and treatment. *Human Services in the Rural Environment, 13*(4), 24-29.

Rolland, M. F., & Hughes, C. S. (2004). Social workers as wisdom seekers: Consulting rural Alaska Native elders. *Rural Mental Health, 29*(3), 19-21

Rossmann, M. R., & Dvorak, J. (2001). The agricultural mental health project. *Rural Mental Health, 26*(4), 18-22.

Rounds, K. A. (1998). AIDS in rural areas: Challenges to providing care. In L. H. Ginsberg (Ed.), *Social work in rural communities* (3rd. ed., pp. 265-276). Alexandria, VA: Council on Social Work Education.

Rural Community Development (2005). U.S. Dept. of Agriculture. Internet Site: http://ocdweb.sc.egov.usda.gov/ Accessed February 24, 2004.

Smith, J. D. (1997). Working with larger systems: Rural lesbians and gays. In J. D. Smith & R. J. Mancoske (Eds.), *Rural gays and lesbians: Building on the strengths of communities* (pp 13-21). NY: Haworth Press.

Snipp, C. (1996). Understanding race and ethnicity in rural America. *Rural Sociology*, 61, 125-142.

Southern Regional Education Board (1998). Educational assumptions for rural social work. In L. H. Ginsberg (Ed.), *Social work in rural communities* (3rd. ed., pp23-26).). Alexandria, VA: Council on Social Work Education.

Watkins, J. M., & Watkins, D. A. (1984). *Social policy and the rural setting*. NY: Springer.

Watkins, T. R. (2004). Natural helping networks: Assets for rural communities. In T. L. Scales & C. L. Streeter (Eds.), *Rural social work: Building and sustaining community assets* (pp. 65-76). Belmont, CA: Brooks/Cole/Thomson Learning.

Websdale, N. (1998). *Rural woman battering and the justice system: An ethnography*. Thousand Oaks, CA: Sage.

White, S. L. (1986). Travel distance as time price and the demand for mental health services. *Community Mental Health Journal, 22*(4), 303-313.

Wilkinson, K. P. (1982). Changing rural communities. In P. A. Keller & J. D. Murray (Eds.), *Handbook of rural community mental health* (pp. 20-28). NY: Human Sciences Press.

Williams, R. T. (2001). The ongoing Farm Crisis: Health, mental health and safety issues in Wisconsin. *Rural Mental health, 26*(4), 15-17).

York, R. O., Denton, R. T., & Moran, J. R. (1998). Rural and urban social work practice: Is there a difference? In L. H. Ginsberg (Ed.), *Social work in rural communities* (3rd. ed., pp. 83-97). Arlington, VA: Council on Social Work Education.

Partial List of Internet Web Sites for Rural Organizations

National Rural Social Work Caucus: http://www.uncp.edu/home/marson/rural/

National Rural Health Association: http://www.nrharural.org/

National Association for Rural Mental Health: http://www.narmh.org/

Center for Rural Affairs: http://www.cfra.org/

Resource Center for Rural Behavioral Health: http://www.apa.org/rural/

Frontier Mental Health Services Resource Network: http://www.wiche.edu/MentalHealth/Frontier/index.htm

Journal of Rural Community Psychology: http://www.marshall.edu/jrcp/

Rural Community Development. (2005) US Dept. of Agriculture. Internet Site: http://ocdweb.sc.egov.usda.gov/

W. K. Kellogg Collection of Rural Community Development Resources

Heartland Center for Leadership Development, Lincoln Nebraska

ttp://www.unl.edu/kellogg/main.html

Notes on Sources for Definitions of Geographic Areas on the Rural-Urban Continuum

USDA Economic Research Service

Rural-Urban Area Commuting Codes (RUCA Codes)

http://www.ers.usda.gov/Data/RuralUrbanCommutingAreaCodes/

Through this site you can obtain the RUCA Codes for your state by census tract. Using the web site below, you can approximate the RUCA Codes using zip codes.

WWAMI Rural Health Research Center

ZIP CODE RUCA APPROXIMATION METHODOLOGY

http://www.fammed.washington.edu/wwamirhrc/rucas/methods.html

USDA Economic Research Service

Rural-Urban Continuum Codes (County "Beale Codes")

http://www.ers.usda.gov/Briefing/Rurality/RuralUrbCon/

These codes place counties on a 10 point ordinal scale from most urban to most rural.

Frontier Education Center

National Clearinghouse for Frontier Communities

2000 Update: Frontier Counties in the United States (Counties meeting the "frontier" definition)

http://www.frontierus.org/index.htm?p=2&pid=6003&spid=6018

At this site you can obtain information about which counties are classified as "frontier."

Information about alternative definitions of rurality can be obtained at the following sites:

Rural Assistance Center

"What is Rural?"

http://www.raconline.org/info_guides/ruraldef/

USDA Economic Research Center

Measuring Rurality

http://www.ers.usda.gov/Briefing/Rurality/

Author's Note

Address correspondence to: Susan A. Murty, M.S.W., Ph.D., Associate Professor, School of Social Work, University of Iowa, 308 North Hall, Iowa City, Iowa 52242-1223. E-mail: susan-murty@uiowa.edu.

THE FUTURE OF AMERICAN FAMILIES:
IMPLICATIONS FOR SOCIAL WORK RESEARCH,
PRACTICE, AND EDUCATION

Karen Kayser

Abstract: *In this article I briefly describe the changing face of contemporary families in America, and in particular focus on four areas of social work practice in which a family-centered approach is needed. I then present future suggestions for social work research, practice, and education. This is not meant to be an exhaustive review of the literature nor is it an in-depth analysis of one particular area of families.*

Keywords: families, future, family-centered, social work

INTRODUCTION

There is little disagreement among researchers and practitioners that American families have changed quite dramatically over the last few decades. Demographic changes include a delay in getting married, a rise in unmarried heterosexual and same-sex cohabitation (with an increase of these households including children), a decrease in fertility, an increase in separating childbearing from marriage among minority group members with less education, and a steady increase of mothers working outside the home (Bianchi & Casper, 2005). Along with these changes in the structure of families, we have seen an increase in the cultural diversity of families, stemming from immigration and continued growth in income inequality between rich and poor in the U.S. Analyzing census data, sociologist Farrell Webb (2005) predicts that the new families will:

- experience severely limited economic growth and growth opportunities,
- be characterized by a semi-extended family form made up of nonbiological kin with some ties to the family members' countries of origin,
- more than likely live in households that have two primary languages for at least two generations,
- consist of people of color as a majority group,
- have social customs, beliefs, attitudes, and communication forms from cultures that researchers have not thoroughly studied,
- probably have some form of major involvement with governmental institutions (e.g., immigration, homeland security, criminal justice, public welfare, and social services), and
- be stigmatized and misunderstood in part because the scientific community will fail to adapt their research and theories in order to understand these families (Webb, 2005).

I would add a final characteristic: the new families will not be helped by our interventions because our current practices will fail to be sensitive and relevant to diverse cultures

Karen Kayser is Professor at the Graduate School of Social Work, Boston College, Boston, MA 02467.
Copyright © 2005 *Advances in Social Work* Vol. 6 No. 1 (Spring 2005), 145-155

and varying forms of families. These social and demographic changes in families have broad implications for many areas of social work practice. While it is beyond the scope of this article to examine all of the challenges that contemporary families now face, I will address four issues related to families—family transitions, child welfare, chronic illness, and poverty.

FAMILIES IN TRANSITION: DIVORCE, SINGLE-PARENTING, AND REMARRIAGE

"Of all the changes in family life during the 20th century, perhaps the most dramatic—and the most far-reaching in its implications—was the increase in the rate of divorce" (Amato, 2000). Partly due to the high divorce rate, at least one-half of all children will spend at least one-quarter of their lives in female-headed households (Webb, 2005). Because there has been a shift from a dominant pattern of lifelong marriage to one of serial marriage, we no longer view divorce as a single, brief event but it is a long-lasting process of changing family relationships. This process begins in the failing marriage, continues through the often distressing period of the marital separation and divorce and its immediate aftermath, and extends often over many years of post-divorce adjustment (Wallerstein, 1998).

The postdivorce years can bring multiple economic, social, and psychological stresses as the single-parent family manages a lowered standard of living, changes in parent-child relationship, and the diminished physical absence of one parent, most often the father. Divorce pushes a significant percentage of families who were living on the threshold of poverty into the depths of poverty. On an emotional level, anger and conflict between the parents persist in an estimated one-third of divorced families (Wallerstein, 1998). Interparental hostility and lack of cooperation between parents during the post divorce phase is a significant predictor of poor outcomes among children (Buchanan, Maccoby, & Dornbush, 1996; Clark & Clifford, 1996; Silitsky, 1996; Vandewater & Lansford, 1998). If one or both parents remarry, there are new challenges of integrating previous children and a new spouse into a family. Because there is a higher rate of dissolution of second (and higher order) marriages than first marriages, it is very likely that the blended family will also breakup (Amato, 2000). As a result, about one out of every six adults experiences two or more divorces (Cherlin, 1992) and one out of ten children will experience at least two divorces of their residential parents before reaching the age of 16 (Hetherington, 1999). It is not surprising that in their adult relationships, children of divorce are at risk for a variety of "sleeper or developmental effects" when they face serious commitments to relationships in late adolescence and young adulthood. Longitudinal studies revealed that young people from divorced families anticipate disappointment in their own adult relationships (Wallerstein & Blakeslee, 1989; Kalter, 1987).

The stresses associated with these various postdivorce phases do not always result in unhappy relationships or psychiatric disorders but the child of divorce is confronted with a set of difficult challenges in addition to the normative tasks of growing up (Wallerstein, 1998). Because of the negative outcomes of divorce and its subsequent stresses, social workers need to actively advocate for the children, especially in the area of court decisions. The courts make decisions regarding custody arrangements and visitations that purport to be based on notions of what is in the best interests of the children. However, many of the decisions are not based on evidence. For example, there is no empirical evidence that either the sole frequency or the amount of contact between noncustodial parent and child is related to a good outcome in the child. What may be more important is the quality of the relationship between the child and parent and the ability of parents to work together for the good of the child after the divorce.

During the 1990s, as the rate of divorce increased, school-based programs for children of divorce became common and in many states, mediation and education courses for divorcing parents became mandatory (Emery, Kitzmann, & Waldron, 1999). Social workers have been playing a major role in these programs. Although there is evidence that compliance with a visitation schedule and provision of child support payments are positive outcomes of these programs, there is no empirical evidence supporting better psychological outcomes for children as a result of them (Amato, 1999; Wallerstein, 1998). Research, using sound methodology, is needed to evaluate these interventions and to develop innovative approaches that support the interests of the children.

CHILD WELFARE: PROMOTING RESILIENT FAMILIES

The social work profession has had a long-standing commitment to the well-being of families. But it is only in the past decade that in the field of child welfare family-based services have emerged as a renewed effort to achieve the goal of a "secure and loving family" (Maluccio, 1991). Indeed, the paradigm of practice in child welfare has shifted from primarily *child rescue* to *family preservation*. This shift is in part due to long-term social and psychological effects of out-of-home placements, including academic, emotional and social adjustment problems and lack of sense of belonging (Rutter, 2000). The financial cost of foster care has also grown.

Federal legislation in the recent decade has supported a family-centered approach to public child welfare. Family-inclusive legislation included PL 96-142, the Adoption Assistance and Child Welfare Act and in 1993, the Family Preservation and Support Act. The subsequent Adoption and Safe Families Act (PL105-89) of 1997 further emphasized the safety of all family members, and not just children. This legislation has lead to the emergence of various family-centered programs which involve a family resilience or competency-based approach to protective services. This perspective refers to an attitudinal, behavioral and organizational approach to families encountering the protective service systems and has the following characteristics: 1. focusing on the family as the unit of attention and as the central context for individuals; 2. maximizing family choice and informed decision-making; 3. assessing with a strengths-perspective versus a pathology perspective; and 4. ensuring culturally and diversity-sensitive interactions and services (Walter and Petr, 2000; Allen and Petr, 1998). Social workers using this approach view themselves as agents of families, strengthening the family's existing skills, promoting acquisition of new skills, and helping families access external resources (Dunst, Boyd, Trivette, & Hamby, 2002). A family-centered approach places social workers in a less adversarial role with the families. Workers are viewed as advocates who will help them keep their children rather than take them out of the family (Byrne, 2003). Research on family-centered practice in child welfare has produced some promising results, including more treatment compliance from families; reduced placement rates; decreased rates of recurring maltreatment (Littell, 2001); more family engagement and families' use of a broader range of services (Walton, 2001).

There are several types of interventions that fall under the rubric of family-centered practice in child welfare. Probably the best known and most controversial among them are the Intensive Family Preservation Services (IFPS). These interventions provide an alternative to removing children from families accused of child abuse and neglect by providing intense services in their homes. These services need to confront problems such as poverty, domestic violence, poor housing, and lack of transportation. Hence, they may include job skills training, finding a local food pantry, applying for Medicaid, obtaining after-school care for their children, teaching positive parenting skills, or scheduling a job interview. The early studies on IFPS in the late 1980s and early 1990s yielded impressive results with fewer out-of-home placements among families utilizing the services. However, many of the studies had weak methodological designs that lacked control groups and relied on only one outcome measure (Blythe, Salley, & Jayaratne, 1994). More recent studies using comparison groups in their designs have produced lower rates of out-of-home placements but the difference between the two groups has not been as great as originally reported in early studies. Some practitioners are questioning if this approach would be considered best practice for these high-risk families and question what we are actually preserving.

Another innovative intervention in child welfare that uses a strengths-based, family-centered model is the family group conferencing. Family conferencing is based on Maori cultural practices in New Zealand and is similar to practices in many other indigenous cultures (Waites, Macgowan, Pennell, Carlton-LaNey, & Weil, 2004). It is a partnership-building model that emphasizes the importance of the family's cultural knowledge for safeguarding children and other family members. The conference provides the larger family group with an opportunity to develop a plan to resolve the child welfare concerns. Checks-and-balances are built in by having the family group formulate a plan that had to be approved by the protective authorities before implementation (Waites, et al., 2004). Following New Zealand's lead, social workers in other countries, including the United States, have adopted the model. Initial outcome studies show that the model is effective in keeping children with their families, kin, or cultural group, stabilizes children's placements, decreases child maltreatment, and increases family pride ("Promising Results," 2003).

A family-centered approach to child protective work may have additional benefits for workers in this highly stressful area. Child welfare traditionally has involved a high level of stress for staff, problems with recruiting and retaining staff, and burnout (Ellett, 2000). It has been suggested that changing the role of workers from an adversarial role to a strengths-based approach with families may have positive outcomes for social workers in terms of their job satisfaction and burnout (Byrne. 2004).

FAMILIES COPING WITH CHRONIC ILLNESSES

Nearly 90 million people in the United States live with a chronic illness (National Center for Health Statistics, 2004). Moreover, as survival rates from life-threatening, chronic illnesses have risen, they are living with illness for a longer period of time. For example, the five-year relative survival rates, for all cancers, have risen from 53% in 1983-85 to 63% in 1992-99 (American Cancer Society, 2004). Individuals with chronic illnesses do not cope with their illness in isolation but, instead, within the context of their interpersonal relationships. Family members are faced with additional caregiving responsibilities, economic stress when the patient is unable to work or has inadequate health insurance, emotional distress such as anxiety and depression, and marital distress (Akamatsu, Stephens, Hobfoll, & Crowther, 1992; Veach, Nicholas, & Barton, 2002). These stresses can negatively affect family members' well-being, but at the same time, family members can positively influence a patient's psychological adjustment and management of illness, including adherence to a treatment regimen, pain management, and facilitating healthy behaviors (Burg & Seeman, 1994).

With the emphasis on managed care and shorter hospital stays, our healthcare system is placing more responsibility on families to care for patients in their homes. This shift in care to the family is occurring at the same time that most women are entering the workforce and are less available to provide care at home. Also, the structure of families is changing due to grandparents and parents beginning to outnumber children. This so-called "beanpole"structure of the American family means that a greater responsibility for caregiving will be placed on fewer people (Bengston, et al., 2005). Especially among some ethnic groups, such as African Americans, family members rely extensively on informal caregivers (Chadiha, Adams, Biegel, Auslander, & Gutierrez, 2004).

The connection between physical illness and family relationships has led researchers to develop psychosocial interventions that include the patient's family. A recent meta-analysis of seventy randomized studies comparing family psychosocial interventions with traditional medical care found positive effects for patients and family members (Martire, Lustig, Schulz, Miler, & Helgeson, 2004). For patients, interventions that included the spouse had positive effects on depression and, in some cases, on mortality. Positive effects were found for family members in decreasing caregiving burden, depression, and anxiety. These effects were strongest for nondemanding illnesses and for interventions that targeted only the family member and addressed relationship issues.

Social workers in healthcare settings rely heavily on peer support groups to help patients adjust to illness. However, given the frequency and intensity of interaction that a patient has with his or her family members, psychosocial interventions within the family context may be more effective than peer group work (Radjovic, Nicassio, & Weisman, 1992). As current changes in the patterns of medical care transfer greater responsibility from health care professionals to the spouse and the couple, it is all the more important to deal with a couple as a unit and include the partner in treatment plans.

FAMILIES IN POVERTY: FAMILY VALUES VS VALUING FAMILIES

In 2002 the overall percent of Americans living in poverty increased to 12.1 percent, up from 11.7 percent in 2001 and 11.3 percent in 2000, reflecting the recession that started in the spring of 2000 and the economic fallout from the September 11, 2001 attacks (National Center for Health Statistics, 2004). These were the first increases in the poverty rate since 1993. Whereas increases in the past were primarily among children and persons 65 years of age, in 2002 the poverty rate increased for all ages (National Center for Health Statistics). Poverty is disproportionately experienced by nonwhites, children, and families head by single-parents. Using data from the Panel Study of Income Dynamics, Rank and Hirschl (1999) found that 34% of children overall will have spent at least one year in poverty; however, for Black children the rate was 69%, for children in single parent households 81%, and for children whose head of household had not completed 12 years of school 63%. While the welfare reform program, Temporary Assistance for Needy Families (TANF) of 1996, demanded that mothers participate in the paid labor force, it has not been successful in lifting their families out of poverty.

By ending the entitlement to welfare benefits, the United States removed a safety net for families, supporting the belief that women and children do not deserve any form of special protection (Hays, 2003). The only indication of concern for the children was the provision of temporary subsidies for paid childcare. Because many politicians view poverty as stemming from the erosion of "family values," policies were created to promote abstinence and decrease out-of-wedlock childbearing. Marriage is promoted as a central path to lifting women and children out of poverty. Recently President Bush has proposed a new model program, Healthy Marriage Initiative, to promote marriage as a part of welfare reauthorization. The proposed program seeks to improve marriages by providing individuals and couples with 1) "accurate information on the value of marriage in the lives of men, women, and children; 2) marriage-skills education that will enable couples to reduce conflict and increase the happiness and longevity of their relationship; and 3) experimental reductions in the financial penalties against marriage that are currently contained in all federal welfare programs" (Rector & Pardue, 2004). Some aspects of this initiative are commendable: First, it is preventative, with emphasis on teaching relationship skills and budgeting skills in high school and, second, it provides low-income individuals and couples with counseling that they may not otherwise be able to afford. At the same time, the Initiative may be shortsighted and inadequate, given the scientific evidence that shows marital breakdown and marital distress are also the *result* of the chronic stress of poverty.

The states with the highest divorce rates in the country also rank near the bottom of the 50 states in terms of employment rate, annual pay, household income, and health insurance coverage and have among the highest rates of poverty in the nation (Karney, Story, & Bradbury, 2005). Empirical investigations by Conger, Rueter, and Elder (2003) reveal that economic pressures increase the risk for emotional distress which, in turn, increases risk for marital conflict. These researchers conclude, "To the extent that these findings have causal implications, we conclude that economic pressure likely has its most significant impact on marriage through its exacerbation of wives' and husbands' emotional problems" (Conger et al, 2003). These findings are further supported by a longitudinal study in which the authors found that during the first years of marriage couples experiencing higher levels of chronic stress experienced steeper declines of marital satisfaction compared to couples who were not experiencing chronic stress (Karney, Story, and Bradbury, 2005). Karney et al. (2005) conclude "it seems that it is harder to maintain even moderate levels of satisfaction when the context of the marriage makes constant demands on a couple's resources (p. 29)." The authors suggest that while skills training and education about relationships may be a valuable beginning, policy makers might consider supporting programs aimed at raising standards of living. If provided with an external context that supports the relationship, couples may be better equipped to maintain their relationships on their own (Karney, et al., 2005).

The Initiative also does not attend to some of the social and demographic characteristics of poor families. For example, at least among poor black women, the high rates of jobless-ness among poor black men may be the single most significant factor causing high rates of unwed parenting (Wilson, 1987). Hence, poor women face a marriage market composed largely of unemployed, underemployed, or only intermittently employed men. Further-more, many African American families in poverty consist of multigenerational families composed of young mothers, grandmothers, and children (Chase-Lansdale, Gordon, Col-ey, Wakschlag, & Brooks-Gunn, 1999). The multigenerational household structure was promoted by the Personal Responsibility and Work Opportunity Reconciliation Act of 1996 when it mandated that unmarried, minor parents live with their mothers or mother figures. The Healthy Marriage Initiative does not offer these types of families much assis-tance in coping with the stresses that young parents face. Another type of family that will likely be excluded from this Initiative is the family headed by a same-sex couple.

DIRECTIONS FOR FUTURE RESEARCH, PRACTICE, AND EDUCATION

In the human services, social workers are often the practitioners who do the lion's share of direct practice with couples and families. However, we have turned over the work of knowledge-building to psychologists and sociologists. For example, out of the 44 articles in last year's volume of *Research on Social Work Practice (2004)*, only four articles con-tained family or families in their titles. Nine articles dealt with a family role (e.g., mother, father, child) or an issue specific to family (such as domestic violence or child abuse). It is also noteworthy that of the 70 studies included in the meta-analysis of interventions with families and chronic illness (Martire, et al., 2004), not one of the studies appeared in a social work journal. Clearly, social workers are not producing the best scholarship in the area of family science. One area of research where social workers could take more leadership is intervention research. By developing innovative interventions with families or evaluating our current practices with families, we would contribute valuable informa-tion on evidence-based practice.

Furthermore, the published social work research on families has methodological short-comings and weak designs. The most common problem is that data are collected from one family member and therefore, the family or couple is not the unit of analysis. We now have statistical techniques that allow us to analyze data from more than one family member or from more than one setting (e.g. school, parents, community). The use of hierarchical linear modeling (HLM) has several advantages in that it analyzes longitudinal trajectories and allows for family members' trajectories to be estimated simultaneously in a model in which the dependencies in family members' data are controlled for. In addition, HLM uses all available data from each individual, even though participants may not have data at every time point.

Our research with families must include longitudinal designs. Families are not static; they change over time with various developmental tasks, stages, and normative and non-normative transitions. To examine the family at one point in time does not allow us to understand fully such things such as the predictors of divorce, consequences of interper-sonal violence, or how families cope with acute stress from trauma, violence, death, or other major stressors.

A common theme that runs throughout our research and work with families is that families face numerous stresses on a daily basis. Balancing work and family roles, dealing with caregiving of children and elderly parents, managing economic pressures, resolving marital conflict, and negotiating family transitions are just few of the types of stresses. Therefore, I strongly suggest that social work researchers, practitioners, and educators focus on applying models of family stress and coping to their research and practice (see Boss, 2002, 2003; Revenson, Kayser, & Bodenmann, 2005). These models are based on the transactional theory of individual stress and coping pioneered by Lazarus and Folkman (1984) but are expanded to include systemic and process-oriented concepts. Boss (2002) describes family stress theory as "an umbrella-like theoretical framework of many ideas to help us understand family stress and crisis within a broader, more culturally sensitive context" (p. 1). She developed a family stress management theory that incorporates the family's external context--its culture, history, economic status, development, heredity, and chronic discrimination--as well as the family's internal context which consists of structural, psychological, and philosophical dimensions (Boss, 2002). This theory offers great potential to inform practice, therapy, advocacy, and public policy.

Finally, there is a trend for students in our graduate schools of social work to pursue an M.S.W. in order to work in private practice. A recent study found that students' interest in working with the poor can actually decrease during graduate school (Perry, 2003). As educators, we should not provide students with clinical training only suitable for work with white, middle-class families. Course content should include theories and practice methods that are also applicable to nonwhite, non middle class families, living in diverse circumstances. For example, theories that focus on resilience instead of dysfunction may provide us with a theoretical lens for understanding the strengths and adaptation of families of color. Furthermore, doctoral-level courses on family theory and research methods are critical to preparing social work scholars who are interested in family research.

Since families are the building blocks of every society, our future depends on the future health of our families. To promote societies that foster the well-being of all people, we need to support and empower our families. To this end, the social work profession must be committed to ensuring that families (however they are defined) are valued, supported, and empowered to have the resources to raise healthy, moral, responsible, and caring members of society.

References

Akamatsu, T.J., Stephen, M.A.P., Hobfoll, S.E., & Crowther, J.H. (Eds.). (1992). *Family health psychology*. Washington, DC: Hemisphere.

Allen, R. & Petr, C. (1998). Re-thinking family-centered practice. *American Journal of Orthopsychiatry, 68*, 4-16.

Amato, P.R. (2000). The consequences of divorce for adults and children, *Journal of Marriage and the Family, 62*, 1269-1287.

Amato, P. R. (1999). Children of divorced parents as young adults. In E.M.

Hetherington (Ed.) *Coping with divorce, single parenting, and remarriage: A risk and resiliency perspective* (pp. 147-164). Mahwah, NJ: Erlbaum.

American Cancer Society (2004). *Cancer facts & figures, 2004*. Atlanta, GA.

Bengtson, V.L., Acock, A.C., Allen, K.R., Dilworth-Anderson, P., & Klein, D.M. (Eds.) (2005). *Sourcebook of family theory & research.* Thousand Oaks, CA: Sage.

Bianchi, S.M. & Casper, L.M. (2005) Explanations of family change: A family demographic perspective. In V.L. Bengston, A.C. Acock, K.R. Allen, P. Dilworth-Anderson, & D.M. (Eds.). *Sourcebook of family theory & research (pp. 93-101).* Thousand Oaks, CA: Sage.

Blythe, B.J., Salley, M.P., & Jayaratne, S. (1994). A review of intensive family preservation services research. *Social Work Research, 18,* 213-224.

Boss, P. (2003). *Family stress: Classic and contemporary readings.* Thousand Oaks: CA: Sage.

Boss, P. (2002). *Family stress management: A contextual approach.* Thousand Oaks: CA: Sage.

Buchanan, C.M., Maccoby, E.E., & Dornbush, S.M. (1996). *Adolescents after divorce.* Cambridge, MA: Harvard University Press.

Burg, M.M. & Seeman T.E. (1994). Families and health: The negative side of social ties. *Annals of Behavioral Medicine, 16,* 109-115.

Byrne, M. (2004). *Strengths-based service planning as a resilience factor in child protective social workers.* Unpublished manuscript, Boston College, Chestnut Hill, MA.

Chadiha, L.A., Adams, P., Biegel, D.E., Auslander, W., & Gutierrez, L. (2004). Empowering African American women informal caregivers: A literature synthesis and practice strategies. *Social Work, 49,* 97-112.

Chase-Lansdale, P.L., Gordon, R.A., Wakschlag, L.S., & Brooks-Gunn, J. (1999). Young African American multigenerational families in poverty: The contexts, exchanges, and processes of their lives. In E.M. Hetherington (Ed.), *Coping with divorce, single parenting, and remarriage* (pp. 165-191). Mahwah, NJ: Lawrence Erlbaum Publishers.

Cherlin, A.J. (1992), *Marriage, divorce, and remarriage.* Cambridge, MA: Harvard University Press.

Clark, R. & Clifford, T. (1996). Towards a resources and stressors model: The psychological adjustment of adult children of divorce, *Journal of Divorce and Remarriage, 25,* 105-136.

Conger, R.D., Rueter, M.A., & Elder, G.H. (2003). Couple resilience to economic pressure. In P. Boss with C. Mulligan (Eds.), *Family stress: Classic and contemporary readings* (pp. 292-320). Thousand Oaks, CA: Sage. (Reprinted from the *Journal of Personal and Social Psychology, 76* (1999), 54-71.

Dunst, C., Boyd, K., Trivette, C., & Hamby, D. (2002). Family-oriented program models and professional help giving practices. *Family Relations, 51,* 221-229. Ellet, A.J. (2000). *Human caring, self-efficacy beliefs, and professional, Organization cultural correlates of employee retention in child welfare.* Unpublished doctoral dissertation, Louisiana State University. Baton Rouge.

Emery, R. E., Kitzmann, K.M., & Waldron, M. (1999). Psychological interventions for separated and divorced families. In E.M. Hetherington (Ed.) *Coping with divorce, single parenting, and remarriage: A risk and resiliency perspective* (pp. 323-344). Mahwah, NJ: Erlbaum.

Hays, S. (2003). *Flat broke with children: Women in the age of welfare reform.* NY: Oxford University Press.

Hetheringon, E.M. (1999). Should we stay together for the sake of the children? In E.M. Hetherington (Ed.), *Coping with divorce, single parenting, and remarriage: A risk and resiliency perspective* (pp. 93-116). Mahwah, NJ: Erlbaum.

Kalter, N. (1987). Long-term effects of divorce on children. *American Journal of Orthopsychiatry, 57,* 587-600.

Karney, B.R., Story, L.B., & Bradbury, T.N. (2005). Marriages in context: Interactions between chronic and acute stress among newlyweds. In T.A.Revenson, K.

Kayser, & G. Bodenmann (Eds.), *Couples coping with stress: Emerging perspectives on dyadic coping*, (pp. 13-49), Washington, D.C.: American Psychological Association.

Lazarus, R.S. & Folkman, S. (1984). *Stress, appraisal, and coping.* NY: Springer Publishing Company.

Littell, J. (2001). Client participation and outcomes of intensive family preservation services. *Social Work Research, 25*, 103-123.

Maluccio, A.N. (1991). Family preservation: An overview. In A.L. Sallee & J.C. Lloyd (Eds.). *Family preservation: Papers from the Institute for Social Work Educators 1990* (pp. 17-28). Riverdale, IL: National Association for Family-based Services.

Martire, L.M., Lustig, A.P., & Schulz, R., Miller, G.E., & Helgeson, V.S. (2004). Is It beneficial to involve a family member? A meta-analysis of psychosocial interventions for chronic illness. *Health Psychology, 23*, 599-611.

National Center for Health Statistics. (2004). *Health, United States 2004.* U.S.Dept. of Health and Human Services, Hyattsville, MD. Perry, R. (2003). Who wants to work with the poor and homeless? *Journal of SocialWork Education, 39*, 321-340.

Promising results, potential new directions: I nternational FGDM research and evaluation in child welfare [Special Issue]. (2003). *Protecting children, 18.*

Radjovic, V., Nicassio, P. M., & Weisman, M. H. (1992). Behavioral intervention with and without family support for rheumatoid arthritis. *Behavior Therapy, 23,* 13-30.

Rank, M.R., & Hirschl, T.A. (1999). The economic risk of childhood poverty in America: Estimating the probability of poverty across the formative years. *Journal of Marriage and the Family, 61*, 1058-1067.

Rector, R.E. & Pardue, M.G. (2004, March). *Understanding the President's Healthy Marriage Initiative.* Retrieved December 15, 2004, from http://www.heritage.org/Research/Family

Revenson, T.A., Kayser, K., & Bodenmann, G. (Eds.), *Couples coping with stress: Emerging perspectives on dyadic coping*, Washington, D.C.: American Psychological

Association.

Rutter, M. (2000). Children in substitute care: Some conceptual considerations and research implications. *Children and Youth Services, 22*, 685-703.

Silitsky, D. (1996). Correlates of psychosocial adjustment in adolescents from divorced families. *Journal of Divorce and Remarriage, 26*, 151-169.

Vandewater, E.A., & Lansford, J.E. (1998). Influences of family structure and parental conflict on children's well-being. *Family Relations, 47*, 323-330.

Veach, T.A., Nicholas, D.R., & Barton, M.A. (2002). *Cancer and the family life cycle: A practitioner's guide.* NY: Brunner-Routledge.

Waites, C., Macgowan, M.J., Pennell, J., Carlton-LaNey, I., & Weil, M. (2004). Increasing the cultural responsiveness of family group conferencing. *Social Work, 49*, 291-299.

Wallerstein, J.S. (1998). Children of divorce: A society in search of policy. In M.A. Mason, A. Skolnick, & S. D. Sugarman (Eds.), *All our families: New policies for a new century.* NY: Oxford University Press.

Wallerstein, J. & Blakeslee, S. (1989). *Second Chances.* NY: Ticknor & Fields.

Walter, U. & Petr, C. (2000). A template for family-centered interagency collaboration. *Families and Society, 81,* 494-503.

Walton, E. (2001). Combining abuse and neglect investigations with intensive family preservation services: An innovative approach to protecting children. *Research on Social Work Practice, 11*, 627-644.

Webb, F. J. (2005). Spotlight on Theory: The New Demographics of Families. In V.L. Bengston, A.C. Acock, K.R. Allen, P. Dilworth-Anderson, & D.M. (Eds.). *Sourcebook of family theory & research (pp. 101-102).* Thousand Oaks, CA: Sage.

Wilson, W. J. (1987). *The truly disadvantaged: The inner city, the underclass, and public policy.* Chicago: University of Chicago Press.

Author's Note

Address correspondence to Karen Kayser, Ph.D., at Boston College, Graduate School of Social Work, Chestnut Hill, MA 02467. Email address: Kayserk@bc.edu.

THE FUTURE OF SOCIAL WORK IN CHILD WELFARE
Jacquelyn McCroskey

Abstract: *Child welfare has always been a volatile and dynamic field of social work practice where policy and practice are continually shaped by attitudes, perceptions and expectations. New developments likely to shift the current balance in the field of child welfare over the next quarter century include: focus on results and performance measures, focus on child and family well-being, and increasing attention to evidence-based practice.*

Keywords: child welfare, outcomes, evidence-based practice, future

INTRODUCTION

Child welfare has always been a controversial and unsettling field of practice. Focusing on child abuse and neglect is bound to be unsettling, raising highly emotional issues that challenge everyone involved because we all have vivid memories of our own childhoods and strong feelings about what is best for other people's children. Controversy on almost every aspect of policy and practice has been the norm ever since late 19th and early 20th century social workers established the key institutions designed to help and support families. Indeed, the different values and assumptions embodied in the Charity Organization Societies (COS), settlement houses and Societies for the Prevention of Cruelty to Children (SPCC) are still very much in evidence today (Halpern,1999; Walkowitz,1999; McCroskey, 2003a).

Social casework methods pioneered by Mary Richmond and other leaders of the COS movement have evolved over time, but they still include investigation, diagnosis, counseling, home visiting and advice for poor, often immigrant, families provided by mostly middle class social workers who may or may not have much experience with child-rearing. Settlement work still focuses on community building, bringing early childhood education, after-school programs, employment opportunities and social activities into poor communities to help families cope in the face of inadequate child care and schools, limited recreational opportunities and the many other devastating correlates of urban poverty. Although the SPCC no longer exists per se, its influence is still felt in both child welfare and law enforcement circles, since SPCC agents were the first protective services workers to police tenement houses, "breaking up families of bad character," rescuing their children, and "becoming the feeders of institutions, both reformatory and charitable" (Folks, 1902, p.176).

Each of these three strands of thought – social casework, community building and child protection – has influenced child welfare policy, practice, training, and research in different ways over the 125 year span of child welfare practice in the United States. Many people in the field use the metaphor of the "pendulum swinging back and forth"—between prevention and remediation, helping families and saving children from bad parents,

Jacquelyn McCroskey is John Milner Professor of Child Welfare at the School of Social Work, University of Southern California, Los Angeles, CA 90089-0411.

community supports and enforcement strategies—to capture the experience of working in this volatile field. While there is no reason to believe that these essential tensions will be resolved during the foreseeable future, it is very likely that new developments will shift the balance once again over the next quarter century. New developments most likely to cause swings in the child welfare pendulum include:

1. Focus on results and performance measures

2. Focus on child and family well-being

3. Evidence-based practice

FOCUS ON RESULTS AND PERFORMANCE MEASURES

Although we sometimes speak of "the child welfare system" as if there was a single system that provides child protection, foster care, adoption and family-centered services in the U.S., actually there are approximately 2610 public child protective services agencies employing an estimated 42,600 caseworkers in state, county and city jurisdictions throughout the country (U. S. Department of Health and Human Services, 2003). All of these agencies are guided by Federal policy, but there is so much latitude for state and local decision-making that they function quite differently in most regards.

Federal support for Statewide Automated Child Welfare Information Systems (SACWIS) was first made available in 1993, and most states now have a functioning SACWIS case management system that regularly reports data to two national data systems—the National Child Abuse and Neglect Data System (NCANDS) and the Adoption and Foster Care Reporting System (AFCARS). State by state comparison data are available from these and other sources [1], but most researchers in the field recognize the profound limitations of existing data sets. In addition to the usual limitations of automated information systems that depend on busy professionals for accurate and timely input, the states have defined basic terms differently and comparisons across jurisdictions are sometimes inherently flawed. For example, some jurisdictions have umbrella agencies that include juvenile justice and mental health along with child abuse and neglect functions, while others have separate agencies for each population. Thus, basic data on children in out-of-home care reported by some states have included all three populations, while others have reported only those children removed from their homes due to maltreatment.

The Child and Family Services Review (CFSR) process is a "comprehensive monitoring review system designed to assist States in improving outcomes for children and families who come into contact with the nation's public child welfare systems" (U.S. Department of Health and Human Services, 2005). This federal process, which has been underway for several years now, requires states to assess their own operations, undergo federal site reviews, and develop specific Program Improvement Plans (PIP) based on seven outcome areas and systemic factors. Taken together, these outcomes and systems factors now effectively define performance expectations for all child welfare jurisdictions across the country. The CFSR thus adds considerable specificity to the three key goals of *safety*, *permanence* and *child well-being* laid out for child welfare services in the 1997 Adoption and Safe Families Act. The outcome areas and systemic factors defined in the CFSR are:

Safety Outcome 1.   Children are first and foremost protected from abuse and neglect

Safety Outcome 2.   Children are safely maintained in their homes when possible

Permanency Outcome 1. Children have permanency and stability in their living situations

Permanency Outcome 2. The continuity of family relationships and connections is preserved

Well Being Outcome 1. Families have enhanced capacity to provide for children's needs

Well Being Outcome 2. Children receive services to meet their educational needs

Well Being Outcome 3. Children receive services to meet their physical and mental health needs

The systemic factors pertain to the following: (1) the Statewide information system; (2) the case review system; (3) training for child welfare staff, foster parents, and adoptive parents; (4) the quality assurance system; (5) the service array; (6) the responsiveness of the agency to the community; and (7) the licensing, recruitment, and retention of foster and adoptive parents. (www.acf.hhs.gov/programs/cb/cwrp/results/statefindings/genfinding04/intro.htm).

The importance of having both clearer definitions of desired results and a process for monitoring performance across the 2600+ public agencies mandated to serve children and families in this complex and controversial arena cannot be overstated. Focus on results and performance measures may become even more important during the next few years if some of the large-scale changes now under discussion at Federal and State levels are enacted. Suggestions have included everything from repealing mandatory reporting laws, separating investigation from service delivery functions, to developing a block grant system (rather than an entitlement) based on key findings from experimentation by states that have Title IV-E waivers (McCroskey 2003a). Clearly, change is in the air around the child welfare system, and having more standardized continuous data on program results will be essential.

Even during the initial rounds, state and local policy makers and administrators have gotten much clearer about where their agencies stand in comparison to others, where improvements are most needed, and where they should focus their efforts in order to meet basic standards. Supervisors and case workers are not only learning about the practice expectations included in their state's PIP, but realizing the importance of accurate reporting and the uses of SACWIS data for program planning, development and improvement. Many local agencies have begun to see these data as critical resources that could guide and support program planning and improvement, not simply as something required by other levels of government for reimbursement purposes.

States like California with state-administered, county-run systems have set similar state-level processes in motion to assure that each county's contribution to statewide progress is measured regularly (Needell & Patterson, 2004). This on-going process requires each of the 58 California counties to carefully align their state-required Self Improvement Plan (SIP) with California's overall plan. In addition to processes mandated at Federal and State levels, some cities and counties are also developing related processes based on the demonstrated value of data-driven planning, performance measurement, and results-based budgeting (Friedman, 1997; Osbourne & Plastrik, 1997; Hogan 1999; McCroskey 2003b), and many local jurisdictions are faced with the challenges of coordinating requirements from multiple levels of government. For example the author is working with the Los Angeles County Department of Children and Family Services to align data requirements from the Federal PIP, the State SIP and the County's performance measurement system so that the data inform planning and service improvement without overwhelming case-workers with more paperwork and reporting requirements, or conflicting with established SACWIS requirements.

Increasing attention to the core data elements included in the CFSR over time should not only improve the validity and reliability of available data, but should increase interest in the potential of data, evaluation and research to improve child welfare services. If accurate, reliable data are not primarily the concern of a small group of child welfare researchers, but a priority for policy makers, agency directors and administrators, the field should see significant improvements in information systems, greater availability of and access to data, and more attention to analyzing these complex data sets. Child welfare has a long way to go, but the fact that policy makers and administrators must now balance attention to the politics of a controversial field with focus on performance measures and results is an important step forward.

As leaders of child welfare agencies across the country take a more proactive stance, there should also be increasing attention to the many gaps in current knowledge, encouraging leaders in practice and research to work together to develop shared research agendas. Research partnerships between universities and public child welfare agencies are well established in some localities [2], but many local agencies, even those in the largest urban areas with the most complex data needs, have not yet formally established such working partnerships. The work of establishing and supporting such university-agency partnerships in states throughout the country has recently begun under the leadership of Fostering Results and the Children and Family Research Center at the School of Social Work, University of Illinois at Urbana-Champaign [3.] These partnerships should also provide significant opportunities for improving both university-based professional education and scholarship in child welfare.

FOCUS ON CHILD AND FAMILY WELL-BEING

Because safety and permanence are clearly essential goals for child protection, much of the initial work on measurement issues has focused on indicators in these two areas. There has been less attention thus far to developing measures reflecting child or family well-being beyond initial measures such as providing services to meet educational, health and mental health needs. In 2000 an advocacy group in Los Angeles noted that:

Efforts to measure child well-being are hampered by the lack of appropriate data on meaningful indicators. It is possible to say, however, that, lacking access to or support for adequate health care, appropriate child care and/or effective education or vocational training, far too many families, particularly families of color, have slipped farther and farther behind economically. The desperation of poverty has driven a disproportionate number to self medication that has deteriorated into substance abuse, further diminishing the families' capacity to meet their children's needs. It is a downward spiral that our lack of will and concerted attention has failed to arrest (Lewis et al, 2000, p. 1).

Well-being is an extremely important area for further exploration for two reasons: 1) we know that maltreatment affects child development, but have not as yet fully incorporated this knowledge into practice; and 2) we know that families involved with the child welfare system usually live in poor communities that do not have many supports for families, and that many of these families have a very broad range of service needs, but few localities have successfully integrated or aligned the supports and services needed by these children and their families.

Impacts of maltreatment on child development. In 2000 when the National Research Council and Institute of Medicine reviewed and summarized the research to date in the science of early childhood development, they noted that:

In sum, the neuroscientific research on early brain development says that young children warranting the greatest concern are those growing up in environments, starting before birth, that fail to provide them with adequate nutrition and other growth-fostering inputs, expose them to biological insults, and subject them to abusive and neglectful care. (National Research Council & Institute of Medicine, 2000, p. 217).

Although this finding is certainly not surprising to experienced caseworkers, the "explosion" of research in the neurobiological, behavioral and social sciences has also led to more nuanced understanding of the interactions between genetics and environment in early childhood. For example, children with prenatal exposure to alcohol may have problems with attention and memory, show poor motor coordination, and have difficulty tuning out excess sensory stimuli (p. 201). Children of depressed mothers also face greater risks including difficulties in school, trouble with peer relationships, heightened aggression and impaired self-control (p. 251). Animal experiments suggest that babies with highly dysfunctional parents may have both short and long-term problems in self-regulation. When stress is overwhelming, the organism must attend to immediate challenges as described by the National Research Council and Institute of Medicine (2000):

When threats begin to overwhelm one's immediate resources to manage them, a cascade of neurological changes that begin in the brain temporarily puts on hold the changes in the body that can be thought of as future-oriented: finding, digesting, and storing food; fighting off colds and viruses; learning things that don't matter right now but may be important some time in the future... (p. 212).

The only peer-reviewed scientific study thus far that has included images comparing the brains of maltreated children with those of non-maltreated children matched for age and sex showed smaller brain volumes and other physiological differences in the brains of maltreated children. These differences were correlated with the duration of trauma, with children who had been abused longer exhibiting greater damage (National Research Council and Institute of Medicine, 2000, p. 257).

Another set of findings which provide important insights both for social workers, and for the relatives, foster and adoptive parents who may assume care for these children, focus on the behaviors and internal models that young children may develop as a result of adverse, disorganized or disrupted parenting. Research shows that 70 to100% of maltreated infants exhibit insecure attachment, and furthermore that the patterns of insecure attachment they exhibit are often atypical. Maltreated infants may "inconsistently employ avoidant and resistant attachment strategies" or exhibit "[b]izarre behaviors, including interrupted movements and expressions, freezing, stilling, and apprehension" (Cicchetti, Toth & Rogosch, 2000, p. 400). Difficulties related to insecure attachment may continue to ripple through later development and "interventions to alter the working models of maltreated children are essential in order to redirect maltreated children on a trajectory toward psychological wellness" (Cicchetti, Toth & Rogosch, 2000, p. 401). Unfortunately very few of the maltreated children known to the child welfare system receive the kinds of treatment they need to develop new mental models of trusting reciprocal human relationships.

A number of authors who have reviewed this literature (National Research Council & Institute of Medicine 2000;Trickett & Schellenbach,1998; Wolfe,1999), conclude that there is reason to believe that natural resilience protects many maltreated children from permanent harm, especially when they are able to develop secure attachments with other caregivers. Even children who have missed key developmental opportunities due to inattentive, disorganized or disrupted parenting can, with loving attention and care, make up for lost time.

But how many of the social workers, foster parents, relatives, guardians and adoptive parents involved in the child welfare system understand the specific physiological and behavioral consequences of abuse and neglect for the children in their care? And how well is the child welfare system preparing them to provide the care needed by children at different developmental stages, with different familial experiences including intensities and durations of abuse? The answer is that we probably are not doing a very good job now, except in some special programs. Hopefully, further development of this research arena will encourage agencies that have focused primarily on child protection to expand their programs in order to include more attention to multidisciplinary treatment programs and family-centered services. Training and support for caregivers is also essential, so they know what to expect from the children they are responsible for and the children stand a better chance of finding the loving attention and care they need.

Service integration and alignment

The challenges of integrating services for children and families have been discussed from many perspectives (Austin 1997; Schorr 1997; Brabeck, Walsh & Latta 2003), but most authors agree that, while challenging, it is possible to work through the barriers of service fragmentation, siloed funding streams, and incompatible organizational cultures in order to better serve vulnerable children and families. Work being done in the Harlem Children's Zone (Tough, 2004), the Atlanta Project (Cutler, 1997) and in Los Angeles County by the Children's Planning Council (McCroskey, 2003b) provide examples of the broad-based prevention-oriented partnerships that are possible, in even the biggest and most complex urban areas.

Given the multifaceted needs of families involved in the child welfare system, and the difficulties of negotiating complex human services systems, some child welfare agencies have devoted considerable attention in recent years to developing community partnerships for protecting children (Zimmerman 2003). Clearly, families who are known to the child welfare system at almost any point – families who are reported for suspected abuse, those who receive voluntary services while keeping their children at home, those who are reunified with their children after foster care, or relatives, guardians and adoptive parents seeking to create new families for these children – have additional needs for support and services that child welfare does not control directly. These include child care, housing, employment, substance abuse treatment, health and mental health services, among others.

One essential element of an effective community partnership for child protection is the agency's capacity to support differential or alternative response strategies. These strategies, described by Waldfogel as core to a new paradigm for breaking the cycle of abuse and neglect place:

> ...greater emphasis on how CPS identifies the families to be served by each part of the child protective services system and how it develops case-specific assessments and service plans, in order to deliver a customized response... [this new paradigm] calls for a community-based system, in which CPS continues to play the lead role but works with the criminal justice system and with other public and private agencies to provide preventive and protective services for the full range of children in need of protection (Waldfogel, 1998, p. 138).

Work to date in communities around the country suggests that community partnerships aligning child welfare with a broad range of other organizations providing essential services to families and children offer considerable promise for the future. Potential partners include public agencies providing early childhood and K-12 education, health and mental health care, substance abuse treatment and income support services; private not-for-profit service providers; grassroots and community based organizations; as well as civic and faith-based groups concerned about families. Creating and supporting such partnerships seems to be a promising approach (McCroskey, in press), augmenting the focus of protective services on *safety* and *permanence* with a third focus on *well-being* that can help to create a shared agenda among a broad range of community partners.

EVIDENCE-BASED PRACTICE

The evidence base to support current child welfare practice is fragmentary at best and irresponsible at worst (Epstein, 1999). Thus, efforts to summarize and evaluate the existing evidence in relationship to specific aspects of practice have been particularly welcome (Cohen, Berliner & Mannarino, 2000; Comer & Frazer; 1998; Davies, Nutley & Smith 2000; Kluger, Alexander & Curtis, 200; Layzer & Goodson, 2001; Marsenich, 2002; McAuley, Pecora & Rose, in press; Thomas et al, 2002).

Finding evidence to support effective practice strategies that address the disproportionate number of children of color in the child welfare system is a very high priority topic for further investigation. Depending on the jurisdiction, children of color in different age groupings are not only referred at higher rates, they are also more likely to be placed in out-of-home care, to remain in foster care for longer periods of times and less likely to be adopted (Geen, 2003). For example in Los Angeles, foster care rates for different racial/ethnic groups differ dramatically. In 2003, African American children were most likely to be placed in foster care with a rate of 49.2 per 1000 children under 18, followed by American Indian children at 20.2. Latino and White children had roughly equivalent rates of 8.2 and 8.3, while Asian Pacific Islander children were least likely to be in foster care at a rate of 2.1 (Los Angeles County Children's Planning Council 2004).

These racial and ethnic group differences also seem to interact with demographic and community factors in ways that are little understood at present. For example, in 2002 the South region of LA County with the highest number of child abuse and neglect referrals (27, 283), also had the highest percentage of children living in poverty (34%), the lowest percentage of third grade public school students reading at or above national averages (22%), and the lowest percentage of high school graduates (66%) [4]. Further investigation of the interactions among such variables is much needed in localities throughout the country.

One promising approach that may help the child welfare field to develop a more substantial evidence base is the widespread use of structured assessment instruments and processes to support decision-making about risk and safety. Although people may overestimate the accuracy of such structured protocols (Munro 2004), they nonetheless offer continuing sources of practical information to support training, supervision and administrative decision-making.

Hopefully, such tentative steps towards evidence-based practice in the child welfare system will provide practical information that is actually used by administrators and caseworkers, reinforcing the need for a deeper and more far-reaching research base to support practice in the field. If so, university-agency partnerships may be used to good effect, improving practice and expanding the knowledge base in a very complex, emotional and political arena of social work practice. Given the sheer number of local child welfare jurisdictions, and the very different demographics, characteristics and political priorities of the communities they serve, these partnerships should be able to explore a broad range of research questions, investing both in rigorous interdisciplinary methodologies and in participative evaluation strategies that can help give voice to vulnerable children and their families. If so, social workers entering the field in the next quarter century will be much better informed than their predecessors, and the field as a whole should be more successful in improving outcomes for children and families.

Notes

1. Sources for comparative data include: 1) NCANDS, National Child Abuse and Neglect Data System (ndacan.cornell.edu); 2) AFCARS, Adoption and Foster Care Reporting System, AFCARS (www.acf.hhs.gov/programs/cb/dis/afcars/publications/afcars.htm); 3) NDAS, the National Data Analysis System run by the Child Welfare League of America (ndas.cwla.org. Data comparing counties is also available from sites such as the University of California Berkeley's Center for Social Service Research, Child Welfare Research Center (www.cssr.berkeley.edu/childwelfare).

2. For example, the Children and Family Research Center at the School of Social Work, University of Illinois at Urbana-Champaign began their partnership with the Illinois State Department of Children and Family Services in 1996.

3. In 2003 The Pew Charitable Trusts initiated support for the Children and Family Research Center at the School of Social Work, University of Illinois at Urbana-Champaign to launch a public education and outreach campaign called Fostering Results. The campaign works nationally and

in selected states to engage influential leaders, using media, reports and meetings around key issues. (www.fosteringresults.org)

4. Los Angeles County uses eight geographic regions, or Service Planning Areas (SPAs), to organize and facilitate coordinated planning and information sharing. See the website of the Children's Planning Council for more detail on the SPAs, and for recent data by SPA and by zip code included in the 2004 Children's Scorecard (www.childrensplanningcouncil. org).

References

Austin, M. J. (ed.). (1997). *Human services integration*. NY: The Haworth Press.

Brabeck, M. M., Walsh, M. E. & Latta, R. E. (eds.). *Meeting at the hyphen: Schools-universities-communities-professions in collaboration for student achievement and well-being*. 102nd yearbook of the National Society for the Study of Education. Chicago, IL: University of Chicago Press.

Cicchetti, D., Toth, S. L. & Rogosch, F. A. (2000). The development of psychological wellness in maltreated children. In D. Cicchetti, J. Rappaport, I. Sandler & R. P. Weissberg (eds.). *The promotion of wellness in children and adolescents*. Washington DC: Child Welfare League of American Press.

Cohen, J. A., Berliner, L. & Mannarino, A. P. (2000). Treating traumatized children, A research review and synthesis. *Trauma, violence and abuse*, 1 (1): 29-43.

Comer, E. W. & Frazer, M. W. (1998). Evaluation of six family support programs:Are they effective? *Families in society: The journal of contemporary human services*, 79(2): 134-148.

Cutler, I. (1997). *Learning together: Reflections on the Atlanta Project*. Atlanta, GA: The America Project.

Davies, H. T. O., Nutley, S. M. & Smith, P. C. (eds.). (2000). *What works? Evidence-based policy and practice in public services*. Bristol, UK: The Policy Press.

Epstein, W. M. (1999). *Children who could have been, The legacy of child welfare in wealthy America*. Madison, WI: University of Wisconsin Press.

Folks, H. (1902). *The care of destitute neglected and delinquent children*. (Classics series). Washington DC: National Association of Social Workers.

Friedman, M. (1997). *A guide to developing and using performance measures in results-based budgeting*. Washington DC: The Finance Project. (See also www.resultsaccountability.com)

Geen, R. (2003). *Who will adopt the foster care children left behind?* Washington DC: Urban Institute. (http://www.urban.org/url.cfm?ID=310809)

Hogan, C. D. (1999). *Vermont communities count, Using results to strengthen services for families and children*. Baltimore, MD: Annie E. Casey Foundation.

Halpern, R. (1999). *Fragile families, fragile solutions: A history of supportive services for families in poverty*. New York: Columbia University Press.

Kluger, M. P., Alexander, G. & Curtis, P. A. (eds.). (2000). *What works in child welfare?* Washington DC: Child Welfare League of America Press.

Layzer, J. I. & Goodson, B. D. (2001). *National evaluation of family support programs*. Cambridge, MA: Abt Associates (http://www.abt assoc.com)

Lewis, L., Aguilar, Y. F., Armstrong, B., Biondi, C. O., Buck, M., Curry, P., McCroskey, J., Olenick, M., Perry, J., Riordan, N. D., Wainwright, M. & Weinstein, V. (2000). *From child welfare to child well-being*. Pasadena, CA: Casey Family Program.

Los Angeles County Children's Planning Council. (2004). *2004 Children's Scorecard. Health, families and income: Key areas of child well-being for school readiness and success.* Los Angeles, CA: author.

Marsenich, L. (2002). *Evidence-based practices in mental health services for foster youth.* Sacramento, CA: California Institute for Mental Health.

C. McAuley, P. Pecora & W. Rose (eds.). (in press). *Enhancing the well being of children and families through effective interventions: UK and USA evidence for practice.* London & Philadelphia: Jessica Kingsley Publishers.

McCroskey, J. (2003a). Child welfare: Controversies and possibilities. In F. Jacobs, D. Wertlieb, & R. M. Lerner (eds.) *Handbook of applied developmental science, Promoting positive child, adolescent and family development through research, policies and programs,* Vol. 2. Thousand Oaks, CA: Sage Publishers: 371-393.

McCroskey, J. (2003b). *Walking the collaboration talk: Ten lessons learned from the Los Angeles County Children's Planning Council.* Los Angeles, CA: Children's Planning Council.

McCroskey, J. (in press). Family-centered community-based supports, services and capacity-building: Effectiveness and promising approaches. In C. McAuley, P. Pecora & W. Rose (eds.). *Enhancing the well being of children and families through effective interventions: UK and USA evidence for practice.* London & Philadelphia: Jessica Kingsley Publishers.

Munro, E. (2004). A simpler way to understand the results of risk assessment instruments, *Children and youth services review,* 26, pp. 873-883.

National Research Council & Institute of Medicine. (2000). From neurons to neighborhoods: The science of early childhood development. In J. P. Shonkoff & D. A. Phillips (Eds.). *Board on Children, Youth and Families, Commission on Behavioral and Social Sciences and Education.* Washington DC: National Academy Press.

Needell, B. & Patterson, K. (2004). *The child welfare system improvement and accountability act (AB 636): Improving results for children and youth in California. A what works policy brief.* Sacramento, CA: Foundation Consortium for California Children and Youth.

Osbourne, D. & Plastrik, P. (1997). *Banishing bureaucracy, The five strategies for reinventing government.* NY: Plume, Penguin Putnam Inc.

Schorr, L. B. (1997). *Common purpose, Strengthening families and neighborhoods to rebuild America.* NY: Anchor Books, Random House.

Thomas, D., Leicht, C., Hughes, C., Madigan, A. & Dowell, K.. (2002). *Emerging practices in the prevention of child abuse and neglect.* Washington DC: Office on Child Abuse and Neglect, US Department of Health and Human Services.

Tough, P. (2004). The Harlem project. *New York Times Magazine,* June 20, pp. 44-73.

Trickett, P. K. & Schellenbach (eds.). (1998). *Violence against children in the family and the community.* Washington DC: American Psychological Association.

U.S. Department of Health and Human Services. Administration for Children and Families/Children's Bureau and Office of the Assistant Secretary for Planning and Evaluation (HHS/ACF & OASPE). (2003). *National study of child protective services systems and reform efforts: A summary report.* Washington DC: U. S. Government Printing Office.

U.S. Department of Health and Human Services, Administration for Children and Families, Child Welfare Reviews. Retrieved April 30, 2005. http://www.acf.hhs.gov/programs/cb/cwrp/index.htm

Waldfogel, J. (1998). *The future of child protection, How to break the cycle of abuse and neglect.* Cambridge, MA: Harvard University Press.

Walkowitz, D. J. (1999). *Working with class: Social workers and the politics of middle-class identity.*

Chapel Hill, NC: University of North Carolina Press.

Wolfe, D. A. (1999). *Child abuse: Implications for child development and psychopathology* (2nd edition). Thousand Oaks, CA: Sage.

Zimmerman, F. (2003). *Doing business differently, Changing policy and practice in the St. Louis Division of Family Services.* NY: Center for Community Partnerships in Child Welfare *and* Washington DC: Center for Study of Social Policy.

Author's Note

Address correspondence to Jacquelyn McCroskey, DSW, John Milner Associate Professor of Child Welfare, University of Southern California School of Social Work, Montgomery Ross Fisher Building, Los Angeles, CA 90089-0411. e-mail: mccroske@usc.edu

THE FUTURE OF SCHOOL SOCIAL WORK PRACTICE: CURRENT TRENDS AND OPPORTUNITIES

Cynthia Franklin

Abstract: *This article discusses information on school social work practice in the United States and summarizes recent trends and their implications for the future of school social work. The number of school social workers and current infrastructure available for the development of school social work practice is also reviewed. Five sociocultural trends are summarized that are affecting public schools along with important school-based practice trends such as standardized testing and high stakes accountability measures. The emerging practice trend of evidenced-based practices is discussed in light of its standards and implications for school-based practice. Finally, essential knowledge for strengthening practice competencies to meet the future challenges of school-based practice is highlighted.*

Keywords: school social work, evidence-based practice, practice standards, accountability

INTRODUCTION

For the past one hundred years social workers have been practicing in school systems. School social workers and other school-based services professionals have evolved into an independent profession that offers specialized knowledge and skills for helping people in the context of schools (Allen-Meares, 2004). This article discusses information on school social work practice in the United States and summarizes recent trends and their implications for the future. First, data are presented on the numbers of school social workers and infrastructure supporting school social work practice. Second, information is provided on the current socio-cultural trends affecting public schools, and the affects of current trends on school-based, practice environments. Some of the major opportunities and challenges facing school social workers are also summarized. Third, this article reviews the importance of evidenced-based practices and how this emerging practice trend is destined to influence the practices of school social workers. Finally, this article suggests essential knowledge for strengthening practice competencies to meet the future challenges of school-based practice.

SCHOOL-BASED SOCIAL WORKERS IN THE U.S.

Current practice in public schools indicates that there are two groups of social workers that practice in the schools. First, are those who are direct employees of the school district and serve as members of the pupil services team. Second are those who are school-based service providers employed by community-based organizations contracting with the school districts (Franklin, 2004). Expanded school mental health services and school-based health centers and other school-based services providers have greatly contributed to this trend (Brener, Martindale & Weist, 2001). For example, Communities in Schools

Cynthia Franklin is Stiernberg/Spencer Family Professor in Mental Health, School of Social Work, University of Texas at Austin, Austin, Texas 78712.

(CIS), a nonprofit community-based agency with 194 programs in some 2600 schools in across 31 states (www.cisnet.org) employs school-based staff including licensed social workers. Typical of this staffing pattern are Houston and El Paso, two of the largest CIS programs in the country, which employ a combined total of some 260 school-based staff, about half of which are not social workers by license or degree (www.cisaustin.org) (cited in Franklin, Harris & Allen-Meares, in press).

The changing climate of education makes it difficult to report an accurate number of school social workers in the U.S. Available data may underestimate the numbers of social workers who work in either full or part-time positions within the schools. The School Social Workers Association of America (SSWAA) completed a survey of state departments of education (www.sswaa.org), which reports 14,636 social workers employed by school districts in 50 states and the District of Columbia. The second survey performed by the Substance Abuse and Mental Health Services Administration (SAMHSA) reports that 8.3% of social worker respondents (4,888 social workers) work in primary and secondary school settings as their primary employer and almost 2% (282 social workers) say school setting are a secondary employer (http://www.mentalhealth.org/publications/allpubs/ SMA01-3537/default.asp). SAMHSA conducted the survey only with social workers who are members of NASW and estimated that the actual numbers are probably twice as large as the survey indicates (Center for Mental Health Services, 2000). Comparing this data to the findings of the SSWAA data might indicate that this estimate was extremely low.

School Social Work Organizations and Infrastructure

School social workers are supported by two strong national organizations, the School Social Workers Association of America (SSWAA) (www.sswaa.org) and the NASW (www. NASW.org). Thirty two state organizations and four regional councils also galvanize the field. SSWAA provides a national, annual conference of some 400 participants, 12 state organizations sponsor annual conferences and training workshops. Texas and Michigan held state conferences in 2003-5, for example, with nearly 500 participants each (Nowicki, 2003). Others participate in regional conferences involving 10 to 12 states, such as the Midwest Council conference (www.sswaa.org).

Social work journals also help to support and inform school social work practice. Children & Schools (http://www.naswpress.org/publications/journals/children/csintro.html) is a journal that provides information on research, practice, and policy issues relevant to school-based practitioners. This journal offers a Practice Highlights Column that encourages practitioners to publish their up-to-date practices. A second journal, The School Social Work Journal (http://lyceumbooks.com/sswjournal.htm) is designed for school social work practitioners, students, and educators. Providing articles on original research, research reviews, conceptual models, and assessment and intervention methodologies, among other topics, the journal encourages effective social work practice in schools.

SOCIO-CULTURAL TRENDS AFFECTING PUBLIC EDUCATION

Most school social workers practice in public education. The educational system is constantly affected by institutional and political trends including local, or federal pressures (Allen-Meares, in press). As Sipple (2004, cited in Allen-Meares in press) states, "The

American public educational system is a beleaguered public institution fraught with relentless criticism…" adding that "…schools are facing ever-challenging and complex educational situations while at the same time an unprecedented inspection and expectation of practice and performance" (p. 1).

Houston (1999) discusses five socio-cultural trends that are impacting public education and have implications for future school social work practice. The first trend is devolution, that is a movement toward decentralizing political authority and placing it in the hands of local leaders and organizations. Trend two is, demasification, which breaks people down into smaller groups and creates more and more choices for our children but fewer and fewer options to unite us into a common set of resources, interests or values. Smaller, exclusive, groups have the potential to create inequities and considerable tensions between interest groups who are left to struggle for waning resources. The third trend is deregulation and all industries have faced this trend, and now education faces it through the eradication of state codes and federal control leading,to increasing choices, vouchers and charter schools.

Trend four is disintermediation, which is occurring through the impacts of technologies on our educational institutions. The Internet, for example, makes it possible to learn anywhere. New technologies are quickly replacing the need for skills learned with those never learned. This creates a continual learning curve and educators have to contend with the fact that skills learned in school today will be antiquated by the time a student graduates. Finally, trend five is the de-emphasis on education for learning's sake. The value of learning for the common good or progress of humanity does not exist in the same proportion as in the 20th century during the progressive era. Corporations and corporate interests, for example, want to know how the skills learned in schools applies to success in the workplace (McLaren,1998).

The future implication for school social workers include an increasing need to give attention to school policy issues so that they can effectively work with educational constituent groups influencing local and national issues that affect the schooling of children. School social workers also need to consider how to keep standards for school social work practice in the face of the changing socio-cultural trends impacting education. For example, at the same time that some states are de-regulating certain educational codes, credentials have become a big issue for compensation in educational systems (Shaffer, 1996). Teachers with more education and who have met the requirements of certain credentials are offered more pay, for example. School social workers have sought to use their credentials in the same manner (Hare, 1996). Unfortunately, however, the education levels and credentials for school social work are the least consistent of any of the school-based services professions. School psychologists, for example, have much more consistent education and credentialing than school social workers. School social work education and credentials vary from Bachelor to Masters degrees, and from requiring specialized certifications and licenses to having no agreed upon credentialing standards (Altshuler, in press). For the future, school social workers must work toward consistent credentials and educational standards. Illinois serves as one of the best states to follow as a model in this quest for consistent credentials.

OPPORTUNITIES AND CHALLENGES FOR
PRACTICE WITHIN PUBLIC SCHOOLS

Current trends indicate that school social work may continue to be a growing profession because populations at risk are increasingly being served within public schools. Studies show that from 12 to 22 percent of all children under the age 18 are in need of services for mental, emotional or behavioral problems (UCLA School Mental Health Project, 2003). Over 70 percent of children receiving mental health care obtain services at school (Center for Health and Health Care in School, 2001) and fall under the care of school social workers and other school-based services professionals. Even conservatively, this means that 10 million school age youth are presenting problems in need of mental health intervention. Unfortunately, the reality on school campuses is that less than one in five children in need of mental health services are receiving treatment (U.S. Department of Health and Human Services, 2000) and this indicates that schools are in great need of school social work services.

When a school social worker practices in a school they are able to use their skills to help youths who are perceived to be most at-risk. Latino and African American children, for example, have the highest rates of need for mental health services and are most likely to go without care or the attention of public schools (RAND, 2001). Latinos are also the fastest growing minority group in the United States. Almost 40 percent of Latinos are between the ages of 5 to 24 and the school-age Latino population is expected to grow by 82% during the next 25 years (Bowman, 2004). In 2000, minority students represented 39% of students in public schools. Latino students represented 17% of students, up from 11% in 1972. Students from minority groups are more likely to attend schools in which most students are from low-income families and high minority enrollment (National Center for Education Statistics, 2004). Children with minority status also receive poorer quality mental health care. Many homeless teens, immigrants, teen parents, and youths that are gay and lesbian are also in great need of mental health services, and may receive care only through institutions such as public schools. Schools also present risks for children and school social workers are needed in areas of crisis intervention and response to these risks. According to survey data collected by the National Center for Educational Statistics, for example, in 1999, 8 percent of students in grades six through twelve reported criminal victimization at school, 8 percent of students in grades nine through twelve reported being threatened or injured with a weapon on school property, and 5 percent of students age twelve through eighteen reported that they had been afraid of being attacked or harmed on school property during the past six months (Kaufman et al., 2001). The implications of these data for the future is that schools will remain a very important practice arena for children's mental health and social services. This also means that school social workers will increasingly be involved in the treatment of complex issues involving an increasingly diverse body of at-risk students.

Standardized Testing and High Stakes Accountability

Increasing standards, greater accountability, and tougher performance measures are being enacted in relationship to the No Child Left Behind (NCLB) legislation (Simpson,

LaCava, and Graner, 2004). Under that legislation, the mandating of standardized testing for evaluating academic preparation has been both praised and criticized. Many constituents in favor of public education, including the NEA, educational researchers, educational groups [including school social workers] view the trends toward standardized testing as being an over-emphasized accountability measure (Faircloth, 2004).

The public debate over how standardized testing is transforming public schools is, perhaps, one of the most pressing current issues facing educators including school social workers. Issues include but are not limited to the following a) how schools shape themselves to teach to the test, b) the inappropriateness of relying on a standardized test as a singular outcome measure, c) the stress of the tests on children, and d) the inequities that standardized measures create in children with learning disabilities, language minority and ethnic-minority groups, for example. Many educators in the policy arena, including school social workers (e.g. SSWAA and NASW), are working diligently to revise NCLB and reverse the trends toward more standardized testing (SSWAA, E-Bell, March 7, 2005). In the meantime, however, school social workers on the front-lines are left to work with tensions, calm those who are anxious, and help schools help children perform well on the tests.

Currently, public schools are held to many new performance measures including both funding penalties for low performance as well as cash incentives for high performance. Incentive structures, cost effectiveness, cost accounting, and benefit verses cost analysis are routine performance measures for all schools. Until these types of management practices are moderated or possibly reversed, school social workers, along with other school employees, must prepare themselves to work in high performance, outcome driven work environments. High stakes accountability in which student achievement and other performance measures (e.g. dropout rate) are directly linked to school funding, and accreditation are becoming standard practice. Kentucky, for example, was one of the first states to enact this type of performance-based system (Linn, 2000).

Critics have argued that NCLB makes many demands of schools without providing enough resources to meet those demands. Yet, schools face serious consequences for falling short of expectations. In the new environment of public school administration, low performing schools are identified in a report card type system, and are sanctioned. If a school fails to improve its' performance stiff penalties are enacted including the replacement of administrators and staff. Some states, also, have cut-off funding and required low performing schools to offer vouchers to students to attend another school (Archer, 2004; Goldhaber and Hannaway, 2004).

NCBL has implications for special education students because it requires that they be administered the same standardized tests that other students are required to take (Faircloth, 2004). Schools that have large numbers of special education students are likely to feel a great deal of additional pressure to ensure that these students are able to pass standardized tests. This affects school social workers because they are heavily involved with special education students from assessment to assisting students with academic, health, and mental health needs (Blair, 1993; Tower, 2000).

Because schools have moved to adopt strict performance measures, school social workers have also adapted by continuing to provide standards for practice, and to link social work practice skills with school-based standards (Lee, 2002; NASW, 2002). The prevailing public view indicates that school social workers must focus on how to meet the concerns of multiple stakeholders (e.g educators, parents, government policy makers, and business) who believe that the success of public schools is their responsibility. Future implication of these trends are not completely known but school social workers must be prepared to help schools meet performance standards, and also be able to document their own performance in relationship to the outcome measures being prescribed.

EVIDENCED-BASED PRACTICE

"The future of school social work is going to be influenced by the emerging practice trend of evidence-based practices" (Allen-Meares, in press). In order to keep the field abreast of this cutting edge issue *Children & Schools* published a special issue on evidenced-based practices in schools in 2004. Raines (2004) discusses the relationship between evidenced-based practices and school social work and offers a thoughtful, practice friendly review of this topic for school social workers.

According to Huang, Hepburn, & Espiritu (2003, cited in Allen-Meares, in press):

> Evidence-based practice is an emerging concept and reflects a nationwide effort to build quality and accountability in health and behavioral health care service delivery. Underlying this concept is (1) the fundamental belief that children with emotional and behavioral disorders should be able to count on receiving care that meets their needs and is based on the best scientific knowledge available, and (2) the fundamental concern that for many of these children, the care that is delivered is not effective care. (p. 1)

Many disciplines currently use the concept of evidenced-based practices and Allen-Meares (in press) reviews two prevailing definitions that have influenced educational researchers and the policy makers who are setting the evidenced-based practices for schools. The first definition comes from the medical field. Medicine describes evidence-based practice as using the best available evidence to inform decisions about patient care. Physicians incorporate this new information into their knowledge built from experience in their practice settings along with the beliefs and experiences of their patients. A second definition is provided by the mental health field that defines evidence-based practice as defines evidenced-based practice as practices that have been established trough a combination of empirical research and standards for practice stemming from that research. Criteria in mental health practice may include standardized treatments, program evaluation, controlled trials evaluating practices, or other outcomes from scientific evaluations (Allen-Meares in press). The main focus here is that the research guiding practice standards must meet a certain set of agreed-upon standards.

Franklin & Hopson, (2004) discuss how evidenced-based practices are also becoming a standard for school mental health services and instructional areas in education. The Department of Education, for example, founded the What Works Clearinghouse (http://www.w-w-c.org), that focuses on the dissemination of the evidenced-based practices in education. Criteria for evidenced-based practices in education are set-by the Institute for Educational Sciences which is the research arm for the Department of Education, in consultation , with a technical services group of distinguished researchers. The four basic criteria include:

1) *employs systematic, empirical methods that draw on observation or experiment; involves data analyses that are adequate to support the general findings; relies on measurements or observational methods that provide reliable data; makes claims of causal relationships only in random-assignment experiments or other designs (to the extent such designs substantially eliminate plausible competing explanations for the obtained results);*

2) *ensures that studies and methods are presented in sufficient detail and clarity to allow for replication or, at a minimum, to offer the opportunity to build systematically on the findings of the research;*

3) *obtains acceptance by a peer-reviewed journal or approval by a panel of independent experts through a comparably rigorous, objective, and scientific review; and uses research designs and methods appropriate to the research question posed.*

4) *uses research designs and methods appropriate to the research question posed.*

The Institute for Educational Sciences sets a criteria for screening studies to decide if they completely meet evidence standards or meet the evidence standards with reservations. This helps the Clearinghouse present the best practices in education. Criteria include: a) *Iintervention fidelity [was the treatment delivered correctly and in a high quality manner]; b) outcomes measures; c) extent to which relevant people, settings, and measure timings were included; d) extent to which the study allowed for the testing of intervenion's effect wihin subgroups; e) statistical analysis and f) statistical reporting. http://www.w-w-c.org/reviewprocess/standards.html*

Every indication suggests that educational institutions may increasingly expect or even possibly guide funding toward the use of evidenced-based practices. This trend would be consistent with practice directions in children's mental health, and the increased emphasis on results and accountability in public schools. Although, it is not known how successfully the evidenced-based practices might be disseminated or monitored for use in education. What is known, is that evidenced-base practices have not been very successfully disseminated within school mental health practice, and the use of effective methods are often not used with the students and families who most need them (Franklin & Hopson, 2004; Hoagwood, 2003). In the future, however, school social workers may be asked to qualify their approaches using a set of standards that meets the criteria for evidenced-based practices in education.

THE FUTURE OF SCHOOLS AND COMMUNITY-BASED SERVICES

Community-based, clinical and health practitioners from diverse disciplines have increasingly linked with schools and are delivering their services on school campuses. This trend has been influenced by related services provisions and demands of the Individual with Disabilities Education Act (IDEA) (Faircloth, 2004), the vanishing autonomy of private practice, and the school-linked services movement (Dryfoos & Maguire, 2002; Streeter & Franklin, 2002). The future implication of this trend is for schools to house and/or link closely with mental health, social services, and other youth development programs. There have been varied projects across the country aimed at increasing the schools involvement with community-based services, and "statewide initiatives were established in California, Florida, Kentucky, Iowa, Missouri, New Jersey, Ohio, and Oregon, among others" (Taylor & Adelman, in press).

Although, partly designed to address fragmentation and to produce more efficient and effective programs, community linkages with school-based services has not resolved these issues. In fact, co-locating services to school campuses may just move the services fragmentation problem from one level to another as practitioners continue to be as disconnected and the services fragmented on school campuses as they were in the community. The UCLA Mental Health project has considerable data and information on the school and community-based services, and how to practice effectively in these types of school-based services programs (http://smhp.psych.ucla.edu/). The long term sustainment of collaboration, and the appropriate policies and infrastructure for practice appears to be significant for all successful, school-linked initiatives.

Franklin (1998) and Streeter & Franklin (2002) addressed the possible implications for an increasingly interprofessional work environment created through school-community programs. Such issues as role overlap and increased competition for service delivery by different services providers were suggested. In 2001 the SSWAA held a national conference in Washington DC focused on resolving related issues between the school-based, services professions, and decreasing job elimination of school social workers due to the co-location of mental health professionals to school campuses. Although, anecdotal reports indicate that the overlap of job descriptions and elimination of jobs may still be an issue for some school social workers, one study has shown that despite the overlapping roles , that the school-based services professionals have also found ways to work cooperatively. Agresta (2004) surveyed school social workers, school psychologists and counselors asking them about twenty-one roles. The results of this survey confirmed that job overlap did occur, and especially in the area of counseling services between social workers and counselors. School Psychologists, however, spent considerable more time on psychometric assessment than other school professionals. Interestingly, all the professionals including school psychologists wanted to do more counseling but the results of this survey indicated that the different professionals were coping well with the overlapping roles. For example, little competitive feelings were reported between the disciplines even with the presence of the interprofessional role overlap.

ENHANCING FUTURE PRACTICE COMPETENCIES

To be effective in the future, school social workers have to continue to position their practice competencies in relationship to the challenges of public schools and its' on-going reforms.

Effective Practices with Diverse, Populations At-Risk

Schools are integrally involved with services delivery of the most at-risk children and many of these children are also ethnic minority and from impoverished backgrounds (NCES, 2002). Many other diverse characteristics of students and families also present challenges to effective practice delivery such as religious diversity, political diversity, and immigration status (Harris & Franklin, 2004). School social workers like all social workers must increase their knowledge for effective practice with diverse populations who also may present more than one risk factor (Altshuler and Kopels, 2003; Caple, Salcido, and Cecco, 1995). This issue overlaps with evidenced-based practices because there is a great need to develop effective practices with co-morbid populations, students of color, and to test these interventions more in the community practice settings including schools, for example (Hoagwood and Johnson, 2003; Schoenwald and Hoagwood, 2001). As school social workers effectively work with these students they can greatly assist schools as a diversity specialist and may also be helpful in training other school personnel in being effective with students of color and other diverse populations. Data indicates that effective service delivery with Latino populations including families with immigrant status may be one of the greatest issues facing public schools both now and in the future (Bowman, 2004).

Preparing for the Challenges of Evidenced-Based Practices

In order for school social workers to prepare for evidenced-based practice it is very important that they learn what are the most effective practices for different student and family issues (e.g. ADHD, substance abuse, parental involvement, facilitating teams, etc.). Fortunately, practice resources are emerging that help the practitioners learn the evidenced-based practices. The What Works Clearinghouse offers evidenced-based reviews of salient practice issues. The School Mental Health Assistant Center (http://csmha.umaryland. edu/; Weist, Evans, and Lever, 2003) also offers many resources for helping practitioners discover evidenced-based practices, and training for school-based, mental health services. Franklin, Harris & Allen-Meares (in press) further provide a comprehensive volume on evidenced-based practices for school-based social workers. As far as practitioners abilities to learn the evidenced-based practices goes, research indicates that reading practice manuals are not as effective as in-service training, and trainings are not as effective as supervision and consultation models (Franklin & Hopson, 2005; Simpson, LaCava, and Graner, 2004). A critical issue for evidenced-based, practice training that must be resolved is the fact that training is extremely expensive, and cost is a major barrier to learning the new methods (Franklin & Hopson, 2005). Shrinking training budgets and lack of provision of effective supervision in schools is an on-going issue for most school-based practices. One future approach to training and supervision might be for school social workers to form alliances with other children's professionals in the community in a strategy to make evidenced-based training and supervision available and more affordable.

Leadership

Rhodes (1999) envisions the new organizational style needed for effective school leadership as a "scaffolding" approach whereby leaders abandon the pyramid style of organization and develop horizontal relationships with their colleagues for the purposes of empowering smaller groups to be more effective. Administrators in schools are increasingly expected to be local problem solvers and capable of developing collaborative relationships, and enhance resources for their school campus. Leadership in school environments requires skills for effective relationship management and coordination. School social workers can take a role in school leadership by working to enhance the importance of differing roles, and helping all professionals work in unity and cooperation.

School social workers can use their knowledge of different systems to increase role autonomy and avoid boundary diffusion between different professionals. Resource mapping and service coordination can also be used to assist schools in maximizing cooperation and decreasing fragmented and overlapping services (Streeter & Franklin, 2002). In schools, for example, case management is a skill emphasized by diverse professionals as school psychologists (Romualdi, V. & Sandoval, 1995; Tharinger, 1995) nurses, (Ross, 1999) and even teachers (Smith & Stowitschek, 1998). The effective implementation of case management in a school, however, requires leadership and coordination. In order to better meet these challenges, school social workers might enhance their competencies as leaders of interprofessional teams and foster additional abilities to facilitate transdiciplinary teamwork among diverse professionals (Streeter & Franklin, 2002).

Increasing Skills for Showing Accountability

Issues of accountability surrounding public schools suggests that school-based services professionals will increasingly be asked to provide outcome data showing that their practices get results. School social workers must enhance their skills in developing ways to measure the effectiveness of their services. There will be a great need for accountability measures that are easy to use and are consistent with the school's expectations for results (Green and Etheridge, 2001). To meet current and future demands for accountability, school social workers might consider measuring outcomes in relationship to the school performance indicators and developing their own report-card type system. Measuring and reporting outcomes require practitioners to have in place a data management and documentation system, that can produce outcome oriented reports that show performance (Franklin, 1999). Report cards for school social work services might be best positioned as marketing oriented tools and placed in the hands of important stakeholders. It is also advisable to provide outcome and positive performances information on a website

Increasing Skills for Using Technologies in Service Delivery

The future of education is intricately intertwined with the increasing use of diverse technologies and school social workers along with other school personnel must become extremely proficient in their use. For example, the Internet and other network and data base technologies will integrate with service delivery. In the future, everything from referrals to progress reports and outcomes measures will be on-line. School-based services professionals, parents and students will communicate with one another on-line. Schools without walls and learning communities may become more prevalent than is imaginable. At a minimum, to meet the future challenges of technology enhancements, school social workers will need to be knowledgeable and possess skills in web-based and Internet technologies, and also be competent in delivering effective and ethical services via these technologies (Giffords, 2003; Pahwa, 2003).

The protection of client records and the struggles to maintain client confidentiality is also likely to magnify with increased use of electronic technologies. The Health Insurance Portability and Accountability Act of 1996 (HIPAA; Center for Medicare and Medicaid Services, n.d.) has been a challenge for school-based practices and schools have been some times slow to accept the implications of increased confidentiality of health and mental health information, for example (Bergren and Pohlman, 2004). Confidentiality of school records and the personal medical information of students have created incidences where school social workers came into conflict with school personnel over how to interpret the increased demands of HIPAA. Like other personnel providing health and mental health services to students, school social workers have an obligation to challenge unethical practices and to develop appropriate policies (Erlen, 2004; Jonson-Reid, 2000).

Marketing and Contract Management Skills

All practitioners need to have excellent marketing and contract management skills because the school-based services funding is increasingly becoming a complex mix of funds from multiple sources (Poirier and Osher, in press). Funding sources are also increasingly coming from outside the public school system (e.g. mental health, health services, juvenile justice, and foundations) and different sources of funding are often combined in creative ways. With so many funding streams, school social workers must be continually prepared to market their own practices, as well as the programs of the school to diverse organizations. In order to be effective in marketing in schools, school social workers need a target approach that as informed by effective practices. Social Marketing theory is one approach that might be useful because it has been successfully used in the school health and school mental health field and the techniques may prove promising for school social workers too. Social marketing theory blends communication tools (e.g. groups, mass media, and individual) to send its' 'message. It takes into consideration three basic questions in formulating messages that can influence people to change their attitudes or behavior. 1) What motivates the person or group? 2) What is in it for the person or group if they change? 3) What are the competing ideas and messages being sent that must be countered? (Kirkwood & Stan, 2004;Rothschild, 1999).

As school social workers become more involved in working with diverse funders such as foundations, managed care organizations and Medicaid, the details of meeting the contract requirements for these funding sources may intensify. It may also be necessary to develop contracts and collaborations with other community services providers in order to fully take advantage of funding sources such as Medicaid, for example. At a minimum, school-based practice may require that school practitioners be knowledgeable about of several funding mechanisms and their issues for reimbursement. Fortunately, social workers often have more training in these types of marketing and contract management issues than other school-based services professionals. The macro training received in schools of social work may become a direct practice strength in practice situations relying on a need for on-going marketing of services, and the management of the diverse contracts.

CONCLUSION

School social workers have evolved into an independent profession and two distinct groups of social workers are currently practicing in schools.. Those who are employs of school districts and those who come from community-based programs. School-based social work has developed a considerable infra-structure of specific practice organizations, conferences and journals to support its' development. Public schools, the principal work environments for school-based social workers are currently experiencing numerous cultural transformations and school reforms aimed at improving these systems. Every indication is that school-based social work will continue to be an important practice arena due to the prominent roles that schools currently have in the delivery of mental health and social services to at-risk students. Public schools are wrestling with the implications of increased accountability standards and this is creating a situation where school social workers must work in performance-oriented jobs.

Educational systems are taking steps to adopt standards for evidenced-based practices and this emerging practice trend has implications for the types of practices that social workers must learn and deliver in schools. Trends indicate that school social work and other school-related services is integrating more with community-based practices and this new service delivery approach is creating a need for resource mapping, coordination, and greater collaboration skills. School social workers can enhance future practice competencies by staying attuned to the current issues confronting educational systems and focusing skills development on those areas. Issues such as the increasing diversity of students, evidenced-based practices, leadership, accountability, increasing use of technologies, knowledge of diverse funding sources, and a need for marketing skills are a few of the pertinent issues that might guide practitioners as they select their continuing education.

References

Agresta, J. (2004). Professional Role Perceptions of School Social Workers, Psychologists, and Counselors. *Children & Schools, 26 (3)*, 151-163.

Allen-Meares, P. (2004). School social work: Historical development, influences, and practices. In P. Allen-Meares (Ed.), *Social Work Services in Schools* (pp. 23-51). Boston, MA: Pearson Education, Inc.

Allen-Meares, P. (in press). The future of school social work practice. In C. Franklin, M. B. Harris, and P. Allen-Meares (Eds.). *School Social Workers and Mental Health Therapist Resource Manual.* New York: Oxford University Press.

Altshuler, S. J., Kopels, S. (2003). Advocating in schools for children with disabilities: What's new with IDEA? *Social Work, 48 (3)*, 320-329.

Altshuler, S.J. (in press). Professional Requirements for School Social Work and Other School Mental Health. In C. Franklin, M. B. Harris, and P. Allen-Meares (Eds.). *School Social Workers and Mental Health Workers Resource Manual.* New York: Oxford University Press.

Archer, J. (2004). Struggling Schools Eyed For Vouchers, Funding. *Education Week, 23 (22)*, 12.

Bergren, M. D., Pohlman, K. (2004). Legal and ethical issues. Privacy questions from practicing school nurses. *Journal of School Nursing, 20(5)*, 296-301.

Blair, K. D. (1993). The Regular Education Initiative and School Social Workers. *Social Work in Education, 15 (4)*, 233-239.

Bowman, D. H. (2004). Latino Optimism High On Children's Schools, National Survey Finds. *Education Week, 23 (20)*, 6-7.

Brener, N.D., Martindale, J. & Weist, M.D. (2001). Mental health and social services: Results from the school health policies and programs study 2000. *Journal of School Health, 71*, (7), 305-312.

Caple, F. S., Salcido, R. M., Cecco, J. Engaging effectively with culturally diverse families and children. *Social Work in Education, 17 (3)*, 159 – 170.

Center for Health and Health Care in Schools. (2001). *Children's mental health needs, disparities and school-based services: A fact sheet.* Retrieved March 10, 2005 from http://www.healthinschools. org/cfk/mentfact.asp.

Center for Mental Health Services. (2000). *Mental Health, United States, 2000.* Manderscheid, R. W., and Henderson, M. J., eds. DHHS Pub No. (SMA) 01-3537. Retrieved March 13, 2005 from http://www.mentalhealth.org/publications/allpubs/SMA01-3537/chapter20.asp. Washington, DC: Supt. of Docs., U.S. Govt. Print. Off., 2001.

Dryfoos, J., and Maguire, S. (2002). *Inside full-service community schools.* Thousand Oaks, CA: Corwin Press.

Erlen, J. A. (2004). HIPAA-Clinical and ethical considerations for nurses. *Orthopaedic Nursing, 23 (6)*, 410-413.

Faircloth, S. C. (2004). Understanding the impact of U.S. federal education policies of the education of children and youth with disabilities. *International Studies in Educational Administration, 32 (2)*, 32-46.

Franklin, C. (1998). One hundred years of innovative ideas about practice. *Social Work in Education, 20(4)*, 211-218.

Franklin, C. (1999). Preparing for managed behavioral health care in children's services. *Social Work in Education, 21 (2)*, 67-70.

Franklin, C. (2004). Special Issue on Evidenced-Based Practice in Schools, *Children & Schools, 26 (2)*, NASW Press.

Franklin, C., Harris, M. B., and Allen-Meares, P. (Eds.). (in press). *School Social Workers and Mental Health Workers Resource Manual.* New York: Oxford University Press.

Franklin, C. & Hopson, L. (2004). Into the schools with evidenced-based practices. *Children & Schools. 67*, 67-70

Franklin C. & Hopson L. (2005). *New Challenges in Research: Translating Community-Based Practices into Evidence-Based Practices.* Paper presented at the Annual Program Meeting of the Council on Social Work Education, New York City, New York.

Giffords, E. D. (2003). Bringing technology to school: an online resource guide for the school social worker. *Journal of Technology in Human Services, 21(1/2)*, 57-83.

Goldhaber, D., Hannaway, J. (2004). Accountability with a Kicker: Observations on the Florida A+ Accountability Plan. *Phi Delta Kappan, 85 (8)*, 598-605.

Green, R. L.; Etheridge, C. P. (2001). Collaboration to establish standards and accountability: Les sons learned about systemic change. *Education, 121 (4)*, 821-828.

Hare, I. (1996). Regulating School Social Work Practice into the 21st Century. *Social Work in Education, 18 (4)*, 250-258.

Harris, M.B. & Franklin, C. (2004). Evidenced-Based life skills interventions for pregnant and parent adolescents in school settings. In A. R. Roberts & . K. R. Yeager (Eds.). *Evidenced-based Practice Manual: Research and outcome measures in health and human services (p.p. 312-322).* New York: Oxford University Press.

Hoagwood, K. (2003 Spring/Summer). Evidence-based practice in children's mental health services: What do we know? Why aren't we putting it to use? *Data Matters, 6*, 4-5.

Hoagwood, K., and Johnson, J. (2003). School psychology: A public health framework I. From evidence-based practices to evidence based policies. *Journal of School Psychology, 41,* 3-21.

Houston, P.D. (1999). A dirty dozen factors reshape our world. *The School Administrator, 56(5),* 45.

Jonson-Reid, M. (2000). Understanding confidentiality in school-based interagency projects. *Social Work in Education, 22 (1),* 33-45.

Kaufman, P., Chen, X., Choi, S.P., Peter, K., Ruddy, S.A., Miller, A.K., Fleury, J.K., Chandler, K.A., Planty, M.G., and Rand, M.R. (2001) *Indicators of school crime and safety: 2001.* Retrieved March 10, 2005 from http://nces.ed.gov. Washington DC: US Departments of Education and Justice.

Kirkwood, A.D. & Stan, B.H. (2004). Confronting Stigma in Idaho. Community-based Social Marketing Campaign.In K. Robinson (Ed.). *Advances in School-based mental health interventions (p.p.21-22).* Kingston, New Jersey, Civic Research Institute.

Lee, B. (2002). Let's Not Get Lost in the Standards! *Children & Schools, 24 (1),* 59-64.

Linn, R. L. (2000). Assessments and accountability. *Educational Researcher, 29(2),* 4-16.

McLaren, P. (1998). Revolutionary pedagogy in post revolutionary times: Rethinking the political economy or critical education. *Educational Theory, 48,* 431-462.

National Center for Education Statistics (2004) *Condition of Education.* Retrieved March 11, 2005 from http://nces.ed.gov//programs/coe/2004/section1/index.asp. Washington, D.C.: U.S. Department of Education Institute of Education Sciences.

NASW (2002). *NASW Standards for School Social Work Services.* Washington,

D.C.: NASW Press. Retrieved March 15, 2005 from http://www.naswdc.org/practice/default.asp.

Nowicki, L.B., Director of Professional Development, The University of Texas at Austin School of Social Work. Interview February, 2003.

Pahwa, B. A. (2003). Technology and school social work services: introducing technology in an alternative school. *Journal of Technology in Human Services, 21(1/2),* 139-60.

Poirier, J. M. and Osher, D. (in press). Understanding the new environment of public school funding: How student support services are funded. In C. Franklin, M. B. Harris, and P. Allen-Meares (Eds.). *School Social Workers and Mental Health Workers Resource Manual.* New York: Oxford University Press.

Raines, J.C. (2004). Evidence-based practice in school social work: A process in perspective. *Children & Schools, 26 (2),* 71-85.

RAND Health Research Highlights: Mental Health Case for Youth (2001). Retrieved March 10, 2005 from www.rand.org/publications/RB/RB4541.

Rhodes, L.A. (1999). Putting union and management out of business. *The School Administrator, 56(11),* 25-27.

Ross, S.K. (1999). The clinical nurses role in school health. *Clinical Nurse Specialist, 13,* 28-33.

Rothschild (1999). Carrots, sticks and promises: A conceptual framework for the management of public health and social issue behaviors. *Journal of Marketing, 63,* 24-37.

Romualdi, V. & Sandoval, J. (1995). Comprehensive school-linked services: Implications for school psychologists. *Psychology in the Schools, 32,* 306-317.

Schoenwald, S.K., and Hoagwood, K. (2001). Effectiveness, transportability, and dissemination of interventions: What matters when? *Psychiatric Services, 52(9),* 1190-1197.

School Social Work Association of America (2005). More people united for more changes in law. *E-bell*(www.sswaa.org), March 7, 2005.

Shaffer, G. L. (1996). School Social Worker Certification in a Climate of Educational Reform. *Social Work in Education, 18 (4),* 195-198.

Simpson, R., LaCava, P., Graner, P. S.(2004). The No Child Left Behind Act: Challenges and Implications for Educators. *Intervention in School & Clinic, 40 (2),* 67-75.

Smith, A.J. & Stowitschek, J.J. (1998). School-based inter-professional case management: A literature based rationale and a practitioner model. *Preventing School Failure, 42,* 61-65.

Streeter, C. L., and Franklin, C. (2002). Standards for School Social Work in the 21st Century. In A. Roberts & G. Greene (Eds.). *Social Workers Desk Reference.* New York: Oxford University Press.

Taylor, L. & Adelman, H.S.. (in press). Want to Work with Schools? What's Involved in Successful Linkages? In C. Franklin, M. B. Harris, and P. Allen-Meares (Eds.). *School Social Workers and Mental Health Workers Resource Manual.* New York: Oxford University Press.

Tharinger, D. (1995). Roles for psychologists in emerging models of school -related health and mental health services. *School Psychology Quarterly, 10,* 203-216.

Tower, K. (2000). Image Crisis: A Study of Attitudes about School Social Workers. *Social Work in Education, 22 (2),* 83-94.

UCLA School Mental Health Project (2003). *Youngsters' Mental Health and Psychosocial Problems: What Are the Data?* Los Angeles, CA: Center for Mental Health in Schools.

U.S. Department of Health and Human Services (2000). *Report of the surgeon general's conference on children's mental health: A national action agenda.* Washington, DC: Department of Health and Human Services.

Weist, M.D., Evans, S.W., & Lever, N. (2003). Advancing mental health practice and research in schools. M. Weist, S. Evans, and N. Lever (Eds.), *Handbook of school mental health: Advancing practice and research (pp. 1-8).* New York: Kluwer Academic/Plenum Publishers.

Author's Note

Address correspondence to Cynthia Franklin, Stiernberg/Spencer Family Professor in Mental Health, The University of Texas at Austin, School of Social Work, 1925 San Jacinto, Austin, Texas 78712. e-mail: CFranklin@mail.utexas.edu.

SOCIAL WORK IN HEALTH CARE IN 2025:
THE LANDSCAPE AND PATHS TO TRANSFORMATION

Kathleen Ell
Betsy Vourlekis

Abstract: *Social work in health care will, over the next 25 years, be transformed in concert with a complex and rapidly changing health care landscape and critical advances in behavioral and social science. Professional practice, research and education will be shaped by evolving patterns of health and illness, changing population demographics, developments in medicine, behavioral and social science, technological innovation and applications, and health care delivery cost and market forces. The profession's practice, research and educational communities must take actions now to guide the necessary transformation of social work in health care and, in the process, significantly influence the delivery of behavioral and psychosocial health care.*

Keywords: health; social work practice; psychosocial care

INTRODUCTION

Over the past decade, health care in the United States has been in rapid transition and frequently in the limelight. Public opinion polls routinely reflect the dramatic rise in consumer health-related expectations coupled with dissatisfaction and anxiety about the state of health care delivery. The media regularly highlights seemingly intractable health policy issues, including lack of insurance for over 40 million Americans, lack of a usual source of care for many, rapidly accelerating cost, a high rate of medical errors and lack of attention to the quality of care, population disparities in access to and receipt of care, and inefficient fragmentation of care across health care systems. In-depth government and private foundation reports document a range of specific problems and explore solutions (CDC, 2005; Kaiser Commission on Medicaid and the Uninsured, 2004; Kaiser/Hewitt, 2004). The Institute of Medicine has focused national attention on serious flaws in the quality of US health care calling for major organizational improvements (IOM, 2001). Among consumers, policy makers, and private industry leaders, policy debates center on the major issues of cost, financing, quality of care, and access to care.

The future of social work in health care will grow and change against this troubling landscape, shaped by evolving patterns of health and illness, changing population demographics, developments in medicine, behavioral and social science, technological innovation and applications, and health care delivery market forces (See Figure 1). The profession's practice, research and educational communities, however, must take actions now to guide the necessary transformation of social work in health care and, in the process, significantly influence the delivery of behavioral and psychosocial health care. Failure to take specific action will leave the transformation of social work and the delivery of behavioral and psychosocial health care to other health professions.

Kathleen Ell is Ernest P. Larson Professor of Health, Ethnicity, and Poverty at the School of Social Work, University of Southern California, Los Angeles, CA 90089-0411. Betsy Vourlekis is Emeritus Professor at the Department of Social Work at the University of Maryland Baltimore County, Baltimore, MD 21250.
Copyright © 2005 *Advances in Social Work* Vol. 6 No. 1 (Spring 2005), 182-192

FORCES OF CHANGE

Powerful forces of change characterize the health care landscape. In some cases these forces exert countervailing expectations and response, while in other cases the forces are synergistic. The imperative of cost reduction filters all forces of change in health care. Examples of counter-valence are particularly likely to revolve around the cost of health care, which for a time was increasing at a rate above the rate of inflation. In the ongoing debate on restructuring Medicare, countervailing forces are evident – greater consumer choice (with an as yet untested assumption of resulting improved access to care), but with increasing consumer out-of-pocket costs. Examples of more synergistic action are evident in the reciprocal effects of medical advances on lengthening life-span and the shift from acute episodic care to long-term management of chronic disease, which together increase consumer expectations of care.

Fig 1: A Changing Health Care Landscape and Trends In Psychosocial Care.

Forces (at times countervailing) of Change

- Advances in medical and genetic science
- Advances in behavioral and social science
- Changing consumer demographics, expectations, preferences, life-span and care needs
- Cost a primary concern
- Market forces - shifting and debated financing - e.g., employers to employees, away from and toward government, basic and limited vs inclusive care
- Changing health care organizational systems
- Monitoring quality of care and access to and disparities in care across

Key Trends in Health Care Delivery

- From individual physician practice to new organizational systems
- Ambulatory care, conveniently located care systems (malls, workplace, schools)
- Growth of non-physician health care providers, e.g., nurse, practitioners, pharmacists
- From single providers to health care teams of providers, e.g., parallel, consultative, collaborative, coordinated, multidisciplinary, interdisciplinary and integrative care models
- Increasing patient/family centered care and emphasis on self-care management/caregiving
- Dissemination of evidence-based care guidelines and outcome monitoring
- Provider quality monitoring, reporting and accountability
- Applications of information technology (IT) - e.g., telecare, patient-provider communication, medical adherence tracking

A critical element in the forces for change is the dramatic change in the demographics of the U.S. population. Over the next 25 years, the nation will experience increases in the number of people who are older (with likely unbalanced gender distribution), who belong to an ethnic minority group, have disabilities and chronic disease, who live in poverty or endure significant periods of marginal economic stability (with the risk of unstable access to health care), and who self-identify as lesbian, gay, bisexual, or transgendered (Yali & Revenson, 2004).

According to the 2000 census, 25-30% of the U.S. population self-identified as a member of an ethnic or racial minority group (U.S. Bureau of the Census). Given that this figure is widely expected to continue to grow and to affect social and racial disparities in health, there will be ongoing need for health care providers to become culturally competent and for health care researchers to study complex contexts (i.e., multi-level systems) of health, illness and health care delivery to identify problems and solutions (Yali & Revenson, 2004).

Medical breakthroughs are improving preventive care, early detection of health risk and disease, and survival from life-threatening illness and trauma. As a result, the average life-span and the numbers of people living longer with chronic illnesses and disabilities is rising as is the cost of health care. However, the latest research takes years to reach medical practices. The uncovering of uneven quality of care across health systems, geographic regions, individual providers and patient demographic groups has spurred the development of quality improvement approaches. Advances in information technology (IT) with the potential to improve the quality of care by empowering patients and health care providers in making choices and managing care is yet to be widely used or tested. Recent cost savings analyses indicate that fully implemented electronic health care information exchange and interoperability would yield a net value of $77.8 billion per year (Walker, Pan, Johnston, Adler-Milstein, Bates & Middleton, 2005).

In recent years, evidence based medicine (EBM) has been widely elevated to something approximating a new paradigm (Timmermans & Mauck, 2005). Accompanying the EBM movement are new government and private institutions concerned with EBM, an increase in randomized controlled trials in medicine and health care research, an increase in care plans, critical care paths and outcomes research, the development of EBM medical education curricula, and a striking array of clinical practice guidelines (leading to questions about their quality) (Timmermans & Mauck, 2005).

KEY TRENDS IN HEALTH CARE DELIVERY

Response to cost, medical advances and consumer challenges are reflected in current trends and evolving changes in health care delivery. This era of rapid and dramatic change might be described as a very large, somewhat incoherent, national experiment with a laundry list of specific and sometimes competing aims, research questions and hypotheses, using an array of structured, pseudo structured and unstructured research designs.

Individual physician practices are evolving into new organizational systems such as independent physician associations, ambulatory care is replacing hospital based care and conveniently located care systems are emerging in local neighborhoods, shopping malls, workplaces and schools. The number of licensed non-physician health care providers is growing (e.g., physician assistants, advanced nurse practitioners, pharmacists, nutritionists, naturopathics, physical therapists, chiropractors (Carlson, 1999). Collaborative, integrated and interdisciplinary health care teams are being tested to address specific patient population needs and to reduce fragmented care (Cashman, Reidy, Cody & Lemay, 2003; Gross, Temkin-Greener, Kunitz & Mukamel, 2004). The proliferation of EBM guidelines include those focused on individual physician decision-making, but increasingly apply to all members of clinical teams (Eddy, 2005).

Increasingly grounded in biopsychosocial evidence and clinical effectiveness trials, quality of care improvements include prevention and health promotion and interdisciplinary disease or case management intervention models (Nasmith, Coté, Cox, Inkell, Rubenstein, Jiminez, 2004; Schaefer & Davis, 2004; Shojania & Grimshaw, 2005; Smith, Orleans & Jenkins, 2005; Suls & Rothman, 2005). Telecare, computer and internet technologies are aimed at improving information transfer, patient/provider and provider/provider communication and tracking care management and patient medical adherence (Garrison, Bernard, Rasmussen, 2002). While cost reduction goals influence health insurance coverage, these decisions are beginning to confront scientific evidence (Gelijns, Brown, Magnell, Ronchi & Moskowitz, 2005). Notably, a recent analysis of Medicare's national coverage decisions for new medical technologies found that coverage determinations were generally consistent with the strength of the evidence (Neumann, Divi, Beinfeld, Levine, Keenan, Halpern, et al., 2005). Patients and family members are increasingly expected to assume more active and extensive self-management and caregiving roles, however, family caregiving incurs human and financial cost that is yet to be factored into overall health care cost estimates.

TRENDS IN THE DELIVERY OF BEHAVIORAL AND PSYCHOSOCIAL CARE

Behavioral and psychosocial care interventions and services have assumed increasingly important roles in the delivery of health care (Borrell-Carrió, Suchman & Epstein, 2004; Nicassio, Meyerowitz & Kerns, 2004). Preventive screening and follow-up and chronic disease management intervention models are multifaceted and routinely incorporate health education, behavioral interventions, interactive case/care management components and patient empowering self-management interventions.

A dramatic shift is occurring wherein primary care physicians and nurses are beginning to provide mental health screening, counseling and pharmacotherapy. Of particular interest are collaborative and integrated care models for depression (in which specialized clinical specialist social workers or nurses provide psychotherapy, medication management, and adherence follow-up) (Dietrich, Oxman, Williams, Kroenke, Schulberg, Bruce, et al., 2004; Gallo, Zubritsky, Maxwell, Nazar, Bogner, Quijano, et al., 2004)), but also for other psychiatric disorders (Bartels, Coakley, Zubritsky, Ware, Miles, Arean, et al., 2004; Felker, Barnes, Greenberg, Chaney, Shores, Gillespie-Gately, et al., 2004).

Professional organizations and government have developed an array of specific practice guidelines that are available on the web and testing of methods to improve implementation of these guidelines in real world practice is growing. A variety of organized monitoring of quality of care programs has been developed in recent years and there is a strong movement to make these reports and data readily available to consumers.

TRANSFORMING SOCIAL WORK PRACTICE AND PRACTITIONERS:
SERVICE SYSTEM, RESEARCH AND EDUCATION ROLES

How will the changing health care landscape shape the future of social work practice, research and education? What is easiest to predict is that transformations of social work and all other health professions will involve the need to effectively address seemingly countervailing forces. For example, cost-conscious/cost-driven administration and policies in proliferating health care settings will interact with the burgeoning need for psychosocial services of an aging and racially/ethnically diverse population with a significant poverty rate. The increased recognition of social/behavioral/environmental components of illnesses and adherence to their treatment will lead to further integration of health and mental health care, interacting both with cost concerns and other psychosocial specialties' (e.g., nursing and psychology) turf claims. All of these forces will interact with increased consumer demand for quality care and organizational demand for evidence-based practice, accountability, and consumer driven cost utility (comparing the monetary value of resources used with health effects such as health-related quality-of-life measures for a defined population) interventions and services (Tovian, 2004).

Further challenging the profession, the historical tensions inherent to social work practice as a part of health care will remain. These include work within host settings where adequate understanding of the social work role and function cannot be assumed; the need to deploy with maximum efficiency a costly professional service and routinely demonstrate its value added; and potential for competition and conflict with nursing and other professionals that can cloud consideration of the real needs of patients and systems. On the other hand, the increased emphasis within medicine on the mind-body synthesis in the health/illness paradigm and policy attention at the national level to health disparities will provide an increasingly strong platform of legitimacy for the psychosocial professional as a member of the health care team. The usefulness of social work's multi-system perspective on problems in health and illness will only continue to grow, with ample opportunities available.

It is unlikely, however, that these opportunities will carry the restricted and specific label "social work." As has long been the case, needs and opportunities within health care will outstrip the social work profession's ability to educate and deploy sufficient person power to create "ownership" of most valued roles and functions. Thus cooperative/collaborative service, educational and research models with nursing and other non-physician and physician providers will be needed (Claiborne & Vandenburgh, 2001; Simpson, 1999).

A Look at Social Work Practice

Key changes are likely to characterize social work practice in the future. Primary among them is the reliance on "sole position" social workers, capable of "self-directed practice" (Volland, Berkman, Phillips & Stein, 2003) as cost constraints continue to eliminate social work administrative and support structures in settings where once they existed, and limit their development in new settings. The independent entrepreneurial "private practice" model of social work, insofar as it requires skills in accountability, autonomous definition and negotiation of role and function, administrative expertise, and a keen eye for shifting financial realities and incentives will be a useful model for social work health care practitioners, often working as the sole social work provider in a larger system or a disease management team. Cost and efficiency considerations will also dictate that these practitioners, whether in nursing homes, primary care clinics, or down-sized hospitals, will need well-honed consultative and supervisory skills so that they can oversee (rather than directly provide) many types of psychosocial services that can be provided effectively by lesser trained (and cheaper) personnel. Highly trained social workers will likely limit their direct practice to a small number of special needs patients and/or highest skill functions.

The increasing integration of mental health within primary care medical settings across the age continuum will be a major trend leading to the transformation of social work practice, as the distinctions between health and mental health social work practice and education blur. Basic clinical mental health assessment, engagement, crisis management, resource negotiation, referral and brief treatment skills will be required for all health direct practitioners. Expertise in mental health, including serious and persistent mental illness, will not be confined to a specialty mental health system. For example, nursing homes today serve as the primary provider of mental health services for the elderly population (Shea, Russo & Smyer, 2000). The staff social worker must be able to provide accurate initial assessment for mental illness, with referral and follow-up.

The demands of EBP will challenge social work education, practice and research in a number of mutually influencing ways, constantly interacting with cost concerns. A comprehensive understanding of the needs of EBP will lead to development and implementation of evidence-based practical program/practice management tools and approaches on the one hand, and on the other social work intervention research that demonstrates the effectiveness and value added of practice interventions to achieve desired health and quality of life outcomes.

Social work practitioners will need to have and use systematic quality management tools and processes to monitor and improve their social work services at the individual case, aggregate case, and facility-wide levels. The essential similarity of key management skills, including planning, organizing, coordinating, and monitoring outcomes for successful direct practice helping as well as system accountability will be explicated in professional education and training (Veeder and Dalgin, 2004).

As sole providers in many settings, direct practitioners will require basic expertise and familiarity with fundamentals of a comprehensive evidence-based practice. Key aspects of evidence-based practice will include the data/information on which to base decisions concerning WHO gets HOW MUCH of WHAT for WHICH problems to effectively achieve certain OUTCOMES, including an efficient allocation of scarce resources. Social workers will need to have expertise in information technologies for documenting, monitoring and evaluating their practice, and will use this expertise in a variety of clinical and services applications.

As a costly service, social work in health care settings will need to carefully target, based on evidence, those health care consumers potentially at highest psychosocial risk and level of need, regardless of setting. Social work's priority clients in health care will be those individuals and their families who are living in poverty, members of minority groups, and medically under-served, regardless of age. Other priority target groups are people with co-existing mental illness and/or substance abuse, those with dysfunctional, extremely limited, or non-existent social support systems, and individuals at points of transition, including discharge, admission to a nursing home, and at the end of life.

Actual assessment of individual patient psychosocial risk and needs will make more use of standardized tools or elements of standardized tools to improve accuracy and to assist in prioritizing goals. Reliable standardized instruments, normed for different populations and conditions, will be available for mental and emotional health, social support, self-efficacy to handle the health problem, patient's knowledge, attitude and beliefs concerning the health problem and treatment, and perceived and actual system and resource barriers.

Social work interventions will be based on evidence-based guidelines or flexible "packages" of such guidelines that are tailored to individual circumstances. Increasingly, evidence-based guidelines are likely to be implemented using a multifaceted approach that seeks input from multiple stakeholders – e.g., multiple members of health care teams, patients and families, and health care administrators (Timmermans & Mauck, 2005). Overarching psychosocial service functions, such as case/care management, will be increasingly needed as chronic disease management assumes growing importance in health care delivery. These functions, when necessary, will be integrated interventions that bundle proven effective strategies to influence multiple system levels; for example, simultaneous use of a patient-empowerment strategy, mediation with another health care provider, and new resource acquisition to achieve results (Vourlekis & Ell, 2004).

Cost constraints and quality practice management will call for demonstrated correctness and efficiency in the provision of social work services. Explicit social work intervention protocols for different psychosocial care levels will guide the intensity (amount or "dosage") of care as well as the nature and required provider skill level of different care routines, once psychosocial assessment has detailed patient and family circumstances.

Establishing the efficacy of a variety of psychosocial interventions will be the task of the social work research establishment, as discussed below. However, demonstrating actual links at a given facility between psychosocial care processes and a variety of outcomes will be an important component of practice and program management, requiring use of practitioner-friendly evaluation tools. These tools will need to be linked conceptually and operationally to facility level, regulatory, and accreditation quality improvement/monitoring processes of overall care provision. Examples of such links could be that case management processes lead to improved facility treatment adherence rates; or that conflict resolution interventions with family members of nursing home residents lead to fewer complaints to corporate headquarters.

The demographics discussed earlier carry the obvious imperative of culturally competent social work practice in health care, as in every other field. While the knowledge, skills and attitudes of this practice will not differ by field, the manifestations of culturally relevant influences will. Patient and family culturally mediated beliefs, attitudes and behaviors in relation to health and illness are potentially potent influences on every aspect of the process of health care. Difference in culture between patients and providers (for example, the prevalence of ethnic minority care staff in nursing homes where the majority of residents are white women; and the growing diversity of the health professional workforce itself) will grow even more pronounced. These realities will call for practitioners' ability to modify and tailor evidence-based interventions, such as cognitively based treatment, for an ethnically diverse clientele, but also the ability to recognize and mediate exchanges and communications troubled by cultural differences for the health care team or facility as a whole.

A Snapshot of Social Work Research

In responding to the challenges in health care, social work research must dramatically accelerate its focus on intervention studies, including comparing interventions with different intensity and diverse team membership and interventions targeted for specific patient populations (Reid, Davis Kenaley, & Colvin, 2004). The development of a strong evidence base for practice in health care will take decades and will require using more advanced research designs, larger sample sizes, and clearly specified interventions (Helfand, 2005; Proctor, 2004). Given the multidisciplinary nature of health care, contributions of social work to intervention research will inevitably require that social workers lead and participate on interdisciplinary research teams. Social work researchers must also become expert in designing intervention studies with attention to real world practice needs (as in adapting psychotherapy models for health care systems and populations) and participate in dissemination and implementation studies. Social work researchers must become expert in conducting both efficacy and effectiveness intervention studies and in evaluating the cost-utility of specified interventions. The latter particularly represents an area of research that is relatively new to social work and will require collaborating with health economist researchers (Kaplan & Groesel, 2005).

Given the likely ongoing disparities in care across populations, social workers will need to design and evaluate interventions to eliminate disparities (Cooper, Hill & Powe, 2002). Research will also need to uncover the critical and minimal elements in cultural competency in diverse contexts (Yali & Revenson, 2004).

The Role of Social Work Education

The practitioner for 2025 will require an education that provides a roadmap to specialized practice that may look very different than what is commonly offered in many programs today. For example, mental health and gerontological competencies will be fundamental to any practitioner working in health care. Familiarity with emerging brain-behavior connections and the operations of both legal and illegal drugs will be essential content, while the specifics of individual diseases, their symptoms, treatments and side effects, and long-term course and management will need to be learned in field practicum or on-the-job. Social workers, who will be practicing independently on health care teams, will require confidence in their knowledge of specifics of medical care. Realistically, social work education can provide the parameters and resources for such expertise, but not the content except in the form of an exemplar.

In addition to teaching evidence-based practice (Howard, McMillen & Pollio, 2003), it will be necessary to prepare students for self-directed and population specific practice

(Volland, Berkman, Phillips, & Stein, 2003; Volland & Berkman, 2004). It is critically important to increase gerontological competence for health care practice (Rosen, Zlotnik, & Singer, 2002). Clinical skill in structured mental health therapies such as Cognitive Behavioral Treatment and Problem Solving Therapy adapted for primary and specialty health care, for diverse patient populations, and for collaborative care program models will be required elements of master's education.

Curriculum on health care delivery models and on the knowledge and skill base of a range of health care professions will also be needed to prepare practitioners for integrative team practice. It is also likely that social work education will test new hybrid education models such as two innovative programs at the University of Southern California School of Social Work—the social work-nurse practitioner specialization under development and a randomized pilot test of a program in which social work graduate students will provide counseling, while students from the dental school provide oral health education designed to meet the needs of those with developmental disabilities and their families. New dual degree programs are likely to emerge and field placements will expand into the array of new health care settings.

CONCLUSION

Behavioral and psychosocial health care over the next 25 years will undoubtedly be characterized by continued advances in behavioral and social science, in evidence of the cost-utility of interventions and services, and in increasing consumer and policymaker demand for these services. The likely advances will present both challenges and opportunities and will be inevitably and inextricably linked to the ongoing external forces described above as well as new forces – e.g., the area of biomedical ethics. However, equally important in determining whether and in what ways social work in health care is transformed will be the direct actions begun now by the social work practice, research and education communities.

References

Bartels, S.J., Coakley, E.H., Zubritsky, C., Ware, J.H., Miles, K.M., Areán, P.A., et al. (2004). Improving Access to Geriatric Mental Health Services: A Randomized Trial Comparing Treatment Engagement with Integrated Versus Enhanced Referral Care for Depression, Anxiety, and At-Risk Alcohol Use. *American Journal of Psychiatry, 161*, 1455-1462.

Borrell-Carrió, F., Suchman, A.L., & Epstein, R.M. (2004). The Biopsychosocial Model 25 Years Later: Principles, Practice, and Scientific Inquiry. *Annals of Family Medicine, 2*, 576-582.

Carlson, B. (1999). The New Health Care Team. *The Physician Executive*, 67-95.

Cashman, S.B., Reidy, P., Cody, K., & Lemay, C. (2004). Developing and measuring progress toward collaborative, integrated, interdisciplinary health care teams. *Journal of Interprofessional Care, 18*, 183-196.

Centers for Disease Control and Prevention. (2005). Health disparities experienced by Black or African Americans – United States. *MMWR, 54*, 1-3.

Claiborne, N.C., & Vandenburgh, H. (2001). Social Workers' Role in Disease Management. *Health and Social Work, 26, 217-225.*

Cooper, L.A., Hill, M.N., & Powe, N.R. (2002). Designing and evaluating interventions to eliminate racial and ethnic disparities in health care. *Journal of General Internal Medicine, 17*, 477-486.

Dietrich, A.J., Oxman, T.E., Williams Jr., J.W., Kroenke, K.H., Schulberg, C., Bruce, M., & Barry, S.L. (2004). Going to scale: re-engineering systems for primary care treatment of depression. *Annals of Family Medicine, 2*, 301-304.

Eddy, D.M. (2005). Evidence-Based Medicine: A Unified Approach. *Health Affairs, 24*, 9-17.

Felker, B.L., Barnes, R.F., Greenberg, D.M., Chaney, E.F., Shores, M.M., Gillespie-Gateley, L., et al. (2004). Preliminary Outcomes From and Integrated Mental Health Primary Care Team. *Psychiatric Services, 55*, 442-444.

Gallo, J.J., Zubritsky, C., Maxwell, J., Nazar, M., Bogner, H.R., Quijano, L.M., et al. (2004). The Prism-E Investigators. Primary Care Clinicians Evaluate Integrated and Referral Models of Behavioral Health Care For Older Adults: Results From a Multisite Effectiveness Trial (PRISM-E). *Annals of Family Medicine, 2*, 305-309.

Garrison, G., Bernard, M., Rasmussen, N. (2002). 21st century health care: the effect of computer use by physicians on patient satisfaction at a family medicine clinic. *Family Medicine, 34*, 362-8.

Gelijns, A.C., Brown, L.D., Magnell, C., Ronchi, E., & Moskowitz, A.J. (2005). Evidence, Politics, and Technological Change. *Health Affairs, 24*, 29-40.

Gross, D., Temkin-Greener, Hl, Kunitz, S., & Mukamel, D. (2004). The growing pains of integrated health care for the elderly: Lessons from the Expansion of PACE. *The Milbank Quarterly, 82, 257-282*.

Helfand, M. (2005). Using Evidence Reports: Progress and Challenges in Evidence-Based Decision Making. *Health Affairs, 24*, 123-127.

Henry J. Kaiser Family Foundation & Hewitt Associates. (2004). Current Trends and Future Outlook for Retiree Health Benefits: Findings form the Kaiser/Hewitt 2004 Survey on Retiree Health Benefits.

Howard, M.O., McMillen, C.J., & Pollio, D.E. (2003). Teaching Evidence-based Practice: Towards a New Paradigm for Social Work Education. *Research on Social Work Practice, 13*, 234-259.

Institute of Medicine (2001). *Crossing the Quality Chasm: A New Health System for the 21st Century*. Washington, DC: Institute of Medicine.

Kaiser Commission on Medicaid and the Uninsured. (2004). T*he Economic Downturn and Changes in Health Insurance Coverage, 2000-2003*. The Henry J Kaiser Family Foundation, Washington, DC.

Kaplan, R.M., & Groessl, E.J. (2002). Applications of Cost-Effectiveness Methodologies in Behavioral Medicine. *Journal of Consulting and Clinical Psychology, 70*, 482-493.

Nasmith, L., Cote, B., Cox, J., Inkell, D., Rubenstein, H., Jimenez, V., et al., (2004). The challenge of promoting integration: conceptualization, implementation, and assessment of a pilot care delivery model for patients with type 2 diabetes. *Family Medicine. 36,:40-5.*

Neumann, P.J., Divi, N., Beinfeld, M.T., Levine, B., Keenan, P.S., Halpern, E.F. et al. (2005). Medicare's National Coverage Decisions, 1999-2003: Quality of Evidence and Review Times. *Health Affairs, 24*, 243-254.

Nicassio, P.M., Meyerowitz, B.E., & Kerns, R.D. (2004). The Future of Health Psychology Interventions. *Health Psychology, 23*, 132-137.

Proctor, E.K. (2004). The search for social work treatments of choice: What intervention work better than others? *Social Work Research, 28*, 67-69.

Reid, W.J., Davis Kenaley, B., & Colvin, J. (2004). Do some interventions work better than others?

A review of comparative social work experiments. *Social Work Research, 28,* 71-81.

Rosen, A.L., Zlotnik, J.L., & Singer, T. (2002). Basic gerontological competence for all social workers: The need to "Gerontologize" social work education. *Journal of Gerontological Social Work, 39,* 25-36.

Schaefer, J. & Davis, C. (2004). Case management and the Chronic Care Model: A multidisciplinary role. *Case Management, 9, 96-103.*

Shea, D.G., Russo, P.A., & Smyer, M.A. (2000). Use of mental health services by persons with a mental illness in nursing facilities: Initial impacts of OBRA 87. *Journal of Aging and Health, 12,* 560-578.

Shojania, K.G., & Grinshaw, J.M. (2005). Evidence-Based Quality Improvement: The State of the Science. *Health Affairs, 24,* 138-150.

Simpson, R.L. (1999). Toward a New Millennium: Outlook and Obligations for 21st Century Health Care Technology. *Nursing Administration Quarterly, 24,* 94-97.

Smith, T.W., Orleans, C.T., & Jenkins, C.D. (2004). Prevention and Health Promotion: Decades of Progress, New Challenges, and an Emerging Agenda. *Health Psychology, 23,* 126-131.

Suls, J., & Rothman, A. (2004). Evolution of the Biopsychosocial Model: Prospects and Challenges for Health Psychology. *Health Psychology, 23,* 119-125.

Timmermans, S., & Mauck, A. (2005). The Promise and Pitfalls of Evidence-Based Medicine. *Health Affairs, 24,* 18-28.

Tovian, S. M. (2004). Health services and health care economics: the health psychology marketplace. *Health Psychology, 23,* 138-141.

U.S. Census Bureau. http://factfinder.census.gov

Veeder, N.W., & Dalgin, R.E. (2004). Social work as management: A retrospective study of 245 hospital care management practice outcomes. *Journal of Social Service Research, 31,* 33-57.

Volland, P.J., & Berkman, B. (2004). Educating social workers to meet the challenge of an aging urban population: a promising model. *Academic Medicine, 79,* 1192-7.

Volland, P.J., Berkman, B., Phillips, M., & Stein, G. (2003). Social work education for health care: addressing practice competencies. *Social Work in Health Care. 37,* 1-17.

Vourlekis, B., & Ell, K. (2004). "Best Practice Case Management for Improved Medical Adherence" presented at the Fourth International Health and Mental Health Congress, Quebec City, Canada, May 23-27.

Walker, J., Pan, E., Johnston, D., Adler-Milstein, J., Bates, D.W., & Middleton, B. (2005). The Value of Health Care Information Exchange and Interoperability. *Health Affairs, 24,* W5-10 – W5-18.

Yali, A.M., & Revenson, T.A. (2004). How Changes in Population Demographics Will Impact Health Psychology: Incorporating a Broader Notion of Cultural Competence Into the Field. *Health Psychology, 23,* 147-155.

Author's Note

Address correspondence to Kathleen Ell, DSW, Ernest P. Larson Professor of Health, Ethnicity, and Poverty, School of Social Work, University of Southern California, University Park, Los Angeles, CA 90089-0411. e-mail: ell@usc.edu.

MENTAL HEALTH SERVICES IN THE 21ST CENTURY:
THE ECONOMICS AND PRACTICE CHALLENGES
ON THE ROAD TO RECOVERY

W. Patrick Sullivan

Abstract: *Since the program was initiated in 1963, little has been stable in Community Mental Health. Not only has this important quasi-public utility fought for survival, but the primary models and philosophies that shape the mission and delivery of services have undergone cycles of reform. There is much to be optimistic about in the mental health treatment arena, particularly in services focused on those with most challenging and debilitating conditions. However, all is not well. As states began to deemphasize institutional care and incrementally build a community infrastructure to care for those most in need, savvy administrators relied less on internal fiscal resources, and more on programs such as Medicaid to accomplish their agendas. Faced with budgetary crises in general, and in the Medicaid program specifically, many states are increasingly forced to consider processes to restrict eligibility, place limits on benefit packages, and cut rates to service providers. Indeed the worlds of economics, policy, and practice are on a collision course. This article explores some of the challenges of providing mental health care in the 21st century, and the continuing quest to address fiscal realities while offering high quality services.*

Keywords: Mental Health, Medicaid, Managed Care, Mental Health Policy

INTRODUCTION

A generation of Americans cannot imagine a world void of Community Mental Health Centers. The availability and accessibility of mental health services, along with a reduction in the stigma associated with seeking care, has resulted in an increased demand from the general population that has stretched the capacity of vendors, and left practitioners gasping for air (Gumz, 2004). Despite the perception that Community Mental Health Centers are a permanent fixture on the healthcare landscape, in reality, the turbulent fiscal and policy context in which they operate, keeps them in a constant state of peril. Indeed, the survival of the community mental health system as we know it remains uncertain.

Since the program was initiated in 1963, little has been stable in Community Mental Health. Not only has this important quasi-public utility fought for survival, but the primary models and philosophies that shape the mission and delivery of services have undergone cycles of reform (Mechanic, 1999; Mechanic, 1998; Foley & Sharfstein, 1983). Indeed, as Mechanic (1998) notes, "these changes often have been more a response to changes in financial structures, social ideologies, and new technologies than they have been to internal practices in the mental health sector itself" (p. 83-84).

Today, there is much to be optimistic about in the mental health treatment arena, particularly in services focused on those with most challenging and debilitating condi-

W. Patrick Sullivan is Professor in the School of Social Work at Indiana University, Indianapolis 46202-5156.
Copyright © 2005 *Advances in Social Work* Vol. 6 No. 1 (Spring 2005), 193-201

tions. Pharmacological breakthroughs continue to offer new hope to those who gained little benefit from an older generation of psychotropic medications, and worse, suffered crippling side effects from an intervention intended to offer relief (Pomerantz, 2001). Rebounding from harsh criticism from all fronts, the last quarter century has seen dramatic improvements in the quantity and quality of community-based services intended to address the psychosocial needs of consumers trying to find their way in a post-institutional world (Mechanic & Bilder, 2004). Furthermore, the concept of recovery, once viewed as wishful thinking at best, has been firmly embraced by consumers, and continues to inform providers and policymakers (Anthony, 1993; Sullivan, 1994).

However, all is not well. The newer psychotropic medications, while effective, are expensive. Given the vast numbers of Americans who are uninsured or underinsured, and resurgent increases in healthcare costs again garnering headlines, difficult choices loom ahead (Zuvekas, 2005). As states began to deemphasize institutional care and incrementally build a community infrastructure to care for those most in need, savvy administrators relied less on internal fiscal resources, and more on programs such as Medicaid to accomplish their agendas. Faced with budgetary crises in general, and in the Medicaid program specifically, many states are increasingly forced to consider processes to restrict eligibility, place limits on benefit packages, and cut rates to service providers (Boyd, 2003). Attempts to maximize Medicaid and Medicare reimbursements, seemingly a wise strategy, can also create difficulties. When organizational behavior is driven solely by available fiscal streams, the range of services offered, as well as the breadth of populations served narrows. Moreover, when an increased percentage of an operating budget is dedicated to providing the match needed to leverage Medicaid, the inherent flexibility of providers is hindered. In turn, chasing the dollar may alter the broad-based mission that has characterized Community Mental Health (Frank, Goldman, & Hogan, 2003). Finally, as the direct federal role in mental health services has been primarily limited to a relatively small block grant to the states, and as providers have depended on Medicaid, Medicare, and private sources to remain afloat, the policy role of State mental health authorities has been reduced (Buck, 2003).

While some professionals would choose to remain blissfully ignorant of these developments, they have a profound impact on how and what kinds of services will be offered, and who will receive them. While veteran practitioners may long for days gone by, as Mechanic (1998) notes, "payment for anything professionals want to do, the long-standing traditional pattern, is no longer realistic and never was ideal" (p. 83). In short, economic realties shape practice, an implicit reality that became increasingly explicit in the early days of managed care. The challenge is to align policy, fiscal, and practice frameworks to support a vibrant and inspirational vision for mental health services. As we enter the 21st century the concept of recovery still offers a compelling vision for our work. However, a disturbing question lurks in the background: Can we continue to find a way to fund the community mental health mission?

THE EVOLUTION OF COMMUNITY MENTAL HEALTH

The birth of the Community Mental Health movement can be traced back to the period immediately following World War II. It is the story of dedicated reformers who hoped to build on the experience they had gathered from the field of battle, and previous work in small local clinics that brought mental health services to places where none had existed previously (Foley & Sharfstein, 1983). Drawing from a public health model, the plan was to develop a network of community based services across the country that not only offered treatment, but also provided consultation and education services and vigorously engaged in prevention (Joint Commission on Mental Illness and Health, 1961).

Ironically, it was the American Medical Association (AMA) who objected loudly to the idea of a nationwide system of Community Mental Health. However, the AMA's energies were diverted by another policy development they considered even more threatening: Medicaid and Medicare. The enactment of these social insurance programs provided the safety net that allowed many psychiatric patients to move from the institution to the community. Through Medicaid and Medicare, mental health authorities, burdened by the high cost of State psychiatric hospitals, now had a method to reduce the census of such facilities. This movement fit hand in glove with a range of important legal decisions that protected the rights of consumers, and made it increasingly difficult to institutionalize people against their will (Foley & Sharfstein, 1983).

In the end, however, Community Mental Health Centers were ill prepared to serve people with the most serious mental health challenges, and simultaneously, the level of sophistication of rehabilitation services, and the limits of primary prevention, was exposed. Faced with a burgeoning crisis and growing criticism, Community Mental Health Centers redoubled their effort to develop an array of services directed to a population then referred to as the chronically mentally ill.

By the late 1970's, the National Institute of Mental Health proffered a new model of care known as the Community Support Program (Turner & TenHoor, 1978). Hogan (1999) suggests, that the community support model, "was the first reform model that viewed serious mental illness as a long term disability requiring both rehabilitation and treatment, rather than a problem that could be avoided by providing only short term acute treatment" (p.107). In response, wide ranging and specialized services directed to those now commonly deemed the seriously and persistently ill have been developed, with case management, housing, and vocational programs in the forefront. State mental health authorities, as always confronted with greater demand for services than were available, increasingly directed their limited funds to those in greatest need by virtue of their illness and poverty.

While no one is prepared to claim victory, it does appear that money and services are being directed to the intended target population, as those in greatest need currently are enjoying greater access to specialty mental health services than ever before (Mechanic & Bilder, 2004). The development of these specialized services, psychopharmacological breakthroughs, the work of the family and consumer movement, as well as the existence of funding streams to support psychosocial interventions, have helped foster a more hopeful and purposeful treatment system.

However, when attention is directed to certain subpopulations, others are left behind. As Mechanic and Bilder (2004) suggest, "many people who need treatment still do not receive it, and most treatment fails to meet reasonable evidence-based standards of care"

(p. 86). In an effort to assess the current state of mental health services, and determine what can be done to improve them, on April 29, 2002 President George W. Bush unveiled the New Freedom Commission, the first presidential mental health commission since the Carter administration (Hogan, 2003). Reflecting on his role as chair of the commission, Michael Hogan noted:

> The one big idea – the headline, if you will in the report to the President is that recovery is possible for anybody, But the system is too fragmented, and the services that are available are inadequate and not of high enough quality to allow recovery to be a realistic promise for many people. So the commission's vision statement for future mental health care is that recovery should be expected because of the accessibility and quality of services that are provided. (Cunningham, 2003, p. 447)

FUTURE OPPORTUNITIES/FUTURE THREATS

As health care costs grew exponentially during the 1990's, managed care programs dramatically altered the delivery of medical services in America. Historically, the unpredictability of mental illness, the lack of specificity in the diagnosis and assessment process, and the relative absence of generally accepted treatment protocols made many proprietary vendors wary of entering the behavioral healthcare market. Although there were, and continue to be some efforts to integrate behavioral health services with primary health care, more often, mental health and substance abuse services have been treated separately, or in the common nomenclature "carved out".

However, the new world of managed care impacted the organization and delivery of behavioral health care. Over a decade ago, Jacobs and Moxley (1993) implored mental health programs to prepare for managed care by adopting a business mindset. Indeed, before long new worlds of management information systems, actuarial analysis, productivity requirements, credentialing, and accreditation was upon us. On the positive side of the ledger, the pressures of managed care have forced provider organizations to be clearer about their processes and outcomes, in a continued effort to improve the quality of care, and to be accountable to the wide range of funding sources that are vital to survival. Given the current state of the economy, the rising costs of Medicaid and Medicare, and the state of individual and employer-based insurance coverage, the pressures for improved quality and greater accountability are not likely to abate. The vexing dilemma facing administrators and practitioners is how to generate needed funds, provide comprehensive services at high quality, and meet accountability requirements?

Drawing from 30 years as a Community Mental Health director, Robert Dunbar (personal communication, October 11, 2004) surmises that:

> I believe that effective Community Mental Health Center directors, and other behavioral health leaders, will need to position their organization to effectively implement evolving evidence based treatments, with very little up front financial support, will need to assess the effectiveness of services by identification and tracking of key performance indicators, will need to employ an increasing diverse and culturally competent staff despite a shortage of professionals seeking a career in behavioral health, will need to integrate services particularly with corrections and physical healthcare in part as a

> means of further revenue diversification, and will continue to seek new and diverse means of funding, particularly of a social enterprise nature. .... The future of community mental health is very uncertain.

All conversations with leaders in mental health begin and end with concerns about funding. The potential crisis in Medicaid is particularly nettlesome, as this one program serves as the foundation for community-based care. Buck (2003) notes, that by 2002, "Medicaid had become the largest single source of revenue for community providers, accounting for 38 percent of their total funding" (p.971). Significantly, non-traditional Medicaid offerings, such as the Rehabilitation Option, have funded key activities, such as case management services, and as the title suggests, this funding stream supports services directed to the broad psychosocial needs of consumers. Vladeck (2003) reports that Medicaid, often viewed as a program for poor mothers and children, actually spends more on the non-elderly disabled (including those with mental illnesses) than any other single group. In part, this is due to a social desire to help a wide range of people who have "real needs for which it is difficult or too uncomfortable to hold them personally responsible" (p.93). However, disability is an illusive term, and the process of determining disability is as much a political process as it is an objective one. As a result, the development of each State's individual Medicaid plan becomes contested turf, with seemingly slight policy adaptations having serious consequences for consumers, families, and providers.

One growing possibility is that Medicaid dollars can become folded into a State's overall block grant, offering greater flexibility, while capping spending. Hogan, the Director of the Ohio Department of Mental Health and Chair of the New Freedom Commission, views this as a reasonable option if the dollars are adequate;

> Because one of the consequences of how Medicaid is often run, given its fee-for-service orientation and categorical approach to eligibility, is that it has made community mental health care into piecework, with an emphasis by case managers and therapists on billable units of service for people who are Medicaid eligible, as opposed to clinically necessary care for people who need that care irrespective of eligibility. (Cunningham, 2003, p. 447)

The growth in Medicaid spending for mental health services will not go unnoticed, and while State and Federal Medicaid officials may be reluctant to eliminate classes of beneficiaries, there will undoubtedly be growing pressure to demonstrate that clinical necessity exists for continued care, and that services deliver a tangible benefit. Not surprisingly, these trends only add to the push to develop evidence based services, As Terry Stawar (personal communication, October 7, 2004), a Community Mental Health director in Southern Indiana predicts, there is a "coming juncture between evidence based practices and funding, in which only evidence based practices will be eligible for Medicaid/Medicare reimbursement."

It is hard to argue against a position that practice should be supported by good science. However, Tanenbaum (2005) suggests that "controversy may reign over fundamental notions of defining evidence, applying evidence, and determining effectiveness." Larry Burch, (personal communication, October 14, 2004) approaching his silver anniversary as a mental health center director, recognizes that dilemmas do exist:

Every provider is challenged to make sure they are engaged in evidence based practices. At the same time we are encouraged to make sure we are focused on recovery and consumer driven services. There are times when these two are contradictory. Consumers do not always choose evidence based services. This will require providers to walk a fine line at least into the distant future.

Consider the concept of recovery. Does recovery mean that a person is symptom free, holding a job and living independently? Or is it a matter of deeper personal meaning, ultimately best-judged by the person facing a challenging condition? These questions are far from trivial, as they may determine what types of services are prioritized, and if linked to social insurance policies, what services are reimbursed?

A move towards evidence-based practice, improved utilization review strategies, and even the quest for insurance parity for those facing mental illnesses leads community mental health and other behavioral health organizations to fall in line with trends seen in the world of physical medicine. If successful, the integration of systems of care for physical and mental health may not be far behind. The specific approach such an integration plan would take is far from clear. Certainly, the primary care gatekeeper model has conceptual coherence, but it will only work to the degree that this system can adequately assess behavioral health challenges, and has secured the proper specialty providers to offer effective services. Given the unpredictability of serious mental illnesses, and the attendant costs, there is always danger that a bifurcated system could return in the form of a narrowly defined medical model – reversing many of the gains of the last 25 years and signal a retreat from the psychosocial model that now prevails.

Few would see this as a desirable trend, but the troublesome question is who will fight this battle? As community mental health centers struggle to diversify funding streams, an increasingly smaller percentage of their budget is comprised of State administered funds. Accordingly, the most important actor in the life of a modern day Community Mental Health director is the not the head of the State mental health authority, but rather the State Director of Medicaid. Medicaid constitutes more than 20 percent of most state budgets, with behavioral health only one of many actors who depend who funds disbursed from this office (Boyd, 2003). Decisions made by a State's Medicaid office, dictates the course of mental health care far more than any other entity. Consider the costs of prescription drugs alone. According to Zuvekas (2005), between 1996 and 2001 prescription drug costs for mental health and substance abuse grew at a rate of 20 percent a year. Remarkably, 80% of this growth was accounted for by selective serotonin reuptake inhibitors and newer antidepressants, and atypical antipsychotics. Few disagree that these newer medications are often critical to the recovery process for consumers, but many wonder if these drugs will remain on a state's Medicaid formulary.

Complicating the lives of mental health directors is that while the press of managed care, and other third party payers, has required the adoption of an insurance model of care, vestiges of the public health, or population-based model remain. State directed funds may support a portion of the cost of serving the most seriously ill, while self paying clients and those with adequate insurance also contribute. Other clients fall into an entirely different group. The working poor, often underinsured, depend on reduced fee schedules to receive services, resulting in a net loss to the provider. Given the pressing demand, practitioners face high productivity standards as all try to maximize their billable units. The worlds of care and finance have collided. The challenge facing administrators is to help guide their organizations through these challenging times without inexorably compromising the primary mission. As Larry Burch notes (personal communication, October 14, 2004):

> It is critical to get the entire organization to buy into a healthy bottom line. The purpose of this bottom line is to serve the mission. But, in order to enhance and protect the mission you must have the capacity to respond to emergencies and opportunities. The final major change in my job has been to develop the skills and organizational commitment for philanthropy/ fundraising.

Burch and his peers have been forced to become social entrepreneurs (Eikenberry & Kluver, 2004). Eikenberry and Kluver (2004) contend that to understand the behavior of a non-profit organization it is first necessary to understand the threats and pressures that emanate from the external environment. Social entrepreneurship requires these leaders to leverage their understanding of the world of business and the market to help improve the lives of consumers while simultaneously respecting the primary mission of the organization (Dees, Emerson, & Economy, 2001).

Adopting a social entrepreneurship model could increase mental health centers' legitimacy with key stakeholders, and consistent with the promise of evidence-based practice, rend organizations more effective, efficient, and accountable. But there are risks. Eikenberry and Kluver (2004) argue that non-profit organizations have been vital to society by serving as "value guardians, service providers and advocates, and builders of social capital" (p. 135). When a non-profit organization unconditionally adopts a market mindset, and becomes driven more by the demands of funders than consumers, these important contributions may be abandoned.

THE UNCERTAIN FUTURE

By virtue of the increased demand for services for problems ranging from interpersonal difficulties at home, to the most difficult psychiatric conditions, Community Mental Health Centers have developed a loyal constituency that should bode well for their survival. The threat of managed care forced even the most traditional of providers to take necessary steps to modernize operations in the area of management information, contract management, and accreditation. In addition, many provider organizations developed networks to share these management functions and fiscal risk, as funding moved from grant-based to a contract-based environment. These centers retain a wealth of expertise in serving the most severely ill, and should be welcome partners should the worlds of physical and behavioral health care merge.

The trends, long sent into motion, have obvious implications for social workers and other mental health professionals. The world of practice has changed. Evidence-based practice, manualized treatment protocols, group modalities, and brief helping techniques have become the rule, not the exception. Increased interdisciplinary work in community settings is on the horizon. For some these changes are unsettling, but as Mechanic (1998) asserts, "mental health professionals have to stop lamenting the changes and devote their energies to better defining good practices and putting into place disease management approaches that are informed by evidence" (p. 93).

References

Anthony, W. (1993). Recovery from mental illness: The guiding vision of the mental health system in the 1990's. *Psychosocial Rehabilitation Journal, 16*(4), 11-23.

Boyd, D. (2003). The bursting State fiscal bubble and State Medicaid budgets. *Health Affairs, 22*(1), 46-61.

Buck, J. (2003). Medicaid, health care financing trends, and the future of State-based public mental health services. *Psychiatric Services, 54*(7), 969-975.

Cunningham, R. (2003). The mental health commission tackles fragmented services: An interview with Michael Hogan. *Health Affairs Web Exclusives*, July-December, 440-448.

Dees, J.G., Emerson, J., & Economy, P. (2001). *Enterprising nonprofits: A tool kit for social entrepreneurs*. New York: Wiley.

Eikenberry, A., & Kluver, J. (2004). The marketization of the nonprofit sector: Civil society at risk? *Public Administration Review, 64*(2), 132-140.

Foley, H., & Sharfstein, S. (1983). *Madness and government*. Washington D.C.: American Psychiatric Press.

Frank, R., Goldman, H., & Hogan, M. (2003). Medicaid and mental health: Be careful what you ask for. *Health Affairs, 22*(1), 101-113.

Gumz, E. (2004). An administrator's perspective of trends in community mental health: An interview with Norman J. Groetzinger. *Families in Society, 85*(3), 363-370.

Hogan, M (2003). The President's New Freedom Commission: Recommendations to transform mental health care in America. *Psychiatric Services, 54*(11), 1467-1474.

Hogan, M. (1999). Public-sector mental health care: New Challenges. *Health Affairs, 18*(5), 106-111.

Jacobs, D., & Moxley, D. (1993). Anticipating managed mental health care: Implications for psychosocial rehabilitation agencies. *Psychosocial Rehabilitation Journal, 17*(2), 15-31.

Joint Commission on Mental Illness and Health (1961). *Action for Mental Health*. New York: Basic Books.

Mechanic, D. (1998). Emerging trends in mental health policy and practice. *Health Affairs, 17*(6), 82-98.Mechanic, D. (1999). *Mental health and social policy*. Boston: Allyn and Bacon.

Mechanic, D., & Bilder, S. (2004). Treatment of people with mental illness: A decade-long perspective. *Health Affairs, 23*(4), p.84-95.

Pomerantz, J. (2001). Atypical antipsychotic agents for the treatment of schizophrenia and mood disorders. *Drug Benefit Trend, 13*(Suppl. D), 5-12.

Sullivan, W.P. (1994) A long and winding road: The process of recovery from severe mental illness. *Innovations and Research. 3*(3), 19-27.

Tanebaum, S. (2005). Evidence-based practice as mental health policy: Three controversies and a caveat. *Health Affairs, 24*(1), 163-173.

Turner, J., & TenHoor, W. (1978) The NIMH Community Support Program: Pilot approach to a needed social reform. *Schizophrenia Bulletin, 4*, 319-348.

Vladeck, B. (2003). Where the action really is: Medicaid and the disabled. *Health Affairs, 22*(1), 90-100.

Zuvekas, S. (2005). Prescription drugs and the changing patterns of treatment for mental disorders,

1996-2001. *Health Affairs, 24*(1), 195-205.

Author's Note

Address correspondence to: W. Patrick Sullivan, Professor, School of Social Work, Indiana University, 902 West New York Street ES 4143, Indianapolis, IN 46202-5156. e-mail: wpsulliv@iupui.edu.

THE FUTURE OF SOCIAL WORK PRACTICE IN ADDICTIONS
Diana M. DiNitto

Abstract: *Few social workers specialize in addictions practice. That number may grow in the years ahead due to demographic changes in the population, an expanding definition of addiction, and other factors. Social workers in all areas of practice see clients with addictions and their family members, but there is a large gap in the numbers who need treatment and receive it. The social work workforce of the future must be better equipped to develop and identify prevention and treatment services that are both appealing to clients and effective. These services may need to be offered in other setting where clients are seen. There is also much work to be done in the years ahead in the political environment to make treatment available and to see that individuals with addictions are treated fairly. Substantial research is being conducted on genetics and the brain chemistry of addiction. Psychosocial factors are also believed to play a substantial role in the development of addictions, thus ensuring social workers place in the addictions field in the years ahead.*

Keywords: future, social work, addictions

INTRODUCTION

Social workers have assisted individuals with addictions and their families since the earliest days of the Charity Organization Societies (COS) and settlement house movement (for a history, see Straussner & Fewell, 1996; Straussner & Senreich, 2002). Though the sin and moral models of alcoholism were prominent, Mary Richmond (1917), a notable COS leader, had a more enlightened view of the problem. She referred to "inebriety" as a disease and encouraged early identification and treatment. Richmond developed an alcoholism assessment instrument that remains a model for those used today. In these early days of the profession, social workers addressed alcohol problems through the temperance movement and their work in public welfare, child welfare, the workplace, and other practice arenas. There was little focus on specialty alcoholism treatment programs until the mid-1900s. Among the most notable accomplishments of social workers during this period was the work of Gladys Price, Margaret Cork, and Margaret Bailey, particularly with families of alcoholics (Straussner & Senreich, 2002).

Developments in the 1970s led more social workers and other helping professionals to enter the field of addictions. The federal government established the National Institute on Alcohol Abuse and Alcoholism (NIAAA); National Institute on Drug Abuse (NIDA); and Alcohol, Drug Abuse, and Mental Health Administration, now the Substance Abuse and Mental Health Services Administration (SAMHSA). These government entities lent legitimacy to work in the field of alcohol and drug problems, and federal financial assistance became available to students interested in preparing for careers in these fields. Today, social workers hold some of the top positions in government agencies like SAMHSA.

Diana M. DiNitto is Cullen Trust Centennial Professor in Alcohol Studies and Education University Distinguished Teaching Professor and Co-Director, Substance Abuse Research Development Program at The School of Social Work, University of Texas at Austin 78712-0358.

In 1995, the National Association of Social Workers (NASW) established a specialty practice section for members specializing in alcohol, tobacco, and other drug (ATOD) problems and more recently began offering an ATOD specialty clinical credential. The first social work journal devoted to addictions, *Journal of Social Work Practice in the Addictions*, was established in 2001. In 2003, a social worker became president of the Association for Medical Education and Research on Substance Abuse. Social workers are taking a more active role in addictions research with the help of initiatives like the NIDA-funded social work research development programs launched in 1999. Their intent is to make social workers more competitive in obtaining federal research funding. These events indicate that social workers will assume more leadership roles in the addictions field in the future.

FUTURE EXPANSION OF THE ADDICTIONS FIELD

The field of addictions practice for social workers and other helping professionals can be expected to grow for at least six reasons. First is population growth and related demographic changes. Life spans are increasing, even for those with alcohol and other drug problems. Given that the baby boomers (those born between 1946 and 1964) are the first generation with wide exposure to illicit drugs, social workers will be seeing more older people with problems related to illicit drug use as well as alcohol and prescription drug use. Another demographic feature of concern is the large number of immigrants coming to the U.S. Many immigrants have been victims of war, genocide, extreme poverty, and other horrific conditions in their homelands or as refugees in other countries (see, for example, Amodeo, Robb, Peou, & Tran, 1996; McNeece & DiNitto, 2005). They may turn to alcohol and drugs, including substances indigenous to their homelands, to assuage the pain from these ordeals (see, for example, Mokuau, 1999). Social work's attention to culturally relevant models of practice can be useful in identifying and treating these problems.

A second reason that social workers will become more involved in the field is that the term addiction is now widely used to include more than substance use disorders. Broadly defined, addictions now include compulsive behaviors such as gambling, sex, eating, shopping, and Internet use (see, for example, van Wormer & Davis, 2003). The Internet has fueled addictions with access to games of chance (like video poker), shopping opportunities (that also abound on TV), and sexual images. Immigrants may bring culturally based addictions to behaviors not previously recognized in the U.S. Undoubtedly the term addiction will come to include even more behaviors, and social workers will be seeing more clients with addictions.

A third reason that social workers' involvement in addictions prevention and treatment will continue to grow is rapid expansion of knowledge in the field. The number of psychosocial treatment approaches has grown to include brief and very brief interventions, the community reinforcement approach (CRA) for treating alcohol dependence and variants of CRA for other drug disorders, voucher reinforcement therapy, network therapy, and other models (for an overview of the range of treatment approaches, see McNeece & DiNitto, 2005). More medications are being tested and approved for use in the addictions field, such as naltrexone for alcohol dependence and buprenorphine for opiate (heroin) dependence. Social workers are contributing to the research done on medications as well as psychosocial treatments (Zweben, 2001). With these new technologies comes the hope that more people with addictions will be attracted to treatment, helping to close the huge gap between those needing and those receiving treatment, and providing more practice opportunities for social workers.

A fourth reason for continuing growth of the field is recognition that addiction often occurs with a wide variety of other diagnoses, including mental and physical disabilities (DiNitto & Webb, 2005). Though clinicians in the fields of mental illness, spinal cord injury, traumatic brain injury, and so on, have often thought that alcohol and other drug problems would remit with adequate treatment for the mental or physical disability, most are now aware that alcohol and drug problems are conditions that require treatment in their own right. This has led to the development of integrated models for treating co-oc-curring disorders and the need for professionals like social workers interested in providing these treatments.

Fifth is the sheer numbers of clients with addictions, primarily alcohol and other drug problems, seen in settings such as child protective services and adult and juvenile correc-tions. Some of the largest addictions treatment programs are now housed in correctional institutions. Many more individuals are being directed to addiction treatment programs in order to keep or have their children returned or to fulfill conditions of probation or parole. Sixth is that most insurance plans include treatment for addictions. With this coverage also comes more demand for the services that social workers provide, including social workers in private practice.

FUTURE OF ADDICTION POLITICS

Despite lip service in the U.S. that addictions should be treated as diseases or public health problems, the political climate remains imbued with a criminal justice perspective (for overviews of this topic, see DiNitto, 2002, 2005; McNeece & DiNitto, 2005). This perspective is commonly called the "war on drugs." Of the $12 billion annual, national drug control budget, about 45 percent goes to "demand side" efforts (treatment, preven-tion, and related research), while 55 percent goes to "supply side" efforts (law enforcement and interdiction) (Office of National Drug Control Policy, 2004). Given evidence that $1 spent on treatment results in $12 saved in criminal justice, health care, and related costs (NIDA, 1999), social workers will continue to make a case for shifting more funds to treatment. Social work is one of the few helping professions in which information on political action and advocacy must be part of the curriculum. NASW's code of ethics includes obligations for advocacy and political participation. In the decades ahead social workers have much to do and "undo" in the political arena in order to see that treatment is readily available, affordable, and more consistent with social work values and ethics.

There are some signs that the U.S. "war on drugs" is abating (DiNitto, 2002). Com-munity drug courts, some with social work staff, offer treatment rather than prosecution, generally to first-time, non-violent drug offenders whose crimes are minor. Proposition 36 in California diverts first- and second-time drug possession offenders to treatment rather than incarceration. In the coming decades social workers have a lot to do in seeing that all incarcerated individuals with addictions have access to treatment and in helping to divert more offenders away from prisons and jails and into treatment.

Other aspects of decriminalization also warrant social workers' serious consideration in the years ahead, such as reduced penalties for possession of small amount of drugs like marijuana and the availability of marijuana for medical purposes. Work is also needed to reduce the penalties for crack cocaine offenses since they are much stiffer than the penalties for offenses involving powdered cocaine. This will bring more equitable treatment for the disproportionate number of poor people and African Americans convicted of crack cocaine offenses (United States Sentencing Commission, 2002).

Political action by social workers is also needed in other aspects of social welfare policy, primarily public assistance and other cash and in-kind benefit programs. Alcohol and drug problems are the only disabilities that can keep otherwise qualified individuals from receiving Supplemental Security Income and Social Security Disability Insurance. Felony drug convictions are the only convictions that can keep otherwise qualified individuals from receiving Temporary Assistance for Needy Families and food stamps. Public housing tenants can be evicted if any member of their household is using drugs. A college or university student with a drug conviction as an adult is ineligible for federal student financial aid for a designated period of time. The Americans with Disabilities Act does not provide individuals who currently use illegal drugs or whose job performance is impaired by alcohol use with same degree of employment protections as individuals with other disabilities. Children may be removed from homes where a parent is using drugs without evidence of child abuse or neglect. Women have been arrested and incarcerated for using drugs while pregnant even though a fetus has no legal standing as a person. Such policies may violate the equal protection and due processes clauses of the U.S. Constitution, requiring social workers' continued vigilance and activism to prevent civil rights infringements.

While trying to reverse or modify public policy that treats individuals with alcohol and drug problems and their families in unjust or punitive ways, there is much proactive work to do in the political arena in the years ahead. Progress has been made in increasing health insurance parity for alcohol and drug treatment, though it lags behind coverage for physical and mental health treatment. Managed care has taken a toll by limiting access to the type and amount of alcohol and drug treatment (see, for example, Hay Group, 2001). Especially problematic is that millions of Americans have no health insurance coverage. Insurance coverage not only affects patients' or clients' access to treatment, it also effects social workers' and other providers' access to reimbursement for their work. Social workers will continue to press for some type of national health insurance program that includes coverage for addictions treatment and for full parity in all insurance plans.

Harm reduction approaches are consistent with the social work philosophy of "starting where the client is" and dignity and worth of the individual. Some harm reduction strategies such as heroin replacement therapy are too radical for the U.S. government to consider, but other approaches are also ignored. For example, the federal government has refused to fund needle-exchange programs despite acknowledging that this approach can reduce HIV transmission and does not promote injection drug use ("Research shows…," 1998). To save more lives, social workers must think of ways to promote harm reduction that are palatable to elected officials and the public.

FUTURE OF THE ADDICTIONS WORKFORCE

An estimated 2 percent of NASW members ("72 Percent Work…," 2001) and 3.3 percent of licensed social workers (Center for Health Workforce Studies, 2005) in the U.S. call addictions their primary practice area. Perhaps more would do so if evidence indicated that social workers are particularly effective in preventing and treating addictions. There are, however, no data to indicate that any particular profession is best suited to treat clients with addictions. It is also difficult to make a case for any particular treatment approach (Project MATCH Research Group, 1997). The limited research on the subject suggests that alcohol and drug therapists' interpersonal skills rather than their credentials are key ingredients in promoting treatment effectiveness (see, for example, Najavits & Weiss, 1994; Project MATCH Research Group, 1998). Nevertheless, Straussner and colleagues (Straussner &Fewell, 1996; Straussner & Senreich, 2002) believe that social work, which is based in systems theory, the person-in-environment perspective, and a biopsychosocial approach, is "an ideal discipline" for work in the field of addictions. This statement is particularly interesting at this juncture when substantial resources are being expended on understanding the genetics and brain chemistry of addiction. In the future, testing for genetic markers may replace criteria found in the *Diagnostic and Statistical Manual of Mental Disorders* (American Psychiatric Association, 2000) and the paper and pencil and verbal assessment tools that social workers and others now use to identify addictive disorders. Gene therapy and medications that alter brain chemistry might also make psychosocial treatments for addictions obsolete.

Social workers espouse a biopsychosocial approach to addictions prevention and treatment but are necessarily heavier on the psychosocial aspects than biological aspects. Though really still in their infancy, psychosocial approaches are the mainstays of the mutual-help movement and addiction treatment programs. Medications to treat addictions are newer still and are only recommended in conjunction with psychosocial services. Many people believe that while genetics and brain biology are important pieces of the puzzle in unlocking the mysteries of addiction, psychosocial factors play equally important roles, thus ensuring a place for social workers in addiction prevention and treatment in the future (Wilcox & Erickson, 2005). It might also be argued that greater efficiency would accrue if a single treatment professional were able to address the biological aspects of addiction (including the prescribing of medications) as well as psychological, social, and spiritual aspects. The addictions workforce of the future may be "up for grabs." On one hand, it may go to the lowest bidder—those who can perform the work at the lowest cost—as often seems to be the case today. On the other hand, highly skilled professionals commanding larger salaries may be needed to address the complex problems of individuals who have addictive disorders and those with co-occurring mental and physical disorders.

Though only a small number of social workers identify addictions as their primary area of practice, their involvement with clients who have addictions is better demonstrated by a survey of NASW members which indicated that 71 percent had "taken one or more actions in relation to clients with substance abuse disorders in the past year" (O'Neill, 2001, p. 10). At a minimum, social workers in all practice settings must be prepared to screen clients for alcohol, drug, and other addictions and refer clients to specialty treatment as necessary. Since there will not likely be sufficient number of social workers or other professionals in specialty addictions programs to meet the demand for services, professionals in a wide variety of settings must be prepared to incorporate treatment for addictions (see Miller & Weisner, 2002). To achieve this goal, AMERSA's Strategic Plan for Inter-disciplinary Faculty Development encourages integration of substance abuse content in all required social work courses and an increase in the number of certificate programs in substance abuse (Straussner & Senreich, 2002). Despite urging, there is no indication that the Council on Social Work Education, the accrediting body for social work education programs, plans to adopt any requirement specific to addictions content.

In 2003, NASW began a workforce initiative "to determine the number of social work-ers; the jobs they perform; credentials they need; compensation and reimbursement; pro-fessional development needs; licensing needs; articulation of practice domains; avenues of administrative, regulatory and legislative advocacy; and other social work workforce issues" (O'Neill, 2003, p. 1). This is an important undertaking as members of the various helping professions, including addictions counselors without degrees in the helping pro-fessions, vie with each other for jobs and prominence. Social workers can help secure their place in addictions prevention and treatment by (1) developing and identifying effective prevention and treatment approaches, (2) obtaining the knowledge and skills needed for work in the field, and (3) providing evidence that they can help clients become abstinent or reduce use and achieve other treatment goals. Clients and third-party payers are expect-ing nothing less.

CONCLUSIONS

The definition of addictions is expanding and along with it the number of individuals needing addictions treatment. Knowledge about addictions and the repertoire of skills needed to practice in the field are also growing rapidly. Social workers are playing a more prominent role in developing new technologies in order to encourage more people to engage in treatment and to improve treatment outcomes. Social workers in all settings are facing increased pressure to ensure rapid transfer of these technologies to practice and also to demonstrate that they can effectively treat clients with addictions. Equally important for the future is for social workers to insure that everyone with an addictive disorder has access to affordable and effective treatment.

References

American Psychiatric Association. (2000). *Diagnostic and statistical manual of mental disorders* (4th ed., text rev.). Washington, DC: Author.

Amodeo, M., Robb, N., Peou, S., & Tran, H. (1996). Adapting mainstream substance-abuse inter-ventions for Southeast Asian clients. *Families in Society, 77*, 403-413.

Center for Health Workforce Studies. (2005, January 7). Survey of licensed social workers in the U.S. Presentation to the National Association of Social Workers. Albany, NY: School of Public Health, SUNY at Albany.

DiNitto, D. M. (2002). War and peace: Social work and the state of chemical dependency treat-ment in the United States. In S. L. A. Straussner & L. Harrison (Eds.), *International aspects of social work practice in the addictions* (pp. 7-29). New York: Haworth Press.

DiNitto, D. M. (2005). *Social welfare: Politics and public policy* (6th ed.). Boston: Allyn and Bacon.

DiNitto, D. M., & Webb, D. K. (2005). Substance use disorders and co-occurring disabilities. In C.

A. McNeece & D. M. DiNitto, *Chemical dependency: A systems approach* (3rd ed., pp. 423-483). Boston: Allyn and Bacon.

Hay Group. (2001, February 15). Employer health care dollars spent on addiction treatment. Retrieved January 23, 2005, from http://www.asam.org/pressrel/hay.htm

McNeece, C. A., & DiNitto, D. M. (2005). *Chemical dependency: A systems approach*, (3rd ed.). Boston: Allyn and Bacon.

Miller, W. R., & Weisner, C. M. (Eds.). (2002). *Changing substance abuse through health and social systems*. New York: Kluwer Academics/Plenum Publishers.

Mokuau, N. (1999). Substance abuse among Pacific Islanders: Cultural context and implications for prevention programs. In B. W. K. Lee, N. Mokuau, S. Kim, L. G. Epstein, & G. Pacheco (Eds.), *Developing cultural competence in Asian-American and Pacific Islander communities: Opportunities in primary health care and substance abuse prevention* (CSAP Cultural Competence Series no. 5, Special Collaborative Edition, pp. 221-248). Rockville, MD: Center for Substance Abuse Prevention.

Najavits, L. M., & Weiss, R. D. (1994). Variations in therapist effectiveness in treatment. *Addiction, 89*, 679-688.

National Institute on Drug Abuse. (1999). *Principles of drug addiction treatment: A research-based guide*. Bethesda, MD: U.S. Department of Health and Human Services.

Office of National Drug Control Policy. (2004, March). *The president's national drug control strategy*. Washington, DC: Executive Office of the President. Retrieved January 25, 2005, from http://www.whitehousedrugpolicy.gov/publications/policy/ndcs04/index.html

O'Neill, J. V. (2001, January). Expertise in addictions said crucial. *NASW News*, pp. 10.

O'Neill, J. V. (2003, March). NASW launches workforce initiative. *NASW News*, pp. 1 & 8.

Project MATCH Research Group. (1997). Matching alcoholism treatments to client heterogeneity: Project MATCH posttreatment drinking outcomes. *Journal of Studies on Alcohol, 58*, 7-29.

Project MATCH Research Group. (1998). Therapist effects in three treatments for alcohol problems. *Psychotherapy Research, 8*, 455-474.

Research shows needle exchange programs reduce HIV infections without increasing drug use. (1998, April 20). Washington, DC: U.S. Department of Health and Human Services press release. Retrieved January 23, 2005 from http://www.hhs.gov/news/press/1998pres/980420a.html

Richmond, M. E. (1917). *Social diagnosis*. New York: Russell Sage Foundation.

72 percent work for private organizations. (2001, January). *NASW News*, p. 8.

Straussner, S. L. A., & Fewell, C. H. (1996). Social work perspectives on alcohol and drug abuse problems. In J. Kinney, *Clinical manual of substance abuse* (2nd ed., pp. 140-146). St. Louis: Mosby.

Straussner, S. L. A., & Senreich, E. (2002). Educating social workers to work with individuals affected by substance use disorders. *Substance Abuse, 23*(3), supplement (*Strategic plan for interdisciplinary faculty development)*, 319-340.

van Wormer, K., & Davis, D. R. (2003). *Addiction treatment: A strengths perspective*. Pacific Grove, CA: Brooks/Cole—Thomson Learning.

United States Sentencing Commission. (2002). *Report to the Congress: Cocaine and federal sentencing policy*. Washington, DC: Author. Retrieved January 25, 2005, from http://www.nicic.org/Library/017829

Wilcox, R. E., & Erickson, C. K. (2005). The brain biology of drug abuse and addiction. In C. A. McNeece & D. M. DiNitto. *Chemical dependency: A systems approach* (3rd ed., pp. 42-60). Boston:

Allyn and Bacon.

Zweben, A. (2001). Integrating pharmacotherapy and psychosocial interventions in the treatment of individuals with alcohol problems. In R. T. Spence, D. M. DiNitto, & S. L. A. Straussner, *Neurobiology of addictions: Implications for clinical practice* (pp. 65-80). New York: Haworth Press.

Author's Note

Address correspondence to Diana M. DiNitto PhD, The University of Texas at Austin, School of Social Work, 1 University Station, Austin, Texas 78712. E-mail: ddinitto@mail.utexas.edu.

THE FUTURE FOR SOCIAL WORK IN
JUVENILE AND ADULT CRIMINAL JUSTICE

Rosemary C. Sarri
Jeffrey J. Shook

Abstract: *Critical contemporary issues in juvenile and adult criminal justice are identified followed by an examination of particular issues for social workers, including the increase in incarceration, the overrepresentation of people of color, and the numerous negative effects on children. The various roles for social workers in the criminal justice systems are presented and discussed. The paper also addresses the decline of social work professionals in the criminal justice systems and why it is imperative that the pattern be reversed now that there is growing interest in the rehabilitation and reintegration of offenders.*

Keywords: Future, social work, juvenile, adult, criminal justice, incarceration

INTRODUCTION

Today there are many opportunities and challenges for social workers in criminal justice despite their relative absence in recent years, but the present systems have greater need than ever before. The United States has the highest rate of incarceration in the world (715 per 100,000 population) and the monies that are being expended in criminal justice have become an impediment to the support of many educational, health, welfare and environment programs.[2] The thrust of social policy has shifted from an emphasis on the provision of social benefits to those in need and at risk to systems of social control that provide little evidence of aiding public safety. Instead they have jeopardized the lives and future of millions of adults and youth, especially persons of color because of their overrepresentation in the criminal justice systems. Before considering the various roles for social work in the future we need to highlight several characteristics of these systems that deserve serious social policy attention because of their society-wide implications.

Moreover, they set the parameters for the roles for social workers.

1. More than 6.9 million adults are under some type of criminal justice supervision – 2 million in prison or jail and over 4 million on probation, parole or some other type of supervision (Harrison and Karberg, 2004).

2. More than 100,000 adjudicated youth are held in institutions, and over a period of a year, a half million youth are held in detention facilities. Many of the latter are abused and/or neglected youth who have "drifted" from child welfare agencies to juvenile detention. In addition, it is conservatively estimated that 85,000 youth annually spend time in an adult jail or prison (Harrison and Karberg, 2004; Lerman, 2002).

Rosemary C. Sarri, Ph.D. MSW is Research Professor Emerita at the Institute for Social Research, University of Michigan, Ann Arbor, MI 48106-1248. Jeffrey Shook PhD, JD & MSW is Assistant Professor of Social Work at the University of Pittsburgh, Pittsburgh, PA.

3. The crime rate has declined nationally and continually since the mid-1990s, as have rates of criminal victimization, but the incarceration and control rates continue to increase. Increased incarceration is the result of mandatory sentencing, "three strikes" laws, zero tolerance school policies, drug laws that require incarceration but not treatment, punitive public attitudes and the decline in availability of community-based programs (Patillo, Weinman & Western, 2004).

4. Overrepresentation of persons of color characterizes both the juvenile and the adult justice systems. Approximately 2 out of 3 offenders is a person of color, with African Americans the largest group (Bonczar, 2003). Recently Petit and Western (2004) reported that with the mass incarceration of African American males, their path to adulthood has been transformed due to their increased probability of incarceration, their decline in human capital development because of incomplete education, and their lack of access to employment in urban communities.

5. There are 1.6 million children with an incarcerated parent currently in prison and overall 10 million children have had an incarcerated parent. These children are traumatized by the loss of their parents and the events surrounding their departure, but they seldom receive adequate health and social services, they are often denied the right to visit their parents, and parents are often not consulted about crucial decisions regarding their children (Mumola, 2000).

6. Placements in community-based programs have declined, although these programs have shown to be more effective in reducing recidivism. Particularly lacking are diversion, alternatives to incarceration and re-entry and reintegration programs for offenders released from prison (Travis and Waul, 2003). Barriers faced by persons with criminal records increasingly inhibit reintegration in the areas of employment, housing, financial benefits, child welfare, family support, voter disenfranchisement and immigration status.

7. Thousands of mentally ill persons and those with drug or alcohol addiction problems are inappropriately confined to prisons and jails because of the lack of appropriate treatment in the community (National Mental Health Association, 2004). Correctional facilities are not able to provide adequate treatment.

8. Most of the persons in all phases and areas of the criminal justice system are poor, young persons of color who have grown up in disorganized and disadvantaged neighborhoods and who experience discrimination, especially in health care, employment, and housing.

9. The numbers of female offenders are increasing rapidly in both juvenile and adult programs, but there has been insufficient attention to gender-specific needs in programming because the majority of offenders are male. Females of color are also seriously overrepresented, with their having a greater probability of incarceration than white females even when one takes seriousness

of crime into consideration (Pimlott & Sarri, 2002).

10. Lastly, the U.S. has been reluctant to ratify and enforce many of the UN Conventions on Human Rights that provide protection to juvenile and adult offenders. This has resulted in toleration of unacceptable conditions of confinement in many jails and prisons such that the U.S. Justice Department has charged more than 20 states with violations (Schiraldi, 2004). Unwillingness of the U.S. to eliminate the death penalty for juveniles was a key factor in our lack of ratification of the UN Convention on the Rights of the Child, but that obstacle is now eliminated by the U.S. Supreme Court decision in Roper v Simmons (543 U.S.____2005) so we can now see if there will be efforts toward ratification.

Given the current situation, it is important to ask: What roles has social work played in recent years and what challenges are there for the future? Early in the 20th Century, social workers were the leaders in juvenile justice reform, the development of the juvenile court, and the development of probation systems. One only has to note the work of Julia Lathrop, Lucy Flower, Edith and Grace Abbott, and Jane Addams (Tanenhaus, 2002). They were instrumental in developing the juvenile court as a model that is found throughout the U.S. today and also in several other countries. Social workers continued to be important professionals in the justice system throughout most of the twentieth century until the 1980s. Between 1950 and 1980, they were key professional leaders in reform in most phases of the criminal justice systems when efforts were made to reduce prison populations. They played critical roles in the development of national policies to reduce incarceration and poverty while increasing resources for education, employment and treatment in the community (Miller, 1991; Rosenheim., 2002). They played significant roles in community work in central cities, in the development of community-based alternatives to incarceration and in developing treatment programs in prisons, jails and residential treatment centers. Many even filled important administrative and policy roles at the state and national levels.

More recently, particularly in the 1990s, many social workers withdrew from participating as professionals in criminal justice. Part of the reason was the withdrawal of funds for community-based and treatment programs during the Reagan administration. There also was a reduction in funds for grants to support training of social workers. At the state level, statutes were passed to emphasize punishment and incarceration and to deemphasize or eliminate treatment programs, particularly in facilities serving adult offenders. Even NASW and other professional social work organizations deemphasized criminal justice as an important field for social workers, arguing that a professional could not function effectively in an environment where punishment and control were priorities. Relatively little attention was given to the fact that more and more poor and disadvantaged persons were ending up in the justice systems and received little or no treatment, despite serious problems of substance abuse and mental illness. Instead it was the courts and human rights attorneys who took up the campaign for reform as is evidenced in a series of federal court decisions about the right to treatment.[3] Also active in recent years on behalf incarcerated offenders have been Human Rights Watch, the American Friends Service Committee, the Youth Law Center, Justice Policy Institute, the Annie E. Casey Foundation, and Amnesty

International.

As a response to the policies of punishment and control, schools of social work reduced their training of social workers and there was also a significant decline in research related to practice in criminal justice by social work faculty. This trend continued throughout the 1990s, and today it is safe to say that the majority of schools of social work no longer have a specialization in social work for criminal justice as most have for mental health.[4] Specialized training for criminal justice roles for social workers is as essential as is training for any other professional role in social work. Further, a noted social worker who revolutionized juvenile justice programs in Massachusetts said that what is needed in addition to knowledge and skill is a passion for caring for the offenders and their families (Miller, 1991). The demands in managing the ongoing conflict between custody and treatment are challenging, but there is a growing awareness of the need for social workers in the criminal justice systems as we shift from systems that focus primarily on punishment and retribution to a concern for rehabilitation.

FUTURE ISSUES IN WHICH SOCIAL WORK CAN PLAY A CRITICAL ROLE

Because of limited space, it is not possible to delineate all of the areas in which social work is needed in criminal justice today; thus, we highlight only a few which appear to be particularly important for the near future and for which social workers are or can be well prepared to provide effective services.

1. *High rates of incarceration.* Reduce incarceration by providing community-based alternative options for diversion, treatment of convicted offenders, family counseling and support, employment and housing programs. In the last two decades, expenditures for correctional programs only have risen from 9 billion dollars to 60 billion dollars, but effectiveness has not improved as recidivism rates are essentially unchanged despite the increase in expenditures. When one investigates why the increased dollars have had so little effect, it is apparent that most monies are spent for custody and control. Through advocacy work, community organization and provision of effective treatment services, social workers can demonstrate that there are alternatives to incarceration.

2. *Juveniles tried as adults.* Since 1990, the numbers of juveniles waived for processing as adults and sentenced to adult prisons has increased substantially, partly as the result of an increased juvenile crime 'blip' in the early 1990s and because of statutory changes in most of the 50 states that mandated or permitted the processing of juveniles into the adult system(Bishop, 2000). The juvenile crime rate has declined continually since 1995, but the number of youth tried and convicted as adults has continued to rise. Little attention has been given to the competence of the juvenile with respect to his/her awareness of culpability and his/her competence in the adjudicative proceedings. Social workers who work in the court can document the failure of these policies and point out that findings from new brain development research require that there be comprehensive assessment of the competence of these juveniles, and they can suggest alternative processing and treatment.

They can also raise issues with respect to the confinement problems for juveniles in adult prisons and jails and present other disposition alternatives to the court. Collaboration with law enforcement and judicial officials as well as treatment professionals will be necessary to effect the many changes that are required in legislation, policies and programming.

3. *Children of incarcerated parents.* Social workers can perform several roles for the children of incarcerated parents and also for the parents themselves. These children are severely traumatized by their parents' incarceration and deserve comprehensive and on-going intervention. Social workers can see that these children are treated sensitively by the child welfare system as persons in need of protection. They can arrange for parental visitation and for facilitating treatment of the children so that parental rights are maintained where that is appropriate. They also can advocate that the rights of these children be acknowledged (San Francisco Partnership, 2003). Since most children face more serious problems when a mother is incarcerated, social workers can advocate for non-custodial sentences for women convicted of property and drug crimes, as they do not provide a threat to public safety in most instances. In instances where grandparents assume custodial responsibility for children of incarcerated parents, social workers can advocate for financial subsidies that other adults would receive as foster parents. They can also ensure the maintenance of continuing support services because the children are at risk for drifting to crime, for suicide, for mental illness and for other maladaptive coping patterns. Some of the most successful intervention programs that have been recently developed including the provision of mentors who provide ongoing caring and support for these children.

4. *Conditions of confinement.* Conditions of confinement in correctional institutions are problematic for incarcerated juveniles and adults. Physical and social conditions in prisons and jails are often seriously damaging to most occupants because of assaultive behavior by custodial staff and other inmates. In addition, unhealthful conditions exist because of overcrowding and insufficient resources. The U.S. Justice Department has charged more than 20 states in recent years for a variety of conditions that violate human rights and required conditions of confinement for prisoners (Schiraldi, 2004). There is also increasing support for action by groups such as Amnesty International, Human Rights Watch and the American Friends Service Committees. Social workers who work in residential facilities and observe violations are obligated by NASW Ethical Standards to take action so that the conditions are remedied and that rehabilitation services are provided (Miller, 1991; Puritz & Scali, 1998; Building Blocks for Youth, 2004; Human Rights Watch, 1999). Effecting changes in these conditions is difficult, so collaboration with other professional groups is important as is seeking redress from the courts for violations.

5. *Overrepresentation of people of color.* One of the most complex problems that urgently needs attention today and in the future is the reduction in

the overrepresentation of persons of color at all stages of the justice systems. There is federal law that mandates states achieve proportional representation, but that is far from reality in all of the states. Many of the practices that result in overrepresentation are institutionalized. Without systematic and ongoing monitoring, problematic decision making goes unrecognized. Persons of color are often covertly discriminated against because of where they reside, problems of family members or associates, racial profiling, poverty, and unemployment (Pettit & Western, 2004). The majority of decision makers are unaware of their own behavior patterns which maintain disproportionality in decision making. Social workers are trained in multicultural practice which is important in treatment intervention, but they also need to be sensitive to institutionalized racism so that it can be corrected. Again, this is a problem that will require sustained collaboration with other officials and professionals if positive change is to result. One example of a social worker who has devoted his career to seeking change toward reducing overrepresentation is Marc Mauer, and he has been very successful in securing national support for many of the policies that he has advocated regarding sentencing, incarceration, and disenfranchisement.[5]

6. *Gender-responsive programming for girls and women.* The majority of offenders in the U.S. are males, primarily under the age of 25 when they are incarcerated for the first time so programming has largely focused on the characteristics and needs of males. However, today female offenders, adult and juvenile, are growing faster in institutional populations and, with few exceptions, there is little recognition of their needs as different from those of men. Social workers need to develop gender-sensitive programming, see that staff are trained to recognize and respond appropriately to the individual and social needs of females. For example, more women offenders are incarcerated because of serious substance abuse problems, but most prisons and jails today do not have adequate programs to treat their problems. Physical and mental health needs of female offenders often differ substantially from those of males, so social workers need to advocate for the provision of appropriate gender-responsive services.

7. *Mental health services.* Because of many unfortunate changes in the mental health systems of most states in the past several decades, it is now probable that thousands of disadvantaged mentally ill persons end up in prisons and jails for extended periods of time because they are picked up on the street or because they commit a crime as a result of their mental illness. Very few receive adequate treatment in correctional institutions with the possible exception of new forensic center programs for persons who are seriously mentally ill. Largely ignored are those with chronic problems where the mentally ill person is the primary victim. All too often they also are homeless, addicted, and without family support. Social workers and other professionals in the mental health system must assert the need for resources for appropriate treatment for these individuals as has been suggested by the

National Mental Health Association (2004).

8. *Substance abuse.* Substance abuse and related behaviors today result in more persons being in jail, prison or under correctional supervision than any other single law-violating behavior. Punitive laws urgently need evaluation and change so that addicted persons receive treatment not just punishment. What is also needed is a comprehensive approach to substance abuse, but it unlikely that this problem will be solved within the criminal justice system. Worthy of attention is the fact that middle-class persons with insurance and other resources can obtain treatment, but the poor are thrust into jails and prisons without treatment.

9. *Child welfare drift.* One of the most disturbing and growing trends is the drift of child welfare clients to the juvenile justice system and then to the adult system (Keller, 2002; Courtney, Terao and Bost, 2004). Child welfare clients are victims whose problems have arisen because of abuse and/or neglect, but without comprehensive habilitation programs, they often end up in the justice system for minor problems and then seldom are removed. It has long been recognized that youth problems come in 'bundles' not as isolated problems, but services have often been specialized and separate. The lack of integrated services to children and youth is at least a contributing factor to those at risk for entering the justice system. What is needed is a comprehensive plan to provide a youth services system that is comprehensive and integrated so that children receive appropriate services promptly and in an optimal environment.

10. *Re-entry and reintegration.* Lastly, and perhaps most important, is the role that social work needs to play in the development and implementation of varied re-entry and reintegration programs for offenders returning to the community from prisons and other institutional settings. It is estimated that approximately 600,000 offenders return to the community each year, but the vast majority are likely to recidivate within two years, primarily because they receive no assistance in reintegration. Research findings have indicated that offenders who have family support, housing, and receive help with employment, education or substance abuse are likely to succeed in reintegration (Travis, 2004). Social workers are well trained for designing and providing the services that are necessary for success because that type of assistance is and has been important for many other clients facing the tasks of reintegration in other fields of practice.

ROLES FOR SOCIAL WORKERS IN THE JUSTICE SYSTEMS

We now identify the crucial roles for which we believe it is imperative to train social workers as soon as possible so that they can have a positive impact. There are opportunities for well-trained social workers who can contribute significantly to the increased effectiveness and humanity in the criminal justice systems

1. Social workers are needed to *organize, develop and administer prevention programs* at the local level but also at the state and national levels, especially in areas of

conflict, high crime, poverty, and racial discrimination (Hawkins & Catalano, 1992). Community organizers can play valuable roles in community education and in mobilizing the public toward more rehabilitative perspectives.

2.   Social workers are needed in police departments to *assist in the training of police* regarding the processing and handling of at-risk offenders, juveniles, mentally ill and disabled, addicted, victims and perpetrators of domestic violence, and non-English speaking immigrants. The actions of law enforcement at the "front-end" of the justice system usually have long-term consequences for the offender.

3.   Social workers could assume responsibility for the *organization and operation of community-based programs* for diversion of offenders from justice system processing, for operating alternatives to incarceration, and for the development and operation of re-entry and reintegration programs.

4.   Social workers can play *critical roles in prosecutors' and judicial offices in the court as well as in probation.* They can assist in the interviewing of victims, in risk assessment and pre-sentence investigation. Increased emphasis on effective assessment of the risk of offenders is of critical importance in disposition decision making and placement so that alternatives to incarceration can be increasingly utilized and not jeopardize public safety or recidivism. Increasing numbers of social workers are completing dual degrees in law and social work, so they are particularly well prepared to work in the courts.

5.   As *advocates,* social workers can support those charged with crime so that they receive the best defense and the most appropriate disposition. Advocates can educate the public for less punitive intervention. They can call attention to the importance of adherence to Human Rights Conventions. They can also advocate for active involvement of offenders in decision making regarding program choices, family matters and other options.

6.   Social workers are needed to *assess juvenile and adult offenders with appropriate procedures and instruments* that acknowledge the differences with respect to mental competence so that those who are incompetent to be tried are placed in treatment-oriented appropriate programs.

7.   Social workers are needed in residential and non-residential programs as *effective treatment specialists* who are trained to meet the different needs of females as well as males, mentally ill or addicted offenders, juvenile as well as adult offenders, violent and/or chronic offenders.

8.   Social workers are needed to *collaborate with family and child welfare agencies* to help them function effectively in serving families and neighborhoods where there is delinquency and crime.

9.   A current national policy priority is the *development and operation of reentry and reintegration programs for both juvenile and adult offenders.* These are particularly challenging tasks because they have received far too little attention up to now with the result that we lack knowledge about what

is required for effectiveness. Returning offenders have significant needs of housing, family reunification, education and employment, but there are too few resources at a time when public resources are declining because of the priorities of budget deficits, defense spending, and health care.

Although this paper has only scratched the surface of the challenges for social workers in the criminal justice systems, we have documented the great need for well-trained social work professionals and the many roles that they can play in important areas of criminal justice. In the past century social workers have demonstrated that their efforts made important differences in policies, programs and services. More than ever today they are needed to take risks to effect major change in the systems at the local, state and national levels. They are needed as treatment agents, as community organizers, as advocates, as challengers to existing law and practice, as trainers, supervisors and administrators, as court officials, as program evaluators and as designers of new and better services for thousands of persons who seek to be assisted to lead law-abiding and successful lives.

Schools of social work have a particular obligation to prepare a new generation of professionals for the criminal justice systems. There are many reasons why they shifted their emphasis to other fields of practice, but with 6.9 million persons under correctional supervision in the United States, it should be a priority to provide well-trained social workers for the variety of roles demanding attention today. In addition, substantial funding is available for program assessment and evaluation so it is hoped that more social work faculty would view this as an important avenue to see that "best practices" program models are adopted in criminal justice. There are role models in social work leaders of the past such as Julia Lathrop, Jane Addams, Jerome Miller, Paul Lerman and David Hawkins, all of whom demonstrated in different times and ways what social workers can accomplish in changing the juvenile and adult criminal justice system. Such leaders are needed now more than ever.

Footnotes

[1] This ignores the influence of organized labor in promoting employee job benefits.

[2] Harrison and Karberg (2004) report that the rate of incarceration averaged 100 per 100,000 of the total population between 1925-1975 and then steadily increased to 715 in 2003. More than half of the inmates are between the ages of 18 and 34 and 58% are persons of color, 8 times the rate of whites for African Americans (Bonczar, 2003).

[3] See federal court decisions in Glover v Johnson 934F.2d 703;1991 U.S. App.Lexis l00900; Haddix v. Johnson 143 F.3d 246 (6th Cir.1998); Bred v. Jones 421 U.S. 519; Morales v Terman 364 F.Supp. 166 (E.D. Tex, 1973). .

[4] In reviewing recently published Handbooks for fields of practice, only one had a chapter related to the justice system and that chapter focused only on juvenile justice.

[5] Marc Mauer has written on a variety of issues related to racial and gender discrimination in the justice systems. See Race to Incarcerate (1999). New York: Doubleday; Invisible Punishment: Collateral consequences of Mass Imprisonment. (2002). New York: New Press; and Losing the Vote. (1999). Washington, DC: The Sentencing Project.

References

Bishop, D. (2000). Juvenile Offenders in the Adult Criminal Justice System. In M.

Tonry (Ed.), *Crime and Justice: A Review of Research* . Chicago and London: University of Chicago Press.

Bonczar, T. (2003). *Prevalence of Imprisonment in the U.S. Population, 1974-2001.* Washington, DC: U.S. Dept. of Justice, Office of Justice Programs.

Building Blocks for Youth . (2004). *Conditions of Confinement.* Washington, DC: Youth Law Center.

Courtney, M., Terao, Y., & Bost, N. (2004) *Midwest Evaluation of the Adult Functioning of Former Foster Care Youth.* Chicago: Chapin Hall, University of Chicago.

Harrison, P., & Karberg, J. (2004). *Prison and Jail Inmates at Midyear 2003.* Washington, DC: U.S. Department of Justice.

Hawkins, J. D., & Catalano, R. F. (1992). *Communities That Care.* San Francisco, CA: Jossey-Bass.

Human Rights Watch. (1999). *No Minor Matter: children in Maryland Jails.* Washington ,DC: Human Rights Watch.

Keller, K. (2002). *Dependency/neglect and delinquency: dually involved minors in the juvenile court.* Chicago, Illinois: Cook County Juvenile Court.

Lerman, P. (2002). Twentieth-century developments in America's institutional systems for youth in trouble. In M. K. Rosenheim, F. E. Zimring, Tanenhaus David S., & B. Dohrn (Eds.), *A Century of Juvenile Justice* (1st ed., pp. 74-110). Chicago: The University of Chicago Press.

Miller, J. (1991). *Last One Over the Wall: The Massachusetts Experiment in Closing Reform Schools.* Columbus, Ohio: Ohio State University Press.

Mumola, C. (2000). *Incarcerated parents and their children.* Washington, DC: U.S. Department of Justice Bureau of Justice Statistics.

National Mental Health Association. (2004). *Mental Health Treatment for Youth in the Juvenile Justice System: A Compendium of Promising Practices.* Alexandria, VA: National Mental Health Association.

Patillo, M. W. D., Weiman, D. & Western, J. (2004). *Imprisoning America : The Social Effects of Mass Incarceration.* Chicago: University of Chicago Press.

Pettit, B., & Western, B. (2004). Mass Imprisonment and the Life Course: Race and Class Inequality in U.S. Incarceration. *American Sociological Review, 69*(2), 151-169.

Pimlott, S., & Sarri, R. (2002). The Forgotten Group:Women in Prisons and Jails. J. Figueira-McDonough, & R. Sarri *Women at the Margins: Neglect, Punishment and Resistance* (1st ed., pp. 55-86). New York: The Haworth Press.

Puritz, P., & Scali, M. A. (1998). *Beyond the Walls: Improving conditions of Confinement for Youth in custody.* Washington, DC: U.S. Department of Justice, Office of Juvenile Justice and Delinquency Prevention.

Rosenheim, M. K. (2002). The modern American juvenile court. In M. K. Rosenheim, F. E. Zimring, D. S. Tanenhaus, & B. Dohrn (Eds.), *A Century of Juvenile Justice* (1st ed., pp. 341-359). Chicago: The University of Chicago Press.

San Francisco Partnership. (2003). *Children of Incarcerated Parents: A Bill of Rights* San Francisco, CA: San Francisco Partnership for Incarcerated Parents.

Schiraldi, I. V. (2004). *Prisoner Abuse.* Washington, DC: Washington Post.

Tanenhaus, D. (2002). The evolution of juvenile courts in the early twentieth century: beyond the myth of immaculate construction. In M. K.. Rosenheim, F.E.

Zimring, D.S. Tanenhaus& B. Dohrn (Eds.). *A Century of Juvenile Justice* (1st ed., pp. 42-73). Chicago: University of Chicago Press.

Travis, J., & Waul, M. (2003). *Prisoners Once Removed: The Impact of Incarceration and Reentry on Children, Families and Communities.* Washington, DC: Urban Institute .

Travis, J. (2004). Reentry and Reintegration of Offenders. In M. W. D. Patillo, & B. Western (Eds.). *Imprisoning America: The Social Effects of Incarceration* (1st ed., pp. 247-267). New York: Russell Sage Foundation.

Author's Note

Address correspondence to Rosemary C. Sarri, Ph.D., Institute for Social Research, University of Michigan, Ann Arbor, MI 48106-1248. e-mail: rcsarri@umich.edu

LOOKING THROUGH THE PRISMS:
A SYNTHESIS OF THE FUTURES OF SOCIAL WORK

James G. Daley

Abstract: *This article synthesizes the twenty-one articles in this special issue and discusses five common themes and three further issues to ponder. The articles reflect an optimistic but precarious outlook that will require new skills and missions, a strong leadership in a society transforming itself, and increasingly facing a multicultural and global context for effective delivery of services. Evidence-based practice (EBP) is growing into the new paradigm of practice but the profession needs to consider its boundaries. Multi-country comparisons are crucial in selecting new strategies to enhance skills and missions as we embrace an international scope of practice. Finally, the complex issue of how society is evolving is intensifying and, as society seems to be resisting change, the role of social workers as advocates is vital.*

Keywords: future, social work, synthesis

INTRODUCTION

With such an array of articles reflecting depth and breadth, I struggle with the best way to synthesize a view of the future. Each article stimulated me to want to delve deeper into each field. The articles as a whole reflect the complexity and diversity of social work and the larger context within which our profession lives.

Each author, as he or she writes about the future, recognizes the fragility of any predictive discussion. One significant change (i.e. the World Trade explosions, managed care, the ethnic restructuring in the United States) can transform a society. The most dramatic changes in the future may not be predicted by people on the "inside" (i.e. within the profession itself) but by outsiders who are not listened to by the insiders. Kuhn (1970) cogently argued that professions live within paradigms, and when the paradigm shifts the insiders are often blindsided. Leonard (2001) has asserted that discussing the future infers a "linear view of history" indicating an "ethnocentric arrogance" that leads to a profound inability to respond creatively to difference, and results in the suppression of the voices of the "Other" (p. 1). Thus, any special issue on the future of Social Work will struggle with the contrast of visions of the future and the likelihood of missing key trends. The social work leaders who have written the articles for this issue must struggle with not being too seduced by the established trends in order to see the potential new directions the future will produce while hopefully hearing the voices of the "Other". The reader and reactions to the issue will reflect how helpful the various visions of the future will be.

I acknowledge that writing about the future of Social Work is not new or novel. Many authors have sought to encapsulate a view of the future into a framework that could help us better adapt to the future our complex profession and the constantly changing societal context we work within (i.e. Adams, Dominelli, & Payne, 2005; Bamford, 1989; Hopps

James G. Daley PhD is associate professor at Indiana University School of Social Work, Indianapolis 46202.

& Morris, 2000; Sowers & Ellis, 2001; Walton,1982). The National Association for Social Work (NASW) for the United States developed a Professional Futures Commission
in 1978 (Beck, 1981) and in 2005 the Social Work Congress created "a vision statement
for the next decade" (Clark, 2005, p.1). Some authors have focused on specialty areas of
social work such as health or field (Pecukonis, Cornelius & Parrish, 2003; Reisch & Jarman-Rohde, 2000) while others have taken a broader stroke and discussed international
or global social work (Johnson, 2004; Kadushin, 1999; Mary & Morris, 1994; Reisch,
1997). A thoughtful synthesis of the various authors' writings would be an article itself.
The purpose of this article is to discuss the common links, themes, and areas to clarify
presented by this issue's articles. I acknowledge the previous discussions and assert that
this special issue joins the gestalt of how we see our profession. My hope is that this collection of different fields of perspective may be seen as a kaleidoscope of futuristic vision.
Seeing many of the different fields of practice may increase our appreciation for the range
and depth that is any future for Social Work.

COMMON LINKS BETWEEN THE ARTICLES

There are several themes or issues that seem to be repeated by several authors. These common links can highlight themes simultaneously occurring in several fields and worthy of
discussion. The links include:

1. *Social work has an optimistic future.* Ginsberg clearly reflected that social
    work, a "mammoth profession" with a strong job growth ahead, will have
    an optimistic future. Demands for more social workers in macro settings
    (Netting), aging (Kroft & Adamek), health care (Ell & Vourleis), addictions
    (Dinetto), and criminal justice settings (Sarri & Shook) are discussed by the
    authors. The other authors acknowledge that, if social workers adapt and
    learn new skills, the needs for social workers can lead to tremendous job
    opportunities. A constant theme through all of the articles is that the client
    needs are increasing, especially as society and politics have not developed
    adequate service delivery systems. The work is needed if we can have the
    skills to compete.

2. *Social work is increasingly facing a multicultural and global context for effective
    delivery of services.* Watkins & Pierce cogently talk about "future relevant
    practice" and the importance of educators teaching skills that can be used in
    a "rapidly globalizing environment". Potocky-Tripodi & Tripodi demom-
    strate clearly that globally-focused social work is needed but the literature
    marginalizes the topic. Fong illuminates the growing multicultural client
    population with massive detailed changes in education and service delivery
    needed. Cournoyer advocates for the utility of evidence-based practice at
    an international level so that best practice choices are done attentive to
    the multicultural context. Canda emphasizes that spirituality must be un-
    derstood in a multicultural and international context. The message from
    the authors is clear: we must prepare for and be attentive to knowledge
    building and application of multicultural and global services. Sadly, Fong
    laments that we have known about this trend for years but there still are a

combination of limited knowledge, insufficient resources, and inadequate curriculum. Whether we prepare or not, this issue is looming like a freight train. The real question is will we be ready or will another profession emerge to meet the need while our opportunities evaporate?

3. *Evidence-based practice (EBP) is growing into the new paradigm of practice.* Cournoyer captures the rapid growth of EBP, not just in social work but within many helping professions. Five other authors (McCroskey, Franklin, Ell & Vourlekis, Sullivan, DiNitto) advocated that EBP is a vital new practice approach crucial to the competitiveness and effectiveness of social workers. Ell & Vourlekis outline massive changes in health care looming and tomorrow's health care social worker using an entrepreneurial model to secure clients and EBP skills being a core element of practice. EBP seems to be emerging as a new paradigm, expanding beyond just a tool. EBP is described by Cournoyer as a growing framework where best practices can be selected, tailored to the specific client, and effectiveness then fed back into the framework as a synergistic process always striving for the best service. A large international collaboration will emerge where clinicians can enter client specifics and select the recommended protocol just like a soda vending machine: research-based, tailor-made interventions for the client. Such a framework may seem fanciful but actually the framework has already been developed for medical treatment of cancer patients. Protocol effectiveness is monitored and a growing pool of tailor-made drug therapies are available. The EBP framework for social workers just needs a serious international commitment to develop a collaborative sharing network of protocols.

4. *New missions and skills will be needed in the near future.* Many authors described urgent client need but social workers not invested or trained. Kroft & Adamek confront us that a rapidly aging population has indifferent social work programs and students who are not training to become gerontologically competent. Ell & Vourlekis alert us that the U.S. health care crisis is growing and a new collaborative and entrepreneurial model of social work intervention is vitally needed. DiNitto points out that addictions is a rapidly growing arena that social work could impact but special skills are needed. Sarri & Shook lament that criminal justice has grown obsessed with sentencing instead of community-based programs and social work needs to roar into the battle to reframe the value of alternatives and re-entry programs. Kayser asserts that the evolving family systems are misunderstood and not helped by traditional social work. Schools, mental health programs, child welfare services, disability services are all going through transforming changes that will dictate new missions and skills. Each author outlines how the profession can evolve to be more on-target and competitive. Authors such as Ell & Vourlekis, McCroskey, Sullivan, Dinitto warn that other professions are reframing their missions and skills. The windows of opportunities are time-limited and, if we do not adapt, we as a profession could wither and be outmoded. Watkins & Pierce, in particular, point out that schools of

social work are growing in number but enrollment nationwide is not growing, and that social work education has a precarious opportunity to connect
with needed new skills or wither.

5. *We live in a transforming society that needs social work in all its fields.* Global
   social welfare is facing grim times (McNutt), a rapid rise in ethnic diversity
   is showing society unprepared (Fong), aging issues demand a transformative
   agenda in how we see positive aging (Kroft & Adamek), new family forms
   are misunderstood and underserved (Kayser), clients with disabilities are
   pushing for empowerment (Patchner), technology is reframing all aspects
   of society (Vernon), countervailing forces demanding cost control and access are tearing health care systems apart (Ell & Vourlekis), mental illness
   and addictions are pushing for needed care (Sullivan, DiNitto), and prisons
   instead of prevention or treatment is traumatizing a sizable portion of our
   growing ethnically diverse population (Sarri & Shook). Each issue demands
   social work leadership and creative solutions. This issue of Advances has
   painted a grim picture of a society confused, evolving, and fearful. The work
   to be done is clearly articulated by the authors. The profession must rally to
   the call for action!

SOME ISSUES TO PONDER

The five potent common issues described above give us much to ponder. The authors have,
in essence, challenged the profession in all fields of interest to energize for action. I wanted
to also include some issues that I felt were still unclear or were not emphasized. Think of
them as missing pieces of the puzzle.

1. *How would a multi-country comparison reframe the issues?* I have one regret in
   my instructions to the authors: I did not ask for multi-country comparisons.
   Most of the authors focused on the United States in defining the issues and
   future. It could be because I did not ask for any international perspectives.
   I grant that covering the issues for the U.S. is complex. But, as I finished
   article after article, I kept thinking: what do other countries have to teach
   us about alternatives to where we are at? McNutt warns of the erosion of the
   occupational welfare system. How do other countries succeed in developing
   welfare systems not link to employment and what tips could we glean from
   them? Spirituality, technology, disabilities, aging, rural settings, family issues, child welfare, schools, health, mental illness, addictions, and criminal
   justice are all subjects that are framed very differently in other countries.
   What lessons can we learn from our colleagues in other countries?

2. *How will our society evolve?* It is clear from the issues previously discussed
   that we as a society are evolving involuntarily. Segments of our population
   are transforming without services or even acknowledgement of the change
   occurring. Aging, ethnic diversification, family structure, globalization
   eroding economic stability and health care coverage are just a few hidden
   cracks in our view of a stable society. The authors warn of the need for skills
   and advocacy in social workers. But the message also seems to say that we

must be advocates because client empowerment is being crushed by society in denial. Social work often is the pulse beat checker of society, even when society is furious at what we find. I suggest that a useful issue to ponder is what is our role in soothing or stimulating society as we ride the roller-coaster of change that is coming?

3. *What are the boundaries of the evidence-based practice paradigm?* EBP seems to be transforming from one of many tools used by a social worker to a dominant paradigm. Several articles emphasize EBP and Cournoyer paints a vivid picture of the potential of and energy generated by EBP. EBP has great promise and has much work left to become actualized. I am intrigued with how rapid and widespread EBP is becoming. Which prompts the question: what are its boundaries? I see little in the literature about dangers or limits of EBP. What is it replacing as a practice paradigm and what price will we pay? Sullivan hinted at some concerns in his article but no other authors seemed to have misgivings. With any given practice paradigm, there should be advocates of an alternative. Trained by Walter Hudson and Bruce Thyer in my doctoral studies in the 1980s, I have heard similar themes for a long time. Empirical social work and practice effectiveness advocates have pushed for EBP as a paradigm. They are now shifting from the outsiders to the insiders. I wonder who are now the outsiders? I do not have an answer. Just have an issue to ponder.

BRIEF OVERVIEW OF EACH ARTICLE'S COMMON THEMES, UNIQUE THEMES, AND AREAS TO CLARIFY

Table 1 strives to briefly describe some common themes, unique themes, and areas to clarify for each article. The table is not intended to be a detailed outline or a complete listing of each article. Instead, this table allows the reader to get a flavor of the key points that I wanted to highlight as I developed this synthesizing article. I hope the reader will peruse the article, consider what I included in each category, and add others that they think of as common or unique themes and areas to clarify.

Table 1. Comparison of articles in special issue

AUTHOR	COMMON THEMES	UNIQUE THEMES	AREAS TO CLARIFY
Ginsberg	Optimistic future, multiculturalism is growing	Need to better capture profession's history, rapid job growth in direct service, political advocacy is vital	What different skills or mission will be needed in future?

AUTHOR	COMMON THEMES	UNIQUE THEMES	AREAS TO CLARIFY
Watkins & Pierce	Challenging future, "rapidly globalizing environment", multiculturalism	Dramatic growth in schools of social work but unchanging enrollment, need to ensure relevant, international education	"future relevant practice" is still not outlined though it is a priority, social work education has a precarious opportunity to connect or wither
Reamer	Maturing profession	Need to recalibrate values & ethics view, shifted from focus on morality to standards and risk management	How will back-to-basics shift link to future relevant practice?
Potocky-Tripodi & Tripodi	International perspective in a globalized society	International content and voice in social work is marginalized, unlikely to change though it needs to	Globally focused social work is advocated but what skills or education that best prepares?
Fong	Multicultural social work	Limited knowledge, insufficient resources, inadequate curriculum hampers growth; rise in ethnic diversity in US; intersectionality is useful tool	Recommended changes are massive. Will the future embrace or marginalize the suggestions?
Netting	Optimistic, versatility of profession is strength	Macro skills are important to all social workers to sustain, change, and advocate for quality of life	How will macro social work transform as we become more globally focused?
McNutt	Transforming society that will need social work	Global social welfare faces grim times; information economy, digital divide, erosion of occupational welfare system stir crisis	Very US focused, how have other countries faced similar issues? Is this transformation unique to US?

AUTHOR	COMMON THEMES	UNIQUE THEMES	AREAS TO CLARIFY
Cournoyer	International focus on EBP shows expanding influence	Evidence-based practice (EBP) is growing as a resource in selecting best practice	Seems to see EBP almost as a paradigm more than a tool of practice. What are its boundaries?
Rapp et al	SBSW has growing influence as a practice approach	Advocates bolstering strengths-based social work (SBSW); needs to refine definition and application standards	Very US focused, how have other countries developed SBSW? Is it generic or are there some situations where SBSW won't work?
Vernon	Technology is shaping practice	Case management systems and geographical information systems converging	Very US focused, how have other countries developed technology?
Canda	Recent rapid growth in focus on spirituality, especially at an international level; globalization is impacting everything	"inclusive approach to spiritual diversity founded in professional values & ethics"	Very broad stroke and visionary view. What skills or education best prepares? Will the initiatives merge into a paradigm?
Patchner	Living with disability (LD) is increasingly empowering with social work serving a key advocate role	Different care systems have been tried shifting from case management to consumer driven service	Very US focused paradigm, how would other countries with national health care evolve their LD empowerment ?
Kroft & Adamek	Rapid aging population, slow social work response, need training and prioritization of aging issues	New paradigms of positive aging and a transformative agenda; wide range of skills needed	Very US focused discussion, how would other countries with different views of aging care and empowerment incorporate social work?
Murty	Community-based practice with generalist view is important for rural areas	Rural social work (RSW) moving in opposite direction of rest: needs generalist not specialist, centralized	More in-depth explanation of RSW effectiveness would help, how do other predominantly rural countries do it?

AUTHOR	COMMON THEMES	UNIQUE THEMES	AREAS TO CLARIFY
Kayser	New format of families misunderstood and not helped by social work	Social work family research needs to be strengthened	how would other countries with different views of family care and empowerment incorporate social work?
McCroskey	Focus on outcomes and EBP urgently needed in child welfare	Inadequate outcome measures, growing research on child effects in high risk settings, and need to integrate services	how would other countries with different views of child care and empowerment incorporate social work?
Franklin	Increased emphasis on EBP, credentialing, and community-based services	Technology and marketing skills need enhancing	how would other countries emphasize school social work?
Ell & Vourlekis	Massive health care reforms as context, EBP and gerontological competence are high priority,	Countervailing forces: cost control vs needs, collaboration, entrepreneurial model useful focused on "priority clients"	how would other countries emphasize health social work? Is the large educational content described feasible?
Sullivan	EBP focus, social entrepreneurship model useful	Collaborative and community-focused care needed	how would other countries emphasize mental health social work?
DiNitto	Optimistic need for social work , culturally relevant models, EBP	Rapid expansion of knowledge, shift from crime to treatment,	how would other countries emphasize addictions care?
Sarri & Shook	High need but reduced SW influence & workforce	Social work role in community-based programs, as trainers, in courts & re-entry transition	how would other countries emphasize criminal justice diversion?

CONCLUSION

My purpose in this article was to synthesize the articles into a discussion of commonalities and issues to ponder. Five common links were found that illuminate both social work's optimistic though precarious future and society's transformation. Clearly social workers in all fields should be hopeful but determined. There is a lot of development of new skills and reforming of our mission to do if we are to be helpful when a very confused society goes into crisis. The authors of the articles in this issue give great advice about what skills and missions on which to focus. We must be committed to be leaders into the future. Our advocacy is vital to an increasingly underserved clientele and confused society.

I have also raised three issues to ponder. One of the common links was the growing global and multicultural society we are becoming. We as a profession need to embrace an international stance. Issues such as child welfare, physical or mental illness, or positive aging should be considered from a global stance. Successful strategies from different countries should be shared in a collaborative, best practice manner. Our society is evolving and we need all the ideas for successful transition we can get. Evidence-based practice shows great promise, energy, and may be a helpful way to foster international collaboration. But we should embrace EBP while still watching for costs or boundaries of its usefulness.

Our profession is complex and massive in its workforce and potential influence. The articles in this special issue help us define the work to do. Our challenge is to adapt and overcome.

References

Adams, R., Dominelli, L. & Payne, M. (2005). *Social Work Futures : Crossing Boundaries, Transforming Practice*. New York: Palgrave Macmillan.

Bamford, T. (1989). *The future of social work*. New York: Palgrave Macmillan.

Beck, B.M. (1981). Social work's future: triumph or disaster? *Social Work, 26*(5), 367-372.

Clark, E.J. (2005). Celebrating past, looking to future. *NASW News, 50*(5), 1. Retrieved August 1, 2005 from http://www.socialworkers.org/pubs/news/2005/05/

Hopps, J.G. & Morris, R. (Eds) (2000). *Critical Reflections on the Future of the Profession*. New York: Free Press.

Johnson, A.K. (2004). The past, present, and future of international social work. *Journal of Community Practice, 12*(1/2): 145-153.

Kadushin, A. (1999). The past, the present, and the future of professional social work. *Arete, 23*(3): 76-84.

Kuhn, T.S. (1970). *The structure of scientific revolutions, 2nd edition*. Chicago: The University of Chicago Press.

Leonard, P. (2001). The future of critical social work in uncertain conditions. *Critical Social Work, 2*(1). 1-6. Retrieved August 1, 2005 from http://www.criticalsocialwork.com/units/socialwork/critical.nsf/

Mary, N.L & Morris, T. (1994). The future and social work: a global perspective. *Journal of Multicultural Social Work, 3*(4): 89-101.

Pecukonis,E.V, Cornelius, L. & Parrish, M. (2003). The future of health social work. *Social Work in Health Care, 37*(3): 1-15.

Reisch, M. (1997). Social work and the new millennium. *Journal-of-Social-Work-Education, 33*(1): 2-3.

Reisch, M. & Jarman-Rohde, L. (2000). The future of social work in the United States: implications for field education. *Journal of Social Work Education, 36* (2), 201-214.

Sowers, K.M & Ellis, R.A (2001). Steering currents for the future of social work. *Research on Social Work Practice. 11*(2): 245-253.

Walton, R.G. (1982). *Social work 2000 : the future of social work in a changing society*. New York: Longman.

Author's Note

Address correspondence to: James G. Daley PhD, Indiana University School of Social Work, 902 West New York Street ES 4115, Indianapolis, Indiana 46202-5156. e-mail: jgdaley@iupui.edu

Advances in Social Work

Advances in Social Work is published twice each year (Fall and Spring) by the Indiana University School of Social Work. An annual subscription is US $30.00 for subscribers in the United States, $40 for international subscribers. Any single issue is $15. The price includes postage by surface mail.

Payment may be made by check or money order payable in US funds to "Indiana University School of Social Work."

Send your subscription request to:

Advances in Social Work
Indiana University School of Social Work
902 West New York Street, Suite ES4115
Indianapolis, Indiana, USA 46202-5156

···

Advances in Social Work
Subscription Request

Name:_____

Address:_____

Address:_____

City,State/Province:_____

Country:_____

Postal Code:_____

Amount Enclosed:_____

e-mail of person to contact if questions:_____

Indiana University School of Social Work, 902 Wes New York Street, ES 4138
Indianapolis, Indiana, USA 46202-5156, USA